WITHDRAWN

DAVID O. McKAY LIBRARY
BYU-IDAHO

P9-AFF-645

DATE DUE

AUG 2 0 1982			
DEC 10 1982			
APR 3 0 1993			
JAN 2 7 1995			
GAYLORD			PRINTED IN U.S.A.

Rhetorical Norms in Renaissance Literature

RHETORICAL NORMS IN
RENAISSANCE LITERATURE

William J. Kennedy

New Haven and London   Yale University Press

1978

Copyright © 1978 by Yale University. All rights reserved.
This book may not be reproduced, in whole or in part,
in any form (beyond that copying permitted by Sections
107 and 108 of the U.S. Copyright Law and except by
reviewers for the public press), without written permis-
sion from the publishers.

Designed by John O.C. McCrillis and set in Press Roman
type. Printed in the United States of America by Halliday
Lithograph Corp., West Hanover, Massachusetts.

Published in Great Britain, Europe, Africa, and Asia
(except Japan) by Yale University Press, Ltd., London.
Distributed in Australia and New Zealand by Book &
Film Services, Artarmon, N.S.W., Australia; and in Japan
by Harper & Row, Publishers, Tokyo Office.

Library of Congress Cataloging in Publication Data

Kennedy, William John, 1942–
  Rhetorical norms in Renaissance literature.

  Includes bibliographical references and index.
    1. European literature–Renaissance, 1450-1600–
History and criticism. 2. Rhetoric–History.
I. Title
PN721.K4   809'.031   78-7391
ISBN 0--300-02263-8

Contents

Acknowledgments

Although this book relates in no way to my Yale dissertation in comparative literature, still it owes most of its conceptual value to the critical acumen, historical insight, and theoretical wisdom of my mentors, Thomas M. Greene, Lowry Nelson, Jr., and René Wellek. At Cornell I have been indebted to two former chairmen and a friend: Wolfgang Holdheim, who supported and encouraged my teaching and writing every step of the way; Edgar Rosenberg, who made me think harder about both endeavors; and Ciriaco Morón-Arroyo, who brought constructive criticism to my inchoate ideas; and to my former students, especially Ann Jones, Barbara Pavlock, and Walter Stephens, who tested and challenged my basic assumptions. I express particular gratitude to A. Bartlett Giamatti for reading and commenting upon the manuscript at a very tender stage in its development. To the editors and staff of the Yale Press, especially Ellen Graham, Lynn Walterick, and Bowden Anderson, I express my sincerest thanks for their painstaking care, infinite resourcefulness, and hard work in conferring upon this book its final form. Most of all, my family has given immeasurably of its time and love, patience and understanding, criticism and joy: my parents, William J. and Ruth Donnelly Kennedy; my wife, Mary Lynch Kennedy; and my children, Liam and Maura, whom I can never thank enough.

Introduction: Rhetorical Criticism
and Literary Theory

Since late antiquity two conceptions of rhetoric have prevailed. One defines it as the art of embellishment and ornamentation; the other, as the art of communication and persuasion. Though not mutually exclusive, these two views have sometimes seemed so through a distorted emphasis on one at the other's expense. The first conception dates back to ancient compendia of elocutionary devices, figures, tropes, and other verbal arrangements with examples drawn from the classical poets. Plato, however, in his *Gorgias* and *Phaedrus*, Aristotle in his *Rhetoric*, Cicero in his *De Oratore*, and Quintilian in his *Institutio oratoria* all expressed deep skepticism about this concept of rhetoric. They defined it instead as the art of communication and persuasion and treated it as a moral act far exceeding the mere arrangement of words that all speech necessarily entails. Though all four (Plato, the least; Quintilian, the most) accorded due attention to elocution, their deeper concern was with other strategies involving the speaker's characterization and his relationship to an audience. The norms governing these strategies in Renaissance literature and their possibilities of interacting to generate larger structures of mode, style, and genre constitute this book's subject.

A focus on the interaction of speaker and audience might imply beginning with a text's verbal structure, but such a study must go beyond superficial elocutionary devices. Too much of recent literary analysis has concentrated on such devices to the neglect of other, more comprehensive strategies. We might instead begin by raising larger, more difficult questions about the nature of literary texts, in particular those of the past. Such texts challenge the reader's understanding of an author's

1

historical meaning, whether through linguistic study or through analogies in generic, modal, and stylistic studies.[1]

Hans Georg Gadamer states the issues squarely:

> The concept of literature is not unrelated to the reader. Literature is not the dead continuance of an estranged being made available to the experience of a later period. Literature is a function of intellectual preservation and tradition and therefore brings its hidden history into every age. . . .
>
> The projecting of the historical horizon . . . is only a phase in the process of understanding, and does not become solidified into the self-alienation of a past consciousness, but is overtaken by our own present horizon of understanding. In the process of understanding there takes place a real fusing of horizons, which means that as the historical horizon is projected, it is simultaneously removed.[2]

On the reader's present horizon, his awareness of various rhetorical strategies must loom large, but precisely how? Does it carry him beyond the local and immediate stylistic effects on the text's surface into the high theoretical realm of modal properties and of abstract but no less real principles of generic organization? If so, what relationships do these rhetorical techniques sustain with the larger systems?

Clearly a concept of rhetoric focusing merely on embellishment or ornamentation provides no answer. The full range of figures, tropes, and other linguistic structures belongs potentially to all verbal expression, and no one device is sovereign in any particular genre, mode, or style. Extended similes, formulaic epithet, elevated diction, and stately rhythms characterize the verbal structure of epic; yet, none is essential to the genre, and one could always find examples, such as Lucan's *De Bello civili* or Ariosto's *Orlando Furioso*, which lack several or even all of those devices. Oxymoronic metaphor, metonymy, and paradox dominate the verbal structure of the Petrarchan lyric from the fourteenth to the seventeenth centuries; the same figures, however, appear and reappear in other modes as diverse as pastoral (Sannazaro) and meditative (Luis de Leon), précieux (Voiture) and metaphysical (Marvell). But certain norms of integration governing the speaker's characterization and his relationship to an audience do seem dominant in various systems of genre, mode, and style. These rhetorical norms include and surpass the elocutionary ones on the text's surface and can be used to characterize a particular system. Genre, the largest category, distinguishes among epic, novel, lyric, drama, and others through formal properties associated with medium (poetry, prose), length (long, short), and voice (dialogue, monologue, mixed). Within each genre are modes such as comic, tragic, satiric, allegorical, and pastoral, determined both by content and theme and by the author's attitude toward them. Finally, within genres and modes, indeed even within individual works, there are several styles ranging from simple and straightforward to complex and allusive.

The speaker's characterization and his relationship to the audience bear greatly upon these generic, modal, and stylistic norms. Generic ones modify the audience's expectations in approaching the text, and they also condition the audience's response to what the speaker or speakers say. Modal norms resulting from the conjunction between subject matter and the speaker's attitude towards it may surface in different genres (such as pastoral eclogues, pastoral dramas, pastoral romances), but in each case they operate on assumptions that link the speaker both to what he says and to his audience. Stylistic norms, it is true, rely to a larger extent on particular verbal structures. However, since stylistic efficacy depends upon the audience's recognition of the speaker's intent, it follows that a rhetorical complicity between speaker and audience must deepen the style.

In defining these norms, I shall try to indicate how they are assimilable to classical and Renaissance concepts of rhetoric and to suggest how the chaos of modern theory and criticism has dimmed their significance. This chaos raises the question of which ancient or modern principles govern the structure (*dispositio*) and style (*elocutio*) of the literary text. The same principles govern other divisions that are either anterior (*inventio*) or posterior (memory and delivery) to the text's production. We must adjust our own historical perspective to understand the classical idea of persuasion,[3] which implies a definite object, a concrete "message" that a speaker is trying to communicate to his audience. But for many modern theorists literary texts posit no such object and instead these texts reify language, making it transcend its merely referential function.[4] This critical focus on the elocutionary, however, confuses poetic discourse with merely gratuitious verbal ornament.

One must return instead to a focus on the *terms* of the referential function, not only the object of the discourse (the persuasive argument) but also its subjects (who is attempting to persuade whom). On the simplest level such an act implicates one who is persuading with another being persuaded. On more complex literary levels it may implicate several, such as a speaker or narrator distinct from the author, fictional characters in turn distinct from both, even a fictive audience distinct from the empirical reader. Moreover, since one seeks to persuade another of the truth or falseness of a given proposition, a certain distance necessarily separates them. Thus, there might ensue a structure of complex, dynamic relationships quite different from the structure of words which it modifies and inflects.[5] In turn this structure may implicate many intermediary members between the historical author on the one hand and the empirical reader on the other.

The first of these intermediaries is already familiar to modern criticism as a speaker or narrator distinct from the author, separately dramatized in his own right.[6] He can be an entirely fictional persona who enunciates a moral vision that may or may not coincide with the author's point of view. The rhetorical speaker's moral life, his inner selfhood, and his social life, the external roles that he plays in relation to others, determine his *ethos*.[7] The humanist formula that man is a moral being who knows and wills implies the existence of a selfhood with controlled reason and volition. Threatening the integrity of the individual's selfhood, however, may be a conflict between reason and will or between will and ability. A rhetorical agent may know what he should do and may even let his audience know, but in action, he may choose not to do what he should; or else he may choose to do something which he subsequently finds himself powerless to execute. If the speaker is even less in control of his reason, will, and ability that he thinks, his private act of delusion or public act of deception may lead to yet a further conflict between what he represents to his audience and what he pretends to represent.

The individual's public life, signaled by the roles that he plays in relation to others in accordance with certain social norms, complicates his character in other ways. No single role ever fully represents or covers his entire fictive nature. He plays instead many roles, some complementary, others contrasting, though even their totality fails to express completely his moral essence. The rhetorical act thus generates a dramatic interest in how the speaker clings to a certain role, shifts to another, moves through a succession of them, or enacts two or more opposing ones simultaneously, and how he squares or fails to square these roles with his moral selfhood.

The second intermediary agent is perhaps less familiar. Just as a speaker distinct from the author can assume a fictive persona in his own right, so too can an audience distinct from the reader. Within the work the author may constrain his reader to play a particular role every bit as fictive as his speaker's or characters' roles. He might oblige the reader to enter into a conspiracy with or against the speaker either by becoming or by refusing to become the kind of audience that he expects it to be, by following or by refusing to follow his cues and commands, by taking or by not taking his addresses seriously—in short, by accepting or by not accepting the specific role as a fictive audience created to respond to the work in a certain way.[8]

The role of fictive audience may make very explicit demands upon the reader to become an "accomplice, communicant, collaborator, or willing suspender of disbelief," in the words of Lowry Nelson, Jr., whose essay on this subject outlines the options with sensitivity and insight.[9] Some of these options lend themselves readily to certain categorizations of genre or mode. In drama, for example, one character addresses another as an immediate audience that is always fictive. In a theatrical performance the spectators function as witnesses, onlookers, and eavesdroppers. In the lyric much the same rhetorical situation prevails, especially when the lyric speaker addresses a specific audience who may be an explicitly fictional character (as the beloved of an amatory poem, including such thinly disguised fictions as Petrarch's Laura, Scève's Délie, and Sidney's Stella) or an implicitly fictional one (such as Donne's various unnamed mistresses or Baudelaire's "hypocrite lecteur"). Even in poems without vocatives or apostrophes (as in descriptive poetry or the poetry of interior meditation, such as Mallarmé's "L'Après-midi d'un faune" and Yeats's "The Tower"), the rhetorical situation implies a potential audience whose willingness to listen justifies the speaker's performance.

In narrative the rhetorical situation is different and the audience's role more complex. Whether in poetry (epic or romance) or prose (novel, tale), the account depends upon a speaker who as storyteller spins out his fiction for a certain audience. It may comprise a particular class of listeners drawn from the speaker's own national or social or intellectual rank (as Ariosto's *donne* and *cavallieri* or Milton's "fit audience, though few"), or it may comprise a general class of readers with an undefined interest in the narrative (as Cervantes's "desocupado lector" or Fielding's "Dear Reader"). No matter what roles he creates for them, the author enjoins his readers or listeners to identify with the fictive audience. Even in an allegedly "objective" fiction the reader must function as an observer of the event rendered in the author's impersonal account.

Several kinds of fictive audience mediate then between the author or speaker on the one hand and the empirical reader on the other, with significant effect on the reader's responses.[10] A specific distance or proximity is imposed which modifies the power of the one to manipulate and of the other to respond.

The distance may entail time (past, present), space (absence, presence), intellectual perspective (differences in factual understanding), and moral awareness (differences in subjective evaluation), as well as emotional factors such as ardor, passion, coolness, detachment. The crucial part of any rhetorical analysis of a literary text involves a judgment on these qualitative varieties. This book offers a model for such judgment.[11]

This emphasis on voice and address crystallizes Renaissance views on the moral purpose of rhetoric.[12] Since the seventeenth century these views have been lost almost entirely, and formal rhetoric has degenerated into a mechanistic catalogue of elocutionary devices and verbal techniques. Earlier creative artists and theorists, however, were acutely conscious of rhetoric's moral and cognitive powers. In fact, they frequently worried about abusing those powers for morally undesirable ends.

This distrust stemmed partly from Plato's *Gorgias* (ca. 395 B.C.?), where Socrates distinguishes between rhetoric and dialectic. There are, he argues, two forms of persuasion, one producing belief without knowledge, the other knowledge (*Gorgias*, 454e).[13] All too often rhetoric guarantees only the former, whereas dialectic always generates the latter. The rhetorician, Socrates claims, has no need to know the truth but merely has to discover an effective technique of persuasion (459c). It is not an art (τέχνη) but an empirically learned routine (ἐμπειρία) aimed at producing gratification and pleasure (462c).

In Plato's *Phaedrus* (ca. 370 B.C.?) Socrates again scorns rhetorical figures and schemes as mere antecedents of true learning (*Phaedrus*, 269c).[14] He does grant limited approval to a rhetorical art in which the speaker knows the truth of his subject as well as the nature of his audience (277b–c). But still, he concludes, dialectic supersedes the written word, just as love of wisdom surpasses rhetorical persuasion, because it is "no dead discourse, but the living speech, the original of which the written discourse may fairly be called a kind of image [ἐίδωλον]" (276a). Socrates thus disparages the place of ethics in the fully developed rhetorical act. To him rhetoric is a mechanical technique not only distinct from, but also counter to, the vitality of ethics.

But rhetoric and aesthetics are not inimical to ethics for Aristotle, nor for the inheritors of his *Rhetoric* (ca. 330 B.C.). Far from viewing rhetoric as the opposite of dialectic, Aristotle classifies it as "the counterpart of Dialectic" (1.1, 1)— a classification that the Renaissance honored by binding together printed rhetorical manuals with dialectic handbooks— and as an offshoot of ethics and politics (1.4, 5).[15] Its directly artistic form of proof is the enthymeme, a kind of syllogism within the province of dialectic, though based on probability rather than on scientific evidence (1.1, 11). Like dialectic, moreover, rhetoric may indifferently prove opposite assertions with either genuine or spurious arguments, according to its speaker's moral purpose (1.1, 12). The successful rhetorician, of course, must know how to analyze various types of character, virtues, and emotions (1.2, 7). Rhetoric, therefore, holds as many ties with ethics and politics as it does with dialectic; its subject matter treats of human actions, and its indirectly artistic forms of proof entail not only emotional appeals to the audience but also manifestations of the speaker's character (1.2, 7).

The concern with voice and address is compatible with Aristotle's seminal concepts of *ethos, pathos*, and *logos.*[16] Rhetoric is "the faculty [power] of discovering in the particular case what are the available means of persuasion" (1.2, 1), and there are three chief means of persuasion:

> The first kind reside in the character [*ethos*] of the speaker; the second [*pathos*] consist in producing a certain [the right] attitude in the hearer; the third [*logos*] appertain to the argument proper, in so far as it actually or seemingly demonstrates [1.2, 3].

Of these means, the last approach through *logos* entails the speaker's selection and use of enthymemes, maxims, example, and their common topoi (2.19–26). It also involves style (elocutionary figures) and arrangement, including invention and disposition (3.1–19). Persuasion through *logos* necessarily governs and inflects persuasion through *ethos* and *pathos*, since the speaker reveals his character and appeals to his audience only in and through language. On the other hand, Aristotle did distinguish the notions of *ethos* and *pathos* from each other and from *logos*, and his scrutiny of them still is worth studying.

Persuasion through the speaker's character Aristotle considers a potent rhetorical strategy (1.2, 4), especially in deliberative performances when the speaker counsels or advises, exhorts, or dissuades his audience on particular issues (2.1, 4). This strategy disposes his audience toward the speaker by evincing his intelligence, virtue, and good will (2.1, 5). He must acquire a mastery of different types of human character and have adequate knowledge of traits associated with youth, age, maturity, fortune, wealth, and power (2.12-17). Above all he must reveal moral conviction in his speech, showing by judicious questions that he knows what options suit him best (3.16, 8).

The speaker persuades through involvement with his audience when he brings them into a state of emotions congruent with his purpose. Rhetoric by its very nature entails the participation of an audience: "'Persuasive' means persuasive to a person" (1.2, 11)—not necessarily to a single individual but to a class of individuals whose identity may in fact be an author's fiction. Even when the speaker proposes an impersonal thesis and does not intend it for a particular audience (as in written discourse addressed to readers at large), he must function as though he were confronting an imagined audience (2.18, 1). Moreover, he should accept the intellectual limitations of his audience, "who cannot grasp many points in a single view, or follow a long chain of reasoning" (1.2, 12), and he should encourage the audience's participation by obliging it to supply missing links and necessary connections in his speech (1.2, 13). He should make himself look good by citing maxims that agree with his audience's preferences (2.21, 15). He should appeal to its members' ironic awareness of the discrepancy between action and intention, will and ability, what one says and what one does: "No other *topos* of paradox is so effective as this" (2.23, 15). Finally, he should attempt to manipulate his audience's sentiments through emotions that he has studied in detail: anger, mildness, love and hate, fear and confidence, shame, benevolence, pity (the most "dramatic" emotion), indignation, envy, and emulation (2.2–11).

Aristotle's influence on subsequent rhetorical theory was decisive. When not direct, as in the early Renaissance before the first printed editions of the *Rhetoric* (in Latin translation, 1478, and in Greek, 1508),[17] it still made itself felt through intermediary sources in the Roman rhetorical tradition, especially through the theories of Cicero and Quintilian. Here the emphasis on voice and address commanded paramount respect. For Cicero in the *De Oratore* (55 B.C.) the theory and practice of rhetoric exert their fullest power "in calming or kindling the feelings of the audience" (1.5, 17).[18] Cicero's essential thesis about the speaker's character asserts, "No man can be an orator complete in all points of merit, who has not attained a knowledge of all important subjects and arts" (1.6, 20). Crassus, his major spokesman in the dialogue, emphasizes the speaker's relationship with the audience by claiming, "The orator's virtue is pre-eminently manifested either in rousing men's hearts to anger, hatred, or indignation, or in recalling them from these same passions to mildness and mercy" (1.12, 53). Elsewhere, in a long passage on winning the audience's favor, another speaker, Antonius, says, "Love is won if you are thought to be upholding the interests of your audience, or to be working for good men, or at any rate for such as that audience deems good and useful" (2.51, 206). Cicero represents these views in full accord with the Aristotelian notion of *ethos* and *pathos*, coloring them with the ancient Roman stress on clear, unpretentious elegance and the primacy of moral character.

In the *Institutio oratoria* (A.D. 92–94) Quintilian was even more explicit than Cicero in adapting Aristotelian terminology and categories. He appropriates the terms *ethos* and *pathos* but suggests their similarities rather than differences, remarking, "*Pathos* and *ethos* are sometimes of the same nature, differing only in degree" (6.2, 12).[19] *Ethos* designates calm and gentle emotions in the speaker, while *pathos* arouses more violent emotions in the audience (6.2, 9); *ethos* is generally continuous, while *pathos* is momentary (6.2, 10). The former includes not only mild and ingratiating signs of good character and courtesy in the speaker, but also "the skillful exercise of feigned emotion or the employment of irony" (6.2, 15) and sometimes even a "feigned submission to our opponents" (6.2, 16). This important association of *ethos* with irony was not lost on Renaissance writers like Petrarch and Sidney, Erasmus and Rabelais, Ariosto and Milton, for whom the discrepancy between what the speaker is and how he appears generates some of the most important meanings.

Pathos for Quintilian is "almost entirely concerned with anger, dislike, fear, hatred and pity" (6.2, 20). To affect his audience the speaker must first have experienced the emotions that he wishes his audience to feel. For this purpose he must be able to present to his imagination things absent "with such extreme vividness that they seem actually to be before our very eyes" (6.2, 29). This all-important power of exhibiting rather than merely narrating is ἐνάργεια, a term from Cicero (*Partitione oratoria*, 6.20) which derives utlimately from Aristotle's use of ἐνέργεια in his *Rhetoric* (2.2, 3, concerning the "active display of opinion," and 3.11, 4, concerning the effects of "lifelike activity" in Homeric description). Ἐνάργεια is the most effective rhetorical means of evoking *pathos*.

The impact of these ancient theories on Renaissance poetics was decisive. Poggio rediscovered the full text of Quintilian's *Institutio* (already known imperfectly by Petrarch) at St. Gallen and published it in 1416.[20] The first complete copy of Cicero's *De Oratore*, with its assertion that "the poet is a very near kinsman of the orator" (1.16, 70), surfaced at Lodi in 1421. Leonardo Bruni rendered the *Gorgias* and the *Phaedrus* into Latin in 1423, fifty-four years before Ficino completed a better Latin translation of Plato's dialogues (1477), and almost a century before Aldus Manutius published Plato's *editio princeps* in Greek (1513). Meanwhile Aristotle's *Rhetoric* appeared in a Latin translation by George of Trebizond in 1478, its Greek edition (and that of the *Poetics*) in the *Rhetores Graeci* of Aldus Manutius in 1508. The combined influence of these editions on literary theory was tremendous, however much the Renaissance theorists revised or adjusted the rhetorical terminology to fit the new and different contexts of their poetics.[21] The earliest commentaries on Aristotle's *Poetics* used the classical rhetoricians' definitions of tropes and figures to amplify Aristotle's brief remarks on the subject. Thus Robortello, commenting on the *Poetics* in 1548, explicated chapters 21 and 22 referring to Cicero's *De Oratore.* He claimed that "the same rhetorical terms can be repeated for the poets, whom Aristotle addressed in this book."[22]

In most cases, however, the accommodation of rhetoric to poetics involved more radical revisions or adjustments of terminology. When Julius Caesar Scaliger defined the poet's four virtues in his comprehensive *Poetices Libri Septem* (1561), he appropriated Quintilian's concept of ἐνάργεια in terms that approach Aristotle's concept of *pathos.* Adopting Aristotle's spelling (ἐνέργεια) and translating the word into Latin as *efficacia,* he defines it as "the rhetorical power of representing words and things which succeeds in causing even an unpopular message to be heard" (3.25).[23] It results from several rhetorical strategies: "exclamations or addresses bear the greatest efficacy" and "there is also such efficacy in apostrophe and interrogation" (3.27).

From a different perspective Minturno in his *Arte Poetica* (1564) synthesized the ancient classical division of elocutionary devices into rhetorical figures and tropes with more recent Renaissance speculations on genre, prosody, literary imitation, and vernacular style, all in the framework of an Aristotelian and Horatian poetics. Book IV focuses upon the speaker's *ethos* and his need to present appropriate details in his characterization "so that he shows enough of the speaker's age, worth, authority, condition, fortune, family, and where he was born and raised." When he adds that the speaker must clarify his audience's disposition—"No less should he show what his audience is like"—he calls attention to Aristotelian *pathos* and the problem of producing the right attitude in the hearer.[24]

In general, the Renaissance was receptive to the Aristotelian concept of rhetoric and to a poetics sharply oriented towards it. Furthermore, rhetoric meant more to the Renaissance theorists than to their medieval predecessors, who regarded it almost exclusively as an art of ornamentation.[25] John of Salisbury (1148), Matthew of Vendôme (1175), and Geoffrey of Vinsauf (1210) characterized it thus in their *artes poeticae*, while in his *Anticlaudianus* (1178–82) Alanus de Insulis showed Lady Rhetoric decorating the vehicle of Prudence and Reason with her various ornaments (3.2–3).[26] By the sixteenth century, however, rhetoric once more had regained the ethical dimension attributed to it by Aristotle and Cicero. Moreover, despite the general adulation of Plato and Platonic philosophy, not everyone was convinced that Socrates' objections to rhetoric in the *Gorgias* and *Phaedrus* were justified. Lodovico Castelvetro, for example, in his brief essay on *Chiose intorno al Gorgia di Platone* (published in 1572) asks whether it is true that rhetoric does not teach one to respond to moral questions, while dialectics does, and he answers with a decisive No. ("Adunque la Rettorica non insegna di rispondere alla domanda, e l'arte del disputare sì? Questo non credeva io.") Rhetoric has the power to persuade audiences to truth and goodness, and he concludes by wishing "that Socrates hadn't defamed rhetoric in such a manner."[27]

Even before Castelvetro's statement, however, the emphasis on elocution that triumphed in Baroque and Neoclassical handbooks was already discernible. In his *Poetica* (1536) Bernardino Daniello of Lucca defined rhetoric as "Speech that is apt and suitable for persuasion" and particularly emphasized elocution as "the form of writing ornately" and "beautiful and ornate speech."[28] Such emphasis gradually reduced rhetoric to nothing more than a mere classification of figures and tropes. Moreover, the new method of logic and rhetoric advocated in Ramus's *Dialecticae Institutiones* (1542) and Omer Talon's *Institutiones Oratoricae* (1544) would contribute to a diminution of personal voice and person-to-person tone, resulting in what Walter Ong has called "the decay of dialogue."[29] At the height of the Baroque, Emmanuele Tesauro in *Il Cannocchiale aristotelico* (1654) called special attention to the figures of *pathos* (*figure patetiche*) which often make false seem true: "The force of these Figures is ever so magical that even when what they say turns out to be false, they could make you think it seem true, inducing your disturbed imagination to yield to it." Tesauro then lists several "figures"—exclamation, interrogation, prosopopoeia, apostrophe, irony, and especially command, request, narration, threat, question, and reply—all of which guarantee the speaker's control over his audience.[30] Reduction of rhetoric to such enumerable elements shows how synonymous it had become with classified elocutionary devices.

Today the older norms of voice and address are largely ignored. Formal rhetoric seems little more than the cadre of elocutionary devices, figures of speech, turns of phrase, tropes, and verbal technique that teachers have been cataloguing since classical antiquity. The notion of defining rhetoric through the speaker's interrelationship with his audience has been lost almost entirely. True, some notable modern attempts to rehabilitate rhetoric have drawn attention to the importance of the hearer or reader. Kenneth Burke, among others, has described it as "the use of language in such a way as to produce a desired impression on the hearer or reader" and has linked rhetoric to poetics by claiming that "all effective literature could be nothing else but rhetoric."[31] But on the whole, rhetorical studies have tended to focus on the author's independent play of creation rather than on his relationship to hearers or readers.[32]

In the more recent structural poetics, Ferdinand de Saussure's radical distinction between *langue* with its homogeneous, hence systematic, character as "the norm of all other manifestations of speech" and *parole* or individual, heterogeneous *actes de parole* as "the executive side of speech" has supplied an important linguistic support for the study of verbal patterns. Saussure warned, however, that an attempt to systematize the study of *parole*, the very basis of poetry, would distort the heterogeneous nature of *parole*, and that in any case a "linguistics of *parole*" does not equal a "linguistics of *langue*" ("linguistics proper") and "must not be confused" with it.[33] Nonetheless, theorists like Roland Barthes have argued that since language is the source of all meaning, the science of language or linguistics might reasonably provide a model for the study of all signs, signals, gestures, and other semiotic phenomena, including the rhetorical use of language.[34] In fact, Barthes even inverts Saussure's assumption that linguistics belongs to the general science of signs when he writes, "Linguistics is not a part of a general science of signs, even a privileged part, it is semiology which is a part of linguistics."

By inverting the apparent order Barthes may have accomplished Saussure's deepest intention in a more profound way.[35] Clearly he appropriates only the scientific model of linguistics, but neither he nor anyone else has ever proved its primacy over others for literary and rhetorical analysis.[36] True, linguistics studies language, the vehicle of literature, but literature itself amounts to much more than language. It uses language (*parole* in Saussure's sense) in a very precise way for effects that far transcend the surface meaning of verbal expression. Structuralist critics forget that each literary utterance adds up to more than the sum of its linguistic parts; the study of those parts at whatever level of abstraction represents only a fraction of the whole. Beyond the binary oppositions and equivalences favored by these critics, there are other rhetorical dimensions that originate metalinguistically in the interaction between speaker and audience, and that furthermore participate in the historical unfolding of the text. The total literary work balances all these rhetorical aspects in subtly nuanced relationships which surpass the structuralist method of analysis.

Significantly, Roman Jakobson, a pioneer in linguistic studies admired by all the structuralist critics, suggests that the mere arrangement of words does not determine literary rhetoric. Jakobson mentions six constitutive factors of the poetic function, only one of which, the code, is language; the other five are the addresser, the message, the addressee, the context, and the contact (medium). In poetry, he says, ambiguity not only heightens the code and message; it also gives special relief to the functions of the addresser and the addressee. "The double-sensed message finds correspondence in a split addresser, in a split addressee, and besides in a split reference." "Split addresser" refers to the difference between the author and the fictive speaker, and "split addressee" denotes the difference between the reader and the fictive audience. "Besides the author and the reader, there is the 'I' of the lyrical hero or of the fictitious story teller and the 'you' or 'thou' of the alleged addressee of dramatic monologues, supplications, and epistles."[37] These terms represent no mere binary oppositions, but highly complex rhetorical relationships that impart a central aesthetic dimension to poetry, generating problems that linguistics alone cannot resolve.[38]

Jakobson's concept of the text evokes the rhetorical importance of voice and address that I have been emphasizing. Other views, such as those of formalist technique and structuralist negativity, risk overextending the freedom of both addresser and addressee; by canceling out each other, they point to the need for a middle ground. The formalists hold that an author may use overt textual mechanisms to limit the reader's freedom of reception, secure a single interpretation, and guarantee the meaning of the text once and for all.[39] The structuralists, however, argue that readers experience their own private interpretations, subjective understanding, and negative comprehension.[40] Against these claims I would assert the positive aspect of the rhetorical situation that endures despite historical accidents, contingencies, and vicissitudes. True, different ages have found different significance in older texts and have hence esteemed them differently according to historical changes in taste or fashion or even in language and rhetoric.[41] The text still remains the same even though the reader perceives it, in Gadamer's phrase, from a new "horizon of understanding" and often registers a new emotional and even intellectual response to the verbal signifiers.

The application of phenomenological theory to rhetorical criticism and literary history, however, raises other issues. Hans Robert Jauss, for example, has tried to square the problem of the reader's role in literary history with the idea of a "productive function of progressive understanding, which necessarily also includes the criticizing and even forgetting of tradition." His "aesthetics of reception" seeks to describe the audience's response to the work "from a previous understanding of the genre, from the forms and themes of already familiar works and from the contrast between poetic and practical language." Thus, Jauss writes that literature has "a sort of grammar or syntax with relatively firm relationships of its own: the structure of the traditional and uncanonized genres, styles of expression, and rhetorical figures. Opposed to this is the more variable field of semantics: the literary themes, archetypes, symbols, and metaphors."[42]

Precisely here, however, difficulties arise which the hermeneutic concept of *Rezeptionsästhetik* cannot resolve.[43] Literary history shows that the "grammar" of genre, style, and mode is no more stable than the apparently variable field of "semantics" (themes, archetypes). Frequently it is even less stable, since themes, archetypes, symbols, metaphors, and myths often persist while the genre, style, or mode that introduced them undergoes transformation. Even within a definable historical period such as the Renaissance the "grammar" of genre, style, and mode changes completely, while the literary "semantics"—the cadre of themes, archetypes, conventional symbols, metaphors, and myths—persists into different periods. The norms of the epic, for example, vary widely from Boiardo's and Ariosto's kaleidossopic chivalric romances to Spenser's and d'Aubigné's sprawling historical allegories, and from Camoens's paean to the voyages of exploration to Milton's tightly organized drama of man's fall. On the other hand, many of Petrarch's favorite symbols and metaphors in the early Renaissance recur in the works of poets so different as Crashaw, Lovelace, Racine, and La Fontaine in the Baroque and Neoclassical ages.[44] The analogy to the linguistic model simply does not epitomize literary history any more than it does literary rhetoric.[45]

Here it is decisive to recognize the intercomplementarity of historical and rhetorical norms. No norm has meaning *in vacuo*. It acquires meaning only by relating to other norms and participating with them in still larger structures. In a particular text the rhetorical norms of voice and address interact and help to define the text's style. That style, in turn, may or may not complement the styles of other texts informed by similar rhetorical norms. If it does, then these norms may interact on a higher level where they come to define a particular modality referring to the theme, content, and author's attitude. Certain modal norms can in turn complement formal laws in whole groups of works where they come to define a particular genre. Each of these larger systems, then, achieves its own integration during a given historical period through a complementarity of norms governing voice and address in such a way that similar rhetorical devices characterize all the texts belonging to a particular system.[46]

The following chapters demonstrate the complementarity of these rhetorical norms in generating larger systems of genre, style, and mode on the one hand and in lending some relief to the course of literary history on the other. The first chapter focuses on the mode of the Petrarchan lyric as it is exemplified through the styles of Petrarch, Ronsard, and Sidney in their contributions to a subdivision of the Renaissance lyric, the fourteen-line sonnet. I begin with the concept of mode because it occupies a middle ground between the concrete particularity of style and the abstract generalization of genre while raising issues pertinent to the rhetorical norms of both. The second chapter focuses on the style of Erasmus's *Praise of Folly*, More's *Utopia*, and Rabelais's *Gargantua and Pantagruel.* All three works participate in the mode of ironic discourse belonging to a genre neither purely narrative nor purely dramatic but mixed in its incorporation of dialogue, monologue, and narrative interchange; perhaps its best historical model is Menippean satire. The weighty problem of genre, however, will fill the third chapter, which addresses the generic problems of Ariosto's, d'Aubigné's and Milton's major poems. Though the mode of Milton's sacred epic would seem radically different from that of d'Aubigné's polemical epic and the modes of both different from the mode of Ariosto's chivalric epic, all three epics, with their idiosyncratic styles, aspire to classical models.

It might be begging the question to assert at the outset that the transformations within all three systems of mode, style, and genre during the Renaissance are historically analogous, but in fact their norms seem to evolve in similar ways. The passage from one historical period to another can be defined by what happens in the rhetorical strategies governing each system, and a critical reading of the texts suggests that in their historical perspective these systems themselves are intercomplementary. Genre is, of course, the broadest classification, but within each genre there operate several different modes, while each mode is further characterized by works in several different styles. But the point at which style determines the norms of a mode or genre, or conversely, the point at which genre or mode determines style, is fluid. That fluidity, as well as the mutual dependence of larger systems upon rhetorical norms governing speakers and audiences, may be the clearest mark of their complementarity.

1

The Petrarchan Mode in Lyric Poetry

The Petrarchan sonnet unites in a single lyric modality the chief rhetorical attributes. Its *ethos* requires a split addresser whose voice as speaker differs from that of the author. Its *pathos* demands a split addressee whose function as fictive audience—usually the speaker's beloved—differs from that of the actual reader. Moreover, its long history from the fourteenth to the sixteenth centuries shows the accommodation of fixed modal characteristics to broad historical change. So narrow are its conventions, finally, that to many critics "Petrarchan" implies nothing more than a limited set of repeated themes and stylistic devices. A closer look, however, reveals that while Petrarchan diction, vocabulary, and elocutionary devices remain unchanged over whole centuries, other rhetorical strategies of voice and address distinguish individual poems, poets, and poetic movements and thereby define the mode more precisely.[1]

The Petrarchan speaker's rhetorical strategy of alternating and suspending contrarieties within his own *ethos* in fact generates structural transformations in each poem. His expression of joy and lament, hope and despair, certitude and doubt characteristically balance thesis against antithesis, statement against counterstatement, and reversal against counter-reversal, allowing a dialectical unity to evolve out of multiplicity through patterns of shading and contrast, challenge and fulfillment, assertion and negation. The result of such a rhetorical patterning is a careful structural proportioning of the poetic utterance into antithetically balanced words, phrases, lines, couplets, tercets, and quatrains, all combining to form antithetically balanced sestets and octaves.

This principle governs the major divisions in various ways. Frequently the largest structural units, the octave and the sestet, stand in symmetrical opposition, paralleling the speaker's tension between opposites. Thus, the tone, attitude, or impression registered in the octave corresponds to a contrasting tone, attitude, or impression registered in the sestet. At other times smaller structural units of the octave (two quatrains rhyming *abba*) or of the sestet (two tercets rhyming *cde*, or three couplets rhyming *cd*) play off each other and develop further nuances in the speaker's *ethos*. Whether the structural strategy is tripartite (quatrain-quatrain-sestet or octave-tercet-tercet) quadripartite (quatrain-quatrain-tercet-tercet, quatrain-quatrain-quatrain-couplet, or quatrain-quatrain-couplet-quatrain), or in irregular five-part or six-part divisions, the last element resolves the first, while the middle elements invert the terminal ones. The speaker's inner life might be so complex that contrasting nuances may mark off still smaller structural units (couplets within the quatrains, or, within the couplet, the first line against the second, or, within the single line, hemistich against hemistich). These nuances can control finally even single words, balancing adjectives against nouns or nouns against verbs. The figure of oxymoron inherent in these relationships thus establishes itself as the normative elocutionary strategy of Petrarchan poetry.

The relationships between speaker and audience are similarly complex. For Petrarch, one means of reinforcing them is through recurrent structures of multiple address. His addresses to the hills and the rills as metonymic landscapes of his soul, to images and memories as synecdochic projections of his mind, and to other objects or personages as direct or indirect audiences enable him to clarify his emotion in different ways for different audiences, circling in on his state of mind from a number of angles, articulating his attitudes with a dialectical tentativeness until he achieves resolution. To a large extent this use of multiple address also controls the distance or proximity between speaker and audience both inside and outside the poem. Its effect is perspectivistic as the speaker seizes upon an idea from a particular angle for one audience, abandons it for another, and tries to explain it a different way for a third.

Of course, there is nothing exclusively Petrarchan about these strategies; they exist in other lyric modes, and one might argue that it is misleading to designate them as norms for the Petrarchan sonnet. True, in poetry older than Petrarch's, especially the Latin lyric and Stilnovisti poetry, and in poetry later than Petrarch's, especially the Baroque lyric, an *ethos* of contrarieties does generate a field of contrasts, reversals, and antitheses. Likewise, a *pathos* mindful of perspectivistic distances between speaker and audience emerges through a rhetoric of multiple addresses. But in Petrarchan poetry these strategies become vehicles for attaining special insight into the moral nature of the speaker and his problem. In Propertius, Ovid, Catullus, or Horace, however, they seem by comparison gratuitous, ornamental, and generally random. Thus, Propertius's speaker in a *poeta-amator* who shares a love-hate relationship with his lady; and yet from first to last he remains submissive, even groveling, without experiencing his contrarieties in full force for very long.[2] In Ovid's love elegies, where the speaker plays the same conflicting roles, the organizing principle of the poetry reflects the ordered, witty, embellished narration of the problem without the sudden reversals that characterize Petrarchan poetry.[3]

Moreover, most Latin poems explore the powerful effects of direct address in only a limited way. Ovid restricts his addresses (if any) to the beloved or to an occasional friend. In a few poems Propertius's speaker transfers to multiple audiences some of his own tensions, as in I.xviii, where he intersperses hortatory addresses to Cynthia with plaintive addresses to trees and streams in the deserted grove he wanders through; or in II.v, where he begins and ends with an address to Cynthia that frames a self-address urging him to withdraw from the amorous yoke. Among other examples, Catullus calls upon "Lesbia," his brother, fellow poets, patrons, and even himself (in VIII.i and LXXVI.v), but within the framework of single poems he never shifts from one audience to another as Petrarch does. Horace tends to call upon one audience in the second person in order to speak about some other subject in the third person. Thus, in

I.xxii ("Integer vitae") the speaker addresses Fuscus in order to declare his love for Lalage. In I.xxiv he addresses a double audience—first Melpomene, then Virgil—in order to lament the death of Quintilius. And in I.xxvii he addresses first his drinking companions (*sodales*) with the story of the love-sick brother of Megilla, then the *miser* himself to offer direct sympathy. But he sustains none of these strategies the way Petrarch and other Petrarchan poets do throughout their entire body of poetry.

Among the sonnets of Petrarch's more immediate predecessors in the Dolce Stil Nuovo, divisions and turns of thought often suggest Petrarchan contrarieties, though they lack the deeper moral dimensions of Petrarch's. Sometimes they are only the merest mechanical contrivances, reflecting the sonnet's derivation from older canzone forms. Following Dante's suggestion in *De Vulgari Eloquentia*, Antonio de Tempo, an early theorist of the sonnet form (1332) and a younger contemporary of Petrarch, pointed to similarities between the sonnet and the canzone.[4] The latter's first two stanzas (generally quatrains) comprise the *fronte* (within which each stanza constitutes a separate *pes*), while a second pair comprise the *sirima* (within which each constitutes a separate *volta*). The sonnets of Giacomo da Lentini (fl. 1233–40) seem clearly divided according to the principles of the canzone. In one typical example the speaker addresses the beloved in the first quatrain recalling the first *pes*, and he initiates a comparison of himself to a butterfly: "Sí como 'l parpaglion, c'ha tal natura, / non si rancura di ferire al foco . . ."[5] ("You have made me like the butterfly, who has such a nature that he does not hesitate to plunge into the flames"). He then develops this comparison in the second quatrain/*pes*. Just as the butterfly does not hesitate to plunge into the brightly burning flame, so he says, in a trope conventional in later Petrarchan poetry, the lover meets his own destruction when he draws closer to his beloved: "come 'l zitello eo oblio l'arsura" ("like a child I forget the heat of the flames"). In the sestet he devises a new metaphor, but not in order to reverse the moral direction of his thought. The turn merely resembles the one from the canzone's *fronte* to its *sirima*. He will die in the flames, he confirms, in the tercet comparable to the first *volta*, but he will lose his life as the phoenix does, only to be born to a new life: "rendendo vita come la finise." For, he concludes in the second tercet/*volta*, love will awaken him, and the lady's beauty restore life to him as to the phoenix: "rendegli vita com'a la finise." In Giacomo's sonnet, therefore, we do not find the truly paradoxical play of opposites or oxymoronic balance of contrasts that characterize the Petrarchan modality; emphasis instead falls upon the aesthetic proportioning and harmonious balancing of parts.

Moreover, the speaker's brief address to his "gentil creatura" suggests how radically his relationships with the audience differ from Petrarch's. The conventional audience up to and throughout the Dolce Stil Nuovo is no more and no less than the speaker's beloved, a relatively impersonal, often uncharacterized *donna*. The only genuine experimentation with different modes of address comes in Dante's poetry. Of the twenty-six sonnets in *Vita Nuova,* eighteen have concrete fictive audiences, but only three are addressed to Beatrice (those in sections XIV, XV, and XVI). The other audiences range from lovers in general (III, VII, VIII, XXXII) and the *donne* associated with Beatrice (XXI, XXII, XLI) to the pilgrims passing through Florence (XL). One sonnet, "Morte villana, di pietà nemica" (VIII), even has a multiple audience: first Death, whom the speaker assails for attacking a young girl, and then those who do not merit salvation, to whom the speaker turns in exhortation at the end of the poem.[6] Still, these isolated examples are exceptions that prove the rule. However much Dante might stand out from his contemporaries in his rhetorical variety, he hardly exploits its potential for developing a relationship with his audience as do Petrarch and others.

A closer look at Petrarch's sonnets with a view towards their later influence on Renaissance sonneteers must acknowledge the speaker's many roles, which complement and complicate each other in their conflicts with his selfhood. The speaker is a courtier and a scholar, a man of affairs at the papal court of Avignon and a man of private sensibility for whom meditation, reflection, and the pursuit of letters at Vaucluse are equally important. He is also a lover by turns teased, rewarded, frustrated, and ultimately deprived of his beloved by her death. He is a Christian who learns resignation, and he is finally a poet who perfects the art of representing his condition. Of all the roles, however, those of poet and lover are most characteristic, and they determine all his strategies of voice and address.

Petrarch's *Canzoniere*

Continually throughout the *Canzoniere* Petrarch (1304–74) depicts his speaker as a poet. In the sequence's first form (1342), containing fourteen poems, both the initial sonnet (now XXXIV) and the second (now XXXV) deal with the themes of poetry; both probably were composed at Avignon between 1326 and 1336. In the second form (1348), the opening sonnet (now I) is also about poetry and was composed at Vaucluse between 1345 and 1347. Thematically these liminary poems emphasize the problems of style and stylistic development. In XXXIV ("Apollo, s'ancor vive il bel desio") the speaker begs Apollo, patron of the muses and lover of Daphne-turned-laurel, to protect his own laurel leaf, the "onorata e sacra fronde" emblematic both of his art and of his beloved Laura.[1] He characterizes himself however as a poet and lover in a simple linear manner similar to the way he also manages the sonnet's general structural movement. The octave merely states his plea, while the sestet elaborates it by comparing him with Apollo "per vertù de l'amorosa speme" ("by virtue of our amorous hope") and promising that he and the god will both view "with wonder" their *donna* sitting on the grass.

The next sonnet, "Solo e pensoso i più deserti campi" (XXXV), reveals a far more subtle self-portrayal with a more deliberate use of formal structure. Here the sestet not only elaborates the octave but answers it. The octave represents the speaker's desperate attempt to flee those who read his amorous dilemma, his role as a frustrated lover, in his very appearance: "di fuor si legge com'io dentro avvampi" ("from the outside one can read how inwardly I burn") By contrast the sestet offers a solution. In his new role as fugitive he will allow the mountains and woods to know the dilemma he hides: "sì ch'io mi credo omai che monti e piagge/e fiumi e selve sappian di che tempre/sia la mia vita ch'è celata altrui." Two lines later in the second tercet *Ma* reverses the argument. No matter how far he travels, the speaker finds himself always accompanied by Amor whose colloquy with him ("ragionando," composing poetry) is continual. This colloquy reasserts his roles as poet and lover, confirms the dependence of one upon the other, and guarantees the failure of his attempt to flee either. Thus, the tripartite stanzaic division allows for a more complex structural evolution than in the preceding poem, and it forecasts the essential form of Petrarch's later poems.[2]

The sonnet "Voi ch'ascoltate in rime sparse il suono" (I) exemplifies even better the mature style, with its inseparability of *ethos* and structure. The speaker refers to his own "vario stile" as an essential component of his art. By "vario stile" one may understand the range of tones, moods, and attitudes that play off one another in balanced patterns of statement and reversal, thesis and antithesis, resolution and dissolution. The fourteen-line structure beautifully captures such a varied evolution. The octave's long periodic sentence begins with an address to the audience, "Voi ch'ascoltate" ("You who hear"), balanced by a self-conscious digression in the first quatrain on the speaker's own "primo giovenile errore" ("first youthful mistake"); then it turns to the major premise, finally enunciated on the last line of the second quatrain: "spero trovar pietà, non che perdono" ("I hope to find pity, not only pardon").[3] The sestet's first word, *Ma*, already suggests a structural reversal. I see, the speaker confesses in a turn to the past, that I have been the subject of everyone's gossip for a long time. Against this admission of his past role he then weighs his present shame: "di me medesmo meco mi vergogno" ("within myself I am myself ashamed of myself"). The conclusion in the second tercet identifies whatever delights the world with a brief dream ("che quanto piace al mondo è breve sogno"). The "vario stile," as the speaker terms it, thus characterizes the sonnet's aesthetic structure as well as the speaker's own *ethos*, his inner structure of thought throughout the collection of his poetry. Furthermore, in the *Canzoniere* as a whole we can perceive just such a movement as the one from XXXIV to XXXV to I, from simplicity and linearity to "vario stile" in both structures.[4]

The speaker's relationship with his audience also becomes more complicated as the poetic mode matures. For example, in XXXIV the speaker addresses one fictive audience, Apollo, while in XXXV he implies, and in I directly states, a wider, intermediate class of readers, "Voi ch'ascoltate in rime sparse il suono." The earliest commentators on the *Canzoniere* were sensitive to the rhetorical complexity inherent in this kind of involvement with the audience. Remarks on it illuminate editions from Antonio do Tempo (1360?, printed 1475) to Ludovico Castelvetro (1545?, published in 1582).[5] The significance of XXXIV, for example, Filelfo (c. 1440, printed in 1476) interpreted as the speaker's inability to hide from his audience or retreat from full public view—"ciechi sono coloro iquali credano occultarsi nella discoverta luce" (25[V]). In XXXIV Fausto da Longiano (1532) underscored the speaker's pragmatic attitude towards his audience: whenever we wish to persuade someone, we must implore him with words that make it difficult for him to refuse ("Quando vogliamo inducere nella nostra sentenza alcuno, cerchiamo con tali parole pregarlo, che gli si disconvengo negare," p. 16).

Of all the commentators, Bernardino Daniello (1549) and Lodovico Castelvetro (1545?, published in 1582) were most sensitive to the implied audience. In his remarks on I, Bernardino claims that the rhetoric of introductions must be either straightforward or oblique (Ai). In the first case the speaker can succeed by skillfully characterizing his own persona, or that of his opponent, his audience, or whomever or whatever he is speaking about (Ai). Otherwise, he can involve his audience obliquely by preempting or upsetting whatever its members might be able to say ("quando si viene a preoccupar quello, che potriano dire gli auditori," Ai[V]). Thus in I, by blaming Love and his own youthfulness, the speaker circumvents his audience's protestation against the frivolity of his theme ("Preocupando

quello, che haverebbono potuto dir gli ascoltanti," Ai^V). Castelvetro, on the other hand, delineates the reader's involvement on
purely grammatical and rhetorical levels by calling attention to
the unusually complicated syntax of the octave's single long
period. The verb governed by *voi*, the poem's first word, is the
infinitive *trovar* on line 8. The space of eight lines between subject and infinitive ought to disturb the reader at the outset and
catch his attention (p. 2). Hence the poem's very grammar
points to the central rhetorical strategy of voice and address
controlling the entire sequence.

One could thus characterize the modality of the Petrarchan
sonnet by how it involves the reader in the speaker's evolution
of thought, feeling, idea, and attitude through multiple statements, shifts, and reversals within a formally limited space of
fourteen lines.[6] Throughout the *Canzoniere* these possibilities
of shift and reversal generate bipartite, tripartite, and even
quadripartite rhetorical divisions which usually parallel stanzaic
divisions into octaves and sestets or quatrains and tercets. In
the first quatrain of "Pien d'un vago penser che me desvia"
(CLXIX), for example, the speaker begins a quadripartite movement by confessing his paradoxical habit of always pursuing the
lady whom he ought to avoid ("pur lei cercando che fuggir
devria"). In the second quatrain he suggests that the lady herself is responsible for generating these contrarieties because she
is both "kind and cruel" and a "beautiful enemy of Love and of
me."[7]

The problem here is to determine just how much the speaker
is willfully projecting the role of *nemica* upon the lady by
fabricating these contrarieties within her, expressing his own
doubts explicitly in the first tercet ("if I do not err"). Still he
admits to discerning a ray of pity on the lady's dark, proud
face, which in part brightens his sad heart: "che'n parte rasser-
ena il cor doglioso." This turn leads to a new development in
the second tercet when he reveals his suffering: "allor raccolgo
l'alma, e poi ch' i' aggio/di scovrirle il mio mal preso consiglio"
("then I call my soul again, and just when I decide to reveal my
badly made choice . . ."). But just when he begins to speak, he

comes to a sudden dramatic halt: "I have so much to tell her that I do not dare to begin." And thus the poem ends with a last-minute reversal of all his expectations.

The open-ended conclusion permits several interpretations of the speaker's sudden lapse into silence. Among Renaissance commentators both Gesualdo (1533) and Castelvetro (published 1582) pointed to two different explanations. While Gesualdo recounts the popular assumption that the speaker retreats to the corners of his own imagination because he doesn't know where to begin expressing his love, Castelvetro portrays him as fearful of offending Laura by revealing too much of his love. Both possibilities are rich in expressive outlets. Whatever motivation, the speaker assigns himself roles that evolve from search in the first quatrain, to hesitation in the second, to encouragement in the first tercet, and then to a final reversal in the second. And accompanying this evolution is a poetic structure that registers various tones in sharply differentiated ways, from the slow halting monosyllables with long vowels in the first quatrain, to the more rapid, spirited pace of the second quatrain, and from the hesitant periodic syntax of the first tercet, to the gathering force and momentum of the second, concluding with the rapid reversal implied in the final words, "che 'ncominciar non oso."

In later poems the speaker's characterization engenders a series of complex transformations and inversions. Not only is he a poet and a lover, but he is also, after Laura's death, one who mourns his beloved, despairs of his own salvation, and even loses confidence in his craft as a poet. "Gli occhi di ch' io parlai sì caldamente" (CCXCII) is a good example of how he plays these roles simultaneously. In the words of Bernardino Daniello da Lucca (1541), the speaker here shows how he has become different from other people, distinct from the mob: "E fatto singular de l'altra gente cioè separato del volgo" (153). The octave's first seven lines catalogue poetic motifs used in his earlier sonnets. The eyes, arms, hands, feet, face, hair, and smile of his beloved, an extraordinary woman, govern the verb that finally appears on line 8: "poca polvere son che nulla sente" ("are now a handful of dust which feels nothing"). The sestet opens with a stark contrast. His beloved is dead, but the speaker remains alive, and his only task now is to weep and mourn: "et io pur vivo, onde mi doglio e sdegno." The speaker therefore lays his former poetic motifs to rest and bids them farewell. His amorous song is at an end, the vein of his imagination is dry, and his lyre is now turned to weeping.

Not only does the immediate condition narrated in the sestet, "Or sia *qui* fine," contrast with the earlier motifs enumerated in the octave, "Gli occhi di ch' io *parlai* sì caldamente" (The eyes of which I so warmly spoke), but a more subtle structure of contrasts within the octave also informs the poem. Of the seven motifs mentioned in four lines (1-2 and 5-6), the two qualities emblematic of the lady in the Dolce Stil Nuovo tradition, the eyes and the smile, appear first and last respectively as a frame for the other qualities. The more earth-bound physical featurres, "e le braccia e le mani e i piedi e 'l viso," provide matter for syntactic contrasts. In both quatrains the first two lines correlate the motifs with the conjunction *e*, while the following lines subordinate them in a dependent *che* clause. Indeed, the syntactic control contrasts oddly with a sense of faltering moral control that affects his *ethos*. The speaker has received a blow from which he has hardly recovered, and the effect is communicated by a syntactic cluster of verbs in rapid succession. The first appears on line 8, "poca polvere son," and is quickly followed by others in the initial tercet: "et io pur vivo, onde mi doglio e sdegno." The concluding verbs also occur closely linked in the second tercet: "Or sia qui fine . . ./secca è la vena . . ./e la cetera mia rivolta in pianto" ("Now let there here be an end . . . dry is the vein . . . and my lyre is now turned to weeping").

The poem's rhythmic patterning allows for a final structure of contrasts. The anapests of the octave ("e le braccia e le mani e i piedi e 'l viso") contrast with the iambs of the sestet ("in gran fortuna e 'n disarmato legno"); while the *a maiore* rhythm of the first quatrain contrasts with the *a minore* rhythm of the second, and the iambic regularity of the first tercet contrasts with the anapestic rhythms of both the octave and the second tercet. The anapestic rhythm of the poem's final line, "e la cetera mia rivolta in pianto," duplicates that of its second line, "e le braccia e le mani e i piedi e 'l viso." Throughout the poem a recurrent pattern of intralinear assonance abets the careful rhythmic patterning. The finely wrought texture of this sonnet, moreover, is not unusual among Petrarch's other sonnets. Its many layers of complexity are only typical of the interlocked orders that underline the Petrarchan mode.[8]

In groups of sonnets considered as a sequence, the rhetorical strategies of voice and address create other interlocked orders. Even the particular arrangement of individual poems within larger units can manipulate the reader's response to the text.[9] The question of response, however, is ultimately a question of the speaker's rhetorical relationship with his audience. That the work is "a work divided between the style of the moderns and the antique style" (XL), makes a strong demand upon its audience. While the speaker, as he claims, is creating a distinctive style for his audience, he is also creating a distinctive audience for his particular style. The strategy is not only to assign a fictive personality to the audience, but also to develop a system of relationships between the speaker and his audience, both of whom mediate between author and reader.

The Petrarchan speaker assigns two kinds of fictive role to his audience. The first is identifiable with some dramatic character within the poem, such as Laura, whom he addresses in thirty-four poems, or friends, whom he addresses in sixteen more poems, or personifications such as those of Amore (nine poems) or the speaker's soul (seven poems) or Death (six poems). Second is the nonspecified role of some more generalized audience such as *voi* (XXVI, LXXXVIII, CCXLVIII) or ladies (LXXXIX, CCXXII, CCCL), or inanimate objects such as certain aspects of nature (CLXI, CLXII, CCXLIII, CCCI), the sun (CLXXXVIII, CCXCI), the Po River (CLXXX) or the Rhone River (CCVIII), the lady's hand (CXCIX), the speaker's own hopes (CCCXX), his poetry (CCCXXXIII), and others. These fictive audiences imply some relationship between them and not only the speaker who addresses them but also the actual reader, who shares in their role. But the speaker's habitation of a persona entirely separate from the author who dramatized him in turn implies yet another important relationship, that between author and speaker. The author's presence finally implies an ultimate relationship with the reader. The latter is crucial in any rhetorical schema where poetry amounts to an act of communication between a real author and a real reader. One consequence is that the author maneuvers the reader to evaluate the speaker's character from the author's critical point of view. The reader joins the rhetorical scheme, and relates to the author, the speaker, and the fictive audiences, functioning with them, sometimes in an ironic conspiracy, sometimes at ironic odds.

Right from the beginning, therefore, every reader enjoys a special relationship with the fictive audience. The most frequently addressed fictive audience is Laura, the speaker's beloved; if not always explicitly evoked by direct address, she is usually implicitly so.[10] In some poems Laura's passage from explicit to implicit fictive audience or vice versa is clearly marked, as in "Lasso, ch' i' ardo et altri non mel crede" (CCIII). Without referring to any audience in the first quatrain, the speaker laments that everyone except Laura (indicated in the third-person pronoun) gives credence to his suffering: "ella non par che 'l creda, e sì sel vede" ("she does not seem to believe it, and yet she sees it"). Suddenly in the next quatrain the speaker shifts to the second-person pronoun and addresses Laura directly. Do you not, he asks, perceive the feeling in my very eyes? "Infinita bellezza e poca fede,/non vedete voi 'l cor nelli occhi mei?" ("Infinite beauty and little faith, do you not see my heart in my eyes?"). And for the rest of the poem he levels his complaint at Laura personally. In other poems, as in "S' una fede amorosa, un cor non finto" (CCXXIV), Laura appears as the explicit audience only on the final line:

> s' arder da lunge et agghiacciar da presso
> son le cagion ch' amando i' mi distempre:
> vostro, Donna, 'l peccato, e mio fia 'l danno.

[If burning from afar and freezing when near are the reasons

why I am distressed in love, yours, Lady, is the sin and mine
the punishment.]

Thus, though not evoked until the very end, she is clearly intended to hear the speaker's declaration of good intentions.

There are more oblique relationships between the speaker
and the fictive audience. Sometimes when Laura seems to be
playing no role in the speaker's meditation she is suddenly
addressed. Thus, in the famous "Movesi il vecchierel canuto e
bianco" (XVI), the pilgrim undertaking an arduous journey to
Rome to behold his redeemer's image on Veronica's veil dominates the octave and the first tercet. But in the second tercet,
after the transitional word *così* establishes all the preceding
words as the mere vehicle of an elaborate simile, Laura intrudes
unexpectedly as the object of a direct address:

> così, lasso, talor vo cercand'io,
> Donna, quanto è possibile in altrui
> la disiata vostra forma vera.

[So, alas, I sometimes go searching, Lady, as much as possible, your true desired form in others.]

The sudden appearance of Laura as the poem's fictive audience accomplishes the transformation from sacred to profane as
a grand coup de théâtre. Indeed, the speaker's words now
appear not as the holy meditation that the figure of the pilgrim implied, but as the recollection of a very secular amorous
experience. As the one who experiences the coup most dramatically, the reader is forced to regard the speaker's lament
from an unexpected perspective.

When the fictive audience is someone or something other
than Laura, the author enlists the reader for a different role.
Sometimes the audience becomes a metonymic extension of
the speaker himself, so that it complements and clarifies his
own role. In these cases the reader may be enjoined to act out
the dramatic situation. In CCVIII, for example, the audience
addressed on the first line is the Rhone River, "Rapido fiume."
Here the speaker draws a comparison between his own spiritual

gravitation (impelled by Love) to Avignon where Laura lives, and the river's natural course there: "notte e dì meco disioso scendi/ov'Amor me, te sol natura mena" (Night and day you descend with me full of desire to go where Love leads me, but where nature alone leads you"). However farfetched, the role brings the reader into the speaker's meditation in an intimate way.[11] By expanding the comparison the speaker contrasts the river's freedom to rush on to Laura's home against his own earth-bound weariness: "Vattene innanzi: il tuo corso non frena/né stanchezza né sonno." His own limitations, his *stanchezza* and his *sonno*, become crucial issues that he iterates on the poem's last line. Meanwhile he moves toward this conclusion when he enjoins his river-audience to stop where the "grass" ("l' erba" = laurel = Laura) is greener and the "air" ("l' aria" = "l'aura" = Laura) is serene. In the first tercet he then specifies the relationship between the river and Laura "ch' adorna e 'nfiora la tua riva manca" ("who adorns and covers with flowers your left bank").

The tone is now set for the final tercet. In it the speaker addresses his river-audience once more and asks it to kiss Laura's feet and act as an intermediary:

> Basciale 'l piede o la man bella e bianca;
> dille, e 'l basciar sie 'n vece di parole:
> Lo spirto è pronto, ma la carne è stanca.

[Kiss her feet or her beautiful white hand; speak to her and use kisses instead of words: The spirit is willing but the flesh is weak.]

The river becomes the intermediary in yet another sense as the receptor of the speaker's articulation. The poem's action in fact dramatizes the speaker's struggle with his articulation, a struggle metrically realized in the syncopated rhythms of the first lines: "Rapido fiume, che d' alpestra vena/rodendo intorno, onde 'l tuo nome prendi . . ." ("Swift river, which running turbulent from your alpine vein, whence you take your name . . ."). And though he concludes with the clear statement "Lo spirto è pronto, ma la carne è stanca," the words themselves are actually from the Gospel of Mark (14:38). Ironically they point to moral problems hovering in the background of the poem, indeed in the background of the entire *Canzoniere*. They suggest how flesh and blood imprison him in his love for Laura, and correspondingly how idolatrous is his love. The audience, then, by supplying an external reference to judge the problem, has enabled the speaker to begin confronting his own moral dilemma.

The implications are similar in poems where a number of different fictive audiences appear in a series of multiple addresses. Frequently such a series aids the speaker in clarifying his own problems. For example, in CCLXXV, "Occhi miei, oscurato è 'l nostro Sole" ("My eyes, hidden is our sun"), he first addresses his eyes to convince himself that even though Laura has ascended into heaven he will see her again where she awaits his arrival. Similarly, he addresses his ears and feet. With a structural shift in the first tercet, he distances himself from these audiences and frames a rhetorical question to argue his innocence regarding Laura's death: "dunque perché mi date questa guerra?" ("Why then do you confront me with this warfare?"). This question reveals an uncertain attitude towards both his audience and his role; even more, his antithetical imperatives in the second tercet, first to blame death, then to praise God who binds and unbinds, reveal uncertainty: "Morte biasmate, anzi laudate lui/che lega e scioglie, e 'n un punto apre e serra."[12] Ironically, however, this final equivocation restores some measure of control. It prepares for the poem's last line, where the speaker recognizes that joy might follow from sorrow: "e dopo 'l pianto sa far lieto altrui." Thus, the audience's participation becomes a key factor in the speaker's acceptance of Laura's death, and the multiple address adds an important dimension to the poem's meaning.

Even while Laura is still very much alive, the speaker uses multiple address to delineate his own frustrations. In the opening quatrain of "O cameretta, che già fosti un porto" (CCXXXIV), for example, he addresses first the *cameretta* and contrasts the way his room, formerly a refuge from the storm, is presently "a fountain of nightly tears." In the second quatrain he addresses his *letticciuol* and complements the shift of audience with a shift in tone. Here in the contrast between the way his bed had been a source of comfort, "O letticciuol, che requie eri e conforto" ("O little bed that was a repose and a comfort"), and the way Amor now bathes it with tears, "ti bagna Amor con quelle mani eburne" ("Love bathes you with these ivory hands"), the speaker becomes more insistent in his complaint. First he involves his audience more closely in the action as the direct object of Amor's bathing (*"ti* bagna Amor)," and second he emphatically shifts the direction of Love's cruelty from *ti* to *me* on the final line of the octave: "solo ver me crudeli a sì gran torto" ("cruel to me alone, so unjustly"). In the sestet he attempts to flee not only from the solitude of his bedroom, but also from himself and his thoughts. Metrically he emphasizes *fuggo* by positioning it as the first word of the tenth line, where it is followed by a strong pause: "Nè pur il mio secreto e 'l mio riposo,/fuggo, ma più me stesso e 'l mio pensero." But he reserves a final surprising reversal for the last three lines when he announces that he will seek his refuge in the crowd, formerly alien and inimical to him. Vellutello in his Renaissance commentary (1525) remarked how elsewhere the speaker explicitly disdained the common crowd: "quello che in altri luoghi ha detto fuggire" (18). The reversal now is so strong that in order to bolster his credibility he appeals to a third audience implicit in the interrogatory exclamation "chi 'l pensò mai?":

> e 'l vulgo, a me nemico et odioso,
> chi 'l pensò mai? per mio refugio chero:
> tal paura ò di ritrovarmi solo.

[And for my refuge I seek, who would ever have thought it?, the crowd, hostile and hateful to me, such fear do I have of finding myself alone again.]

Thus, by addressing a series of three audiences the speaker announces his frustrations ("O cameretta"), emphasizes them ("O letticciuol"), and gropes toward a resolution ("chi 'l pensò mai"). And through each successive shift he provides a new perspective on his emotional life and its complexities.

Sometimes the speaker moves through a series of multiple audiences, finally evoking Laura as his ultimate audience.[13] In the sonnet after her death "Or ài fatto l' estremo di tua possa" (CCCXXVI), he first addresses *Morte* in sharply accusatory tones with the rebuke that Death has despoiled the kingdom of Amor: "Now you have exercised the worst of your power." The fourfold repetition of "or ài" in the octave (lines 1, 2, 3-4, 5), the broken staccato rhythms on the third and fourth lines, two enjambments on the second and third lines, and the clipped economy of four paratactic sentences all convey the agitation in his voice. Nor are the speaker and Amor the only victims of Death's action, for the plural *nostra* (*vita*) on line 5 suggests a potentially wider audience and expands the circle of Death's victims to include everyone. Thus, not only Death but also all Death's victims constitute a second audience. A radical shift in tone follows in the seventh line, however, as the speaker tempers his emotion. Now he taunts Death with the recognition that it has claimed only Laura's bare bones, while Heaven has the rest; he heightens this irony as he passes into the sestet, with no pause from the seventh to tenth lines:

> ma la fama e 'l valor che mai non more
> non è in tua forza: abbiti ignude l' ossa;
> ché l' altro a' 'l cielo, e di sua chiaritate,
> quasi d' un più bel sol s' allegra e gloria.

[But fame and valor which never die are not in your power; you have the bare bones, for heaven has the rest, and with its splendor it rejoices and does glory in itself as with a fairer sun.]

Here the rhythm of line 7 expands *a maiore* in marked contrast with the *a minore* rhythms of the six opening lines, and as a beautifully managed periodic complexity enriches the syntax, the verse attains its full harmony. Reaching a momentary resolution at the end of the first tercet, the speaker solves his problem in the final tercet by turning to a new audience, to Laura

herself, the victor over Death and now an "angel novo" recent-
ly arrived in heaven:

> Vinca 'l cor vostro in sua tanta vittoria,
> angel novo, lassù di me pietate,
> come vinse qui il mio vostra beltate.

[May pity for me conquer your heart in such great victory,
my new angel, in heaven, just as here below your beauty
conquered me.]

In his Renaissance commentary, Gesualdo appropriately noted
here the speaker's first direct address to Laura since her death
(350). The new address generates a transposition in tone and
attitude. The poet hopes that "di me pietate" will win over her
heart just as her beauty has won over his. With the sharp contrast between Laura *lassù* and the speaker *qui*, between her
heart and his, and between his wish that pity *may* conquer
("vinca") and the reality that her beauty has already conquered
("vinse"), the speaker attains equilibrium. The shift of address
from Death to Laura, now an "angel novo," thus signals the
resolution and effectively enforces it.

The eventual return to Laura as the poem's final audience
suggests one last rhetorical aspect central to the modality of the
Petrarchan sonnet. Laura is an audience who dominates the
entire sequence, even when not directly evoked. She is critic
and judge presiding over the speaker's performance. But if the
speaker assigns her these roles, the author assigns the actual
reader coextensive ones. Early in the sequence he enjoins the
reader to gauge Laura's sentiments, indeed even to adopt them
outright in the poems addressed to her as a fictive audience. He
also enjoins the reader to share her moral perspicacity by judg-
ing the speaker explicitly as she does implicitly.[14] For just as
Laura's roles as critic and judge come to dominate her role as
beloved, so the speaker's role as man of many failings, a role
indicated as the very beginning of the sequence in his cry
"favola fui gran tempo" (I, 10), comes to dominate his roles
as poet and lover. And the author of the *Canzoniere* not only
records this drama but also presses the reader to judge the

speaker's *ethos* from the viewpoint of Laura, his major fictive audience. This viewpoint moreover is fully congruous with the author's.

The role that the author asks the reader to play vis-à-vis the speaker is identical, then, with the role of Laura, the chief fictive audience. The poet involves the reader in a dialectic affecting his relationship to the poem both as a performance and as an artifact. This dialectic characterizes Petrarchan poetry at its best. It operates even in poems with no explicit fictive audience. In "Or che 'l ciel e la terra e 'l vento tace" (CLXIV), for example, there is none, and yet the reader is drawn into the author's conspiracy against the speaker.[15] This poem is archetypally Petrarchan not only in its perfect fusion of classical allusions (it echoes Virgil, Ovid, and Tibullus throughout key lines of the octave and first tercet), but also in its deployment of the dramatic motif of the lover's sleeplessness. Several major Petrarchists later appropriated this motif in one way or another, and I shall refer to some of their accomplishments in the pages on Ronsard and Sidney. Here, however, I would like to conclude my observations on Petrarch by pointing to the poem's synthesis of rhetorical strategies unifying speaker and audience, voice and address.

The octave turns on a contrast between nature's peacefulness at night and the lover's inner restlessness, a contrast that stands unresolved rhythmically, grammatically, and syntactically at the end of the second quatrain. The speaker juxtaposes the calmness of three of nature's four elements—earth and the animals that inhabit it immobilized in sleep; air and the heavens covered with the starry train (the line echoes Tibullus 2.1. 87); and water and the sea in waveless repose—all against the turbulence of the fourth element, fire—specifically the fire of passion within him: "vegghio, penso, ardo, piango, e chi mi sface/sempre m' è inanzi per mia dolce pena" ("I see, I think, I burn, I weep, and she who undoes me is always before me as my sweet torment"). The rapid succession of the four active intransitive verbs conveying this turmoil provides in turn a foil to the slowly unfolding paratactic period of

the first quatrain where each line ends with the statement of
a single verb ("tace ... affrena ... mena ... giace"). The first
and last words of lines 7 through 8, *guerra* and *pace*, finally,
indicate the oxymoronic contrarieties and antithetical conflicts which the speaker as lover experiences inwardly: "guerra
è il mio stato, d' ira e di duol piena, / e sol di lei pensando ò
qualche pace " ("My state is warfare, full of wrath and grief,
and only thinking of her do I have some peace").

In contrast to the literal statement of the octave, the sestet
turns on two similes, both of which heighten the speaker's
irresolution. In the first, like a source of sweet and bitter
water, the hand of Laura cures and irritates him; here the classical allusion is to Ovid's *Remedia amoris* 44:

> Così sol d' una chiara fonte viva
> move 'l dolce e l'amaro ond' io mi pasco;
> una man sola mi risana e punge.

In the second, like a storm-tossed sailor who fails to reach
port, the speaker dies and is reborn a thousand times each day;
here the word *salute* with its moral and religious overtones
conveys fitting gravity:

> e perché 'l mio martir non giunga a riva,
> mille volte il dì moro e mille nasco:
> tanto da la salute mia son lunge!

> [And so that my suffering may not arrive on shore, a thou-
> sand times daily I die and a thousand times I am reborn;
> so far am I from my salvation.]

Thus, the speaker confirms his essential moral folly. Yet the
reader participates in this admission, following all the proclama-
tions, all the turns, all the hesitations. The reader comes to
appreciate the distance that he ought to maintain between himself and the speaker. From Laura's perspective the speaker is
following a reckless course of action and the reader must weigh
each of his words with caution. Only by adopting Laura's perspective will the reader attain what the author wishes: a moral
judgment of the speaker's folly and error.

All the poet's artistic distance and proximity, finally, only serve to heighten the central Virgilian echo of the sonnet's opening lines (*Aeneid* IV, 522–31: "Nox erat, et placidum carpebant fessa soporem . . ."). Here, as Bernardino Daniello da Lucca saw in 1541, by imitating lines associated with Dido's passionate noctural soliloquy, Petrarch deepens and dignifies the tone of his own speaker's lament: "Quanto sia grave, misero, i inquieto lo stato de gli amanti descrivendone" (II.97). Manipulating the rhetorical means of the Petrarchan poem is a poet in control of his craft, capable of making and handling allusions to the Classical and Christian traditions and of transforming all that he approaches into a creative moral synthesis that is at once definitive and artistic.

The moral dimension of this synthesis would often be lost in the later development of the Petrarchan mode, and certainly many minor quattrocento poets would trivialize it beyond recognition. But it is at any rate integral to the strategies of voice and address through which Petrarch created and rendered so effective his own poetic mode. If later generations saw only the technical finesse in Petrarch's poetry, there was still no guarantee that they would be able to reproduce it. The inextricable union of character and audience, the one mirroring the other and contributing to its aesthetic advancement, is Petrarch's particular art and his legacy to the lyric tradition that sprang from the *Canzoniere*. Aside from the purely formal features of the fourteen-line sonnet, it is this union which gives the Petrarchan mode its distinctive quality.

Ronsard's *Les Amours*

While it was easy to select "Or che 'l ciel" as typical of Petrarch's poems, no single sonnet exemplifies Ronsard (1524–1585). The reason stems partly from Ronsard's more varied and extensive corpus of poetry and partly from his changing attitude towards voice and address. In the early decasyllabic poems addressed primarily to Cassandre (*Les Amours*, 1552–53), where he focuses on the attainment of balance, harmony, complex musicality, and mythopoetic precision, there is very little characterization of the speaker and almost no sense of an immediate audience. In the later sonnets composed in alexandrines and addressed to such diverse audiences as Marie (in the *Continuation des Amours*, 1555, and the *Nouvelle Continuation des Amours*, 1556), Sinope (*Le Second Livre des Meslanges*, 1559), and Astrée (*Sonnets pour Astrée*, 1578), there is substantially more characterization of the speaker, but still not very much sense of an immediate audience. In the *Sonnets pour Hélène* (1578), however, the characterization of both speaker and audience is strong and their interaction is fully explored.

Ronsard's adaptation of the Petrarchan mode reflects his changing attitude towards voice and address. In the liminary sonnet of the *Continuation des Amours* (1555), the speaker addressed his friend and fellow poet, Pontus de Tyard, expressing frustration over the audience's reception of his poetry. His previous compositions, presumably those in the first *Les Amours*, the public judged too difficult; his more recent poetry, presumably the *Continuation des Amours*, it judges as too low and undistinguished.

> Thiard, chacun disoit à mon commencement
> Que j'estoi trop obscur au simple populaire:
> Aujourd'hui, chacun dit que je suis au contraire,
> Et que je me dements parlant trop bassement.[1]

He devises two figures for this audience: one is a "monstre testu, divers en jugement" ("a many-headed monster, varying in its opinion"), which forever resists his best approaches; the other is a Proteus which may yield to the poet's constraints: "De quel estroit lien tiendrai-je, ou de quels clous,/Ce monstrueux Prothé, qui se change à tous cous?" He concludes that Tyard's stoic resignation to their intractability is healthy: "Paix, paix, je t'enten bien: il le faut laisser dire,/Et nous rire de lui, comme il se rit de nous" ("Peace, peace, I hear you: we must let them speak their opinion, and we must laugh at them as they laugh at us").

In the *Elégie à son livre*, published in the *Nouvelle Continuation des Amours* (1556) and printed as the introduction to the

Second Livre des Amours after 1560, however, he arrives at a more important accommodation with his audience. Despite its private genesis, his work lies in the public domain and it acquires a real existence only when an audience responds to it. As an event, it becomes the property of others who comprehend it from the horizons of their own understanding; as his own personal utterance it is like a breath of wind, always in motion and never returning to its origin. Thus, the speaker addresses his own book, echoing Horace's *ars poetica* (*Ad Pisones* 390):

> Quand tu seras party, sans jamais retourner,
> Il te faudra bien loing de mes yeux sejourner,
> Car ainsi que le vent sans retourner s'en vole
> "Sans espoir de retour s'echappe la parole".
>
> [5-8]

By the same token, however, Petrarch's poetry can become his. Purists will object that he violates the Tuscan poet's thematic norms by not honoring one woman in a single elevated style, and by singing of many women in several different styles. No matter, says the speaker. He is responding to the poetry as but one audience: "Je suis de tel advis, me blasme de ce cas/Ou loue qui voudra, je ne m'en soucy pas" (65-66) ("This is my opinion: whoever wishes may blame or praise me in this matter, I don't care"). Ronsard's adaptation of the Petrarchan mode is thus a difficult and complex matter to assess. It amounts to much more than the appropriation of elocutionary devices inherent in diction, tropes, and other verbal figures; it concerns instead the rhetorical methods that we investigated in the *Canzoniere*. In his adaptations, therefore, we must see how Ronsard achieves a union of external structure and internal rhetoric in a way that carries a definition of the Petrarchan mode and its history a step further.[2]

As an archetypal sonnet, perhaps "Pren cette rose aimable comme toy" best illustrates Ronsard's technique. Although he first published it in *Le Septiemme Livre des Poèmes* (1569), he later included it among the Cassandre poems of the *Premier Livre des Amours* in every edition of *Les Oeuvres* after 1571.

He continued to revise it for each edition of *Les Oeuvres* (1572-73, 1578, 1584), until the posthumous edition of 1587, when Muret, his commentator, wrote, "Ce Sonnet n'a besoin de commentaire."[3] It is thus a late sonnet in Ronsard's canon, and yet it nonetheless accords in mode and style with the earlier sonnets.[4] The association is understandable because its decasyllabic verse form harks back to the decasyllables of the first *Les Amours* (1552-53), even though Ronsard had long since turned to alexandrines after *Le Bocage* (1554). Despite its retreat from the later verse form, however, it displays the full rhetorical complexity of the mature poems. In this discussion I will follow the earliest text of the poem.

Structurally the sonnet's quatrains and sestet anticipate modulations in the speaker's rhetorical character and in his distance from the central fictive audience, the beloved. In the first quatrain he urges her to accept the rose, which he compares to her in beauty. Here the neatly parallel verses enforce the coherence of the stanza and the seeming simplicity of his intent, and they lend weight to the *pathos* of his request. In the second quatrain he repeats the request and adds a new element: accept the rose, he urges, and also accept "my heart which has no wings at all." With the poem's inward turn comes an accompanying shift in tone from the hortatory toward the expository and argumentative. In the later versions (1584-87) he accelerates this turn by exclaiming the effect on himself of the beloved's first fragrance; thus "Qui sers de Muse aux Muses & à moy," which in the original version preserves the parallelism of verses ("Qui sers de rose . . . /Qui sers de fleur . . . /Qui sers de Muse . . ." becomes "Dont la senteur me ravist tout de moy," which calls attention to his own inner attitudes (1584-87). The latter motif in turn comes to dominate the second quatrain, for there the speaker argues that his heart has suffered a hundred cruel wounds from its fidelity to the beloved: "Il vit blessé de cent playes cruelles,/Opiniastre à garder trop de foy." On the ninth line, however, he turns from the comparison between the lady and the rose to a comparison between himself and the rose. His tone becomes yet more argumentative:

La rose & moy differons d'une chose,
Un Soleil voit naistre & mourir la rose,
Mille Soleils ont veu naistre l'amour
Qui me consome & jamais ne repose.

[The rose and I differ in one respect. A single sun sees the
rose be born and die; a thousand suns have seen new-born
the love which consumes me and which never relents.]

Setting the life-span of the rose against the longer life-span of
his fidelity to the lady, the speaker solicits pity for his own
amorous fate. In the final lines, with an implied turn to a new
audience, he laments that his suffering has outlived the rose: if
only it had pleased God that his love, and hence his suffering,
had endured no longer than a single day: "Que pleust à Dieu
que telle amour esclose,/Comme une fleur, ne m'eust duré
qu'un jour."

The speaker has thus subtly shifted the focus from the beloved
to his own inner self. The rose remains at the center of the
sonnet, but it acquires a new rhetorical significance. He considers it no longer an emblem of his own amorous agony, but
an expression of his own character. This expression leads
directly to the final unflattering exclamation that he doubtless
intends his beloved to overhear. Is she really worth all that he
has suffered for her? Perhaps, but the final ambiguity prevents
any certainty.

Most striking about the sonnet in its full performance is the
speaker's gradual modulation of tone from the laudatory opening to the deprecatory conclusion. The use of the familiar
address only heightens this tonal ambiguity. In his poems to
Cassandre, Ronsard generally employed the *tu* form in keeping
with conventional poetic usage for addressing gods or superior
beings. By the time he wrote this sonnet, however, he had
begun to employ it as the form for ordinary familiar address.
The effect of the reader's not knowing at what level the speaker
assesses his *toy* is witty. At least in the case of this sonnet,
Ronsard's wit betrays the influence of the newly renascent
Greek and Roman classicism, particularly the epigram, the

poetry of the *Greek Anthology*, and the Latin elegy.[5] Here Ronsard differs sharply from Petrarch. Moreover, especially after 1555, Ronsard grafts on to the essential Petrarchan rhetorical strategies others from the Neo-Latin poetry of Marullus, Jean Second, and Navagero in the fifteenth century, the vernacular poetry of the Italian Petrarchisti in the quattrocento, and the vernacular poetry of Marot, Scève, and Saint Gellais in his own century. The result is that though Ronsard participates in the Petrarchan mode, he does so with several differences.

The major difference is in tone. In Petrarch it is varied though never discordant, and the final thematic element usually resolves the initial one. In Ronsard the central shift in tone is often so extreme that the final element completely inverts the preceding ones. This radical inversion of the speaker's attitude, however, does not necessarily derive from a more complex characterization on his part, at least not in the early poems. There the speaker is much less mature than his counterpart in the *Canzoniere*. Whereas the latter usually draws complicated contradictions into some sort of oxymoronic unity, pointing to a moral capacity for discipline and restraint, Ronsard's speaker either experiences no such inner contradictions, or else he allows himself to pass without remorse from one attitude to its opposite. In later poems Ronsard would elaborate the characterization of his speaker, and in the *Sonnets pour Hélène* he would manage a complex relationship between him and the audience. But even then he would seldom fabricate structures with multiple inversions. His sonnet pivots only on one crucial turn, while Petrarch habitually allows minor reversals of tone and attitude to modify further his central shift of thought.

A good example is one of Ronsard's sonnets from the first *Les Amours* (1552), "Qui vouldra voyr dedans une jeunesse" based on Petrarch's "Chi vuol veder quantunque po natura" (CCXLVII). In Petrarch the speaker urges whoever would see Laura to come soon, affirming that the observer will weep forever if he arrives too late. There may be some ironic weight to Gesualdo's assertion that the speaker is less concerned about forecasting Laura's mortality than about demonstrating the adequacy of his own style and his claim to poetic talent: "havendo invitato color a cui peradventura parea errante forse il suo stile in loder M.L. che à veder l'andassero" (294). In any case, a genuinely ironic perspective in Petrarch's sonnet renders Laura's earthly beauty ambiguous and problematic.

Ronsard pursues a different rhetorical route. His sonnet begins with an invitation, "Qui vouldra voyr" ("Whoever would see"), centers in an assertion, "De ceste Dame oeillade la beaulté,/Que le vulgaire appelle ma maistresse" ("he should regard the beauty of this woman whom the crowd calls my mistress"), and concludes with two predictions which are laudatory rather than foreboding, oriented towards compliment rather than moral vision: "Il apprendra comme Amour rid & mord . . . /Puis il dira voyant chose si belle . . ." ("he will learn how Love smiles and bites, . . . then seeing such a beautiful thing he will say . . ."). If the speaker's motivation for offering praise and compliment is straightforward and simple, so too is the structural strategy of his poem, which never ventures beyond a simple contrast. Thus, the major assertion, located at the poem's exact midpoint, acts as a fulcrum between its first and last parts. The hypothesis dominating the octave allows the speaker to effect a parallel between the quatrains by beginning each with "Qui vouldra voyr." The conclusion, in turn, filling the sestet, allows him to pair a couplet that predicts what the observer will soon learn, "Il apprendra, . . ." with a quatrain that predicts how the observer will respond, "Puis il dira. . . ." These parallelisms and repetitions contribute above all to the linearity and *a legato* musicality of the sonnet's structure.[6]

Even when he later revised his work, Ronsard tried hard to preserve its original musicality. He managed to do so a quarter of a century later, when for the edition of 1578 he changed this sonnet's last four lines to suggest a more philosophical self-awareness in the speaker's voice. The new ending emphasizes the paradoxical presence of heavenly beauty on earth:

> Puis il dira, quelle estrange nouvelle!
> Du ciel la terre empruntoit sa beauté,

La terre au ciel a maintenant osté
La beauté mesme, ayant chose si belle.

[Then he will say, what a strange new thing! That earth should borrow its beauty from heaven, that in having something so beautiful, earth has now taken beauty itself from heaven.]

The movement from earlier emphasis on figures of words (punning, echoes, forms of verbal wit) to later figures of thought (irony, paradox, other forms of conceptual wit) shows the direction Ronsard's work would take over the years, both in composition and revision.[7] Still, the speaker's mature characterization does not alter the balanced symmetry of the earlier version in any way. One could conclude that Ronsard's penchant for structural parallelism usually overrides his concern for achieving serious moral effect. Balance and harmony of form remain his key preoccupations.

The movement of Ronsard's interest away from verbal towards conceptual wit dominates his later career. A typical example is "Sinope, baisez moy: non: ne me baisez pas," which originally appeared in the *Second Livre des Meslanges* (1559). Since *Le Bocage* (1554), Ronsard had been using the alexandrine meter to deepen the flavor of his distinctive style. The bantering to and fro movement of the full, rich alexandrine line is traceable to classical topoi from Theocritus's idylls and Propertius's elegies. Remy Belleau asserted that the sonnet's particular beauty owes to *gentille* repetitions and contrasts: "Ce Sonnet est des plus beaux que se puisse trouver, pour estre tout plein de gentilles repetitions contraires." Here the play of mannered oppositions begins in the octave with borrowings from Ronsard's neo-Latinist contemporary, Jean Second. The strategy is to issue a request, then immediately to revise it for one better. The speaker asks the lady to kiss him, then recants and asks her instead to draw out his heart with her sweet breath: "Sinope, baisez moy: non: ne me baisez pas,/Mais tirez moy le cueur de vostre douce halene." He recants a second time and asks her to suck out his soul. And in the next quatrain he changes his mind once more. At this point the unusual latinate diction (*semblance, demeine, feintes*) and syntactic obscurity complicate the expression:

> Non: ne la sucez pas, car apres le trespas
> Que seroi-je, sinon une semblance veine,
> Sans corps de sur la rive où l'amour ne demeine,
> Comme il fait icy haut, qu'en feintes, ses esbas.

[No, don't suck it out, for after death what would I be if not an empty shade without a body on the shore where Love (as it does up here) conducts its revels only in shadows.]

This complexity seems alien to the idiomatic directness and colloquial simplicity of the poet who in the *Suravertissement* of his *Odes* (1550) vigorously defended "le naif dialecte de Vandomois," after the example of "tous les poëtes Grecs, qui ont ordinairement ecrit en leurs livres le propre langage de leurs nations."[8]

It is short-lived, however. The speaker opens the sestet with a new strategy from classical poetry, in this case by adapting the *carpe diem* argument from Catullus (*Carmen* V). The twist that Ronsard gives the topos comes in a single stark metaphor where the sleep of death becomes an iron thread that pierces eyelids and sews them tight; the metaphor derives from the practice of binding the eyes of young hawks in training for falconry: "Amour ne regne point sur la debile trope/Des morts, qui sont sillez d'un long somme de fer." The binding is doubly appropriate, for in addition to consigning the dead to eternal sleep, it blocks the conventional access of love "through the eyes." So strong is the speaker's conviction that Amour does not dwell in the realm of the underworld that he goes on even to revise the myth of Pluto's love for Proserpina.[9] According to his own conception, no infernal god or creature could ever feel love for another: "Love would not know how to live among the dead in hell."

The grotesque turn that the speaker's wit takes in this poem is indeed atypical of Ronsard's poetry, but it does suggest the more complicated representation of his character that recurs in later poems. Its forceful imagery evokes the speaker's inner life, so that he seems to be evolving some sort of attitude towards death. And yet it does not complicate his character for sustained moral effect as in Petrarch's poetry. The effect is theatrically mannered, more apt to reveal the theme's decorative potential than its problematic consequences.

Similar concerns dominate the *Sonnets pour Hélène* (1578). This collection, along with *Sur la mort de Marie* and the *Sonnets pour Astrée* composed close on each other, represents the poet's first major contribution to the mode since the sonnets for Sinope (1559). Here the speaker characterizes himself in an intense, sometimes stormy relationship with a new beloved. He plays the customary role of the poet-lover, but he does so with a difference. Though his beloved is a young lady, he is now an older man. Yet while ironies of situation rendered in highly charged figurative language increase the sonnet's dramatic vitality, nothing in the drama shows the moral effect on the speaker of his debilitating love affair. The speaker proves in fact to be not the slave of his beloved but rather her equal in every way, matching insult for insult, scorn for scorn, and often with such subtlety that his annoyance is only barely perceptible.[10]

In "Je m'enfuy du combat, ma bataille est desfaite" the rhetorical structure of complaint and attack is highly subtle. At the opening the speaker acknowledges defeat in his lifelong battle against Amour; he is now too old to win the lover's game, and so he signals his retreat. Since he has always derived most of his poetic inspiration from Amour, he is implicitly resigning from the field of poetic activity. Thus, he begs Hélène to pardon his artistic flaws: "If your glory is not as perfect as I had wished, don't blame my spirit, blame my age". Ironically, he adds that he is only obeying the norm of nature in growing old: "Je ne suis ny Pâris, ny desloyal Jason:/J'obeïs à la loy que la Nature a faite." At the beginning of the sestet he explains more precisely how Amour has been a kind of muse for him. It has generated within him emotional (Petrarchan) antitheses that have sharpened his perception, intensified his feeling, and polished his verses: "Entre l'aigre & le doux, l'esperance & la peur,/Amour dedans ma forge a poly cest ouvrage" ("Between the bitter and the sweet, hope and fear, Love has polished this work in my own forge"). Then follows the reversal, which registers his changed attitude towards the audience. He now complains about himself and her proud heart: "Je me plains de moymesme & de ton fier courage." And in the poem's closing lines he reinforces his annoyance with her first by abandoning the present for the future tense (*repentiras*); then by qualifying it with a *si* clause, thus casting doubt on her willingness to repent; and finally by quoting a trite proverb, as though to affirm that her repentance would not be worth the effort anyway: "Tu t'en repentiras, si tu as un bon coeur,/Mais le tard repentir ne guarist le dommage" ("You will repent of this deed if you have a good heart, but late repentance does not heal the injury"). Far from suffering the consequences of his lady's disdain, he thus emerges as a victor over amorous circumstance.

Another major difference between Ronsard and Petrarch is in their use of direct address. Petrarch manipulates the reader into the fictive world of the sonnet in order to evaluate the speaker's moral performance; Ronsard never makes the reader a critic or judge. For one thing, he provides no sure center for evaluation, at least no such center as there is in Petrarch's sonnets. The ladies in Ronsard's poetry function as beloveds always and everywhere, indeed even to the point of monotony and colorlessness, and they never criticize or judge, as Laura does.[11] That Ronsard was able to eradicate the names of Sinope, Isabeau, Genevre, and Astrée or to interchange them with those of Cassandre or Marie when he integrated the later sonnets into the earlier cycles confirms their limited individuality.

The absence of specifying traits among the beloveds has a direct effect on their roles as fictive audiences, therefore, and with these limitations come others. Although Ronsard makes no critical demand on the reader to adopt the perspective of the fictive audience, he does require that the reader acknowledge the audience's lyric presence. The result is an evident appropriation of the central Petrarchan strategy with some narrowing restrictions. To be sure, there are the same Petrarchan devices—the direct address to a fictive audience, the shift from one audience to another, the use of multiple address—but the author's intention is not a representation of the speaker's moral character but rather an elegant, eloquent, often humorous portrayal of the speaker's amorous frustrations.

One example from the first edition of Les Amours in 1552 illustrates the point. I have already spoken of how in "Or che 'l ciel e la terra e 'l vento tace" (CLXIV) Petrarch manipulates the reader to judge the speaker's performance from Laura's high moral perspective. In "Or que le ciel, or que la terre est pleine" Ronsard uses no comparable strategy to achieve a poetic effect. Instead of devoting the octave to a description of nocturnal placidity vibrant with classical, especially Virgilian echoes as Petrarch had done, Ronsard evokes the coldness and harshness of winter, with its ice, hail, and rough winds. In the initial tercet, then, the speaker opposes the coldness of outer nature to the ardor burning within him: "Amour me brusle." In contrast to the moral urgency of Petrarch's addresses, Ronsard's speaker apostrophizes other lovers in the concluding tercet only to underscore his pervasive oxymoronic wit:

> Voyez, Amantz, comme je suis traitté,
>   Je meurs de froid au plus chault de l'Esté,
>   Et de chaleur au cuoeur de la froidure.

[See, lovers, how I am treated: I die of cold on the hottest of summer days, and of heat in the midst of winter.]

The spiritual overtones of Petrarch's plea for *salute* at the end of his sonnet have no valid place in Ronsard's secular transformation.[12] As Muret implied, the sonnet has no ethical valence: "Il est assez aisé de soy" (I.265).

The speaker's preoccupation with himself at the expense of his beloveds seems often throughout Les Amours to motivate his appeal to a larger, more inclusive audience than the ladies themselves.[13] Indeed, even when he directly addresses Cassandre,

Marie, Sinope, Isabeau, Genevre, and Astrée as fictive audiences, he represents them so ineffectually that he seems to be speaking past them to a public audience more attuned to his fine sensibility. In the *Sonnets pour Hélène*, however, he has no need to appeal to other audiences. There he incorporates his own subjective preoccupation into a remarkably objective dramatic representation of his last love affair. Hélène is certainly not so colorless as the other beloveds, but she is at various removes from the speaker, despite his ardent interest. This distance renders plausible her many minor betrayals, while it also affords him an excuse for retreat at the end of their affair.

A direct comparison with Petrarch will elucidate the point. The first ten lines of "Le Soleil l'autre jour se mit entre nous deux" from *Sonnets pour Helène II* rework an ambiguous narrative situation from *Canzoniere* CXV.[14] Petrarch's speaker finds himself competing for his beloved with Apollo, the sun god who rules over men and other gods and who himself loved a *laura*. Differences in rhetorical situation distinguish the two sonnets. In Petrarch the speaker contemplates the relationship between Laura and Apollo; suddenly in the sestet Laura smiles on him, and the sun god falls prey to jealousy. Recorded entirely from the speaker's perspective, with no direct address, Petrarch's sonnet conveys a straightforward, unambiguous sense of delight at the favorable outcome. In Ronsard, the speaker directly addresses Hélène and yet manages to remain aloof while registering his own bemused attitude about the way things turn out. The outcome of Ronsard's poem entails a complication unforeseen in Petrarch's. In the first quatrain the sun had been the rival for Hélène's attention, but dazzled by Hélène's "vive lumiere," it now retreats from the field of competition. In the second quatrain the speaker boasts directly to Hélène of his own victory in conquering the god because he now hears from his lady how much she prefers him to the other: "Quand regardant vers moy tu me dis, ma guerriere,/Ce Soleil est fascheux, je t'aime beaucoup mieux" ("Whenever looking at me you say, my warrioress, this Sun is tiresome; I prefer you much more"). The rhetorical shift to the direct report of the lady's speech reinforces the validity of the speaker's boast. He becomes, in effect, the audience of his own audience's address to him.

This form of self-preoccupation continues until the speaker abruptly discards his Petrarchan model: "Mais longuement cest aise en moy ne trouva lieu" ("But this happiness within me did not last long"). In the last three lines, he then laments that Hélène has subsequently shifted her affection to an attractive younger man without regard for his own earlier triumph. The reversal is ironic, certainly, but it is also crisp and facetious. In the address, the speaker conveys to his audience no great sense of loss, nor does he arraign the lady for her change of heart. The result is an uncertainty in his regard toward Hélène. Does he blame her? Himself? Fate? The sense of bemusement covers a variety of attitudes and lends strength to them all, and the poem ends in a state of ironic suspension as the speaker reflects on the course that events have taken: "You leave me all alone so that you might caress him".

In the Hélène cycle Ronsard intensifies his speaker's relationship to the audience through similar strategies of direct and multiple address. The effect is almost always comic, with sometimes an echo of brilliant Hellenistic irony, sometimes a twist of sardonic Roman wit. With the rueful humor comes a distancing of the speaker's perspective, at times a philosophical detachment. The attitude is one of poise and confidence, betokening an awareness of a gifted speaker addressing his beloved and several public audiences at the same time and secure in his relationship to each. It has now become a moral attitude, though not moralistic in any conventional Petrarchan sense with the Tuscan's emphasis on spiritual crisis and the discovery of self. It conveys instead the speaker's resignation to the situation, his triumph over the opinions of others, his acceptance of his own limitations and strengths with wordly grace.

This kind of poise calls attention to a substantial difference between Ronsard's earlier and later poetry. It finds its ancient parentage in the Anacreontics and the *Greek Anthology*, the latter published in the same year (1554) that the former was rediscovered by Henri Estienne. Ronsard's poetry more and more comes to evoke the tone of the Greek and Roman lyric, with slightly irreverent drinking songs and abundant reference to lightly erotic myths. His penchant for Anacreontic poems and the *Greek Anthology* had been noticeable since his sonnets for Marie in the *Continuation des Amours* (1555), and it comes into full maturity in the *Amours Diverses* of 1578. Ironically, as Ronsard veers away from mere Petrarchistic echo of tropes, topics, themes, and elocutionary devices, and as he approaches an original and creative evolution of his own vision, he comes closer to exploiting the dramatic and rhetorical spirit of Petrarch than any of his contemporaries in Italy or France. He does so by transcending the merely mechanical norms of diction and figures of speech that other poets mistook for the essence of Petrarchism. The norms that Ronsard respects are the central ones of voice and address that more surely affect the structure and rhetorical vitality of his poetry. Ronsard's career thus shows the systematic rejection of superficial verbal strategies in favor of a greater and deeper absorption of Petrarchan irony, antithesis, and contrast, fully achieved by the careful imitation of Petrarch's own rhetorical norms.

The high degree of involvement by the reader in fathoming the speaker's irony amounts to a final decisive difference between the rhetoric of Ronsard's *Sonnets pour Hélène* and that of his earlier sonnets, and it marks the climax of Ronsard's poetic development in the Petrarchan mode over a period of twenty-six years. In *Les Amours* (1552–53), *Le Bocage* (1554), and *Les Meslanges* (1554), his rhetorical strategy grants the reader a free field to explore his poetic counterpoints and musical harmonies without involving the reader in the role of his fictive audiences. In the poems to Marie and Sinope in *La Continuation des Amours* (1555), *La Nouvelle Continuation des Amours* (1556), *Le Second Livre des Meslanges* (1559), and to others in various occasional poems written between 1563 and 1573, *Sur la mort de Marie* (1578) and *Sonnets pour Astrée* (1578), the reader has a greater involvement, partly because the characterizations of speaker and audience are inherently more interesting than in the earlier poems, and partly because their relationships are more complex. In the *Sonnets pour Hélène*, however, the dominant rhetorical strategy fully identifies the audience, and it invites the reader to participate in the speaker's continuing relationship with that audience.

"Quand vous serez bien vieille, au soir à la chandelle" from the second book of the *Sonnets pour Hélène* (1578) offers one of the most celebrated examples of Ronsard's achievement in the Petrarchan mode. Its rhetoric carries one step further the relationships implicit in the *Canzoniere* and throughout Ronsard's career. The poem's audience, addressed as *vous*, is actually a double audience: the "you" in the future whom the speaker represents as an old lady, "sitting beside the fire, spooling and spinning," and "you" in the present whom the speaker invokes in the last two lines: "Vivez, si m'en croyez, n'attendez à demain:/ Cueillez dés aujourdhuy les roses de la vie." This "you" in the present is young and attractive, an object of the speaker's seduction; the "you" in the future is deformed and unhappy: "You will be an old woman crouched by the hearth, missing my love and sorry for your proud scorn".

Ironically, the image of the audience as "une vieille accroupie" contrasts dramatically with her own image of herself when she was young in words that the speaker assigns her: "Ronsard me celebroit du temps que j'estois belle." This contrast serves to motivate the urgent shift to present tense, "si m'en croyez," and imperative mood, "Vivez, . . . n'attendez à demain:/Cueillez . . ." at the end of the poem. Today soon slips into tomorrow, when youth turns into old age and old age into death. Thus the speaker exhorts his audience both now and in the future to forget her "fier desdain" and to enjoy her youth while she may. And by relating to his audience from these several points of view, addressing her first in the future, then in the present tense, and finally in a hortatory imperative, he applies the Petrarchan strategy of multiple address to his involvement with a single audience.

The supreme rhetorical achievement of this sonnet, however, is the speaker's own act of self-praise. When he foretells Hélène's exclamation, "Ronsard me celebroit," he is more than putting words into her mouth; he is creating a new rhetorical situation that brings yet another fictive audience into the poem. Thus, the servant who happens to overhear Hélène will praise her for the reputed beauty of her past youth and, more important, will praise the poet whose song rendered that beauty immortal.

> Lors vous n'aurez servante oyant telle nouvelle,
> Desja sous le labeur à demy sommeillant,
> Qui au bruit de Ronsard ne s'aille resveillant,
> Benissant vostre nom de louange immortelle.

[Then you will not have a single servant hearing such news already half asleep over her work, who won't spring awake at the sound of "Ronsard," blessing your name with immortal praise.]

The ironic contrast between his name, "Ronsard," and "vostre nom" reinforces the point that even in her praise of Hélène the servant is in effect according greater honor to the poet who celebrated Hélène. Ronsard will have, after all, the last laugh.

The poet's words are therefore full, rich, and potent. They have the power to immortalize Hélène in all her youthful beauty, to reveal her to the world at the height of her charms; they also have the power to suggest a pragmatic course of action which can mitigate for the poet the sadness of the "ombres Myrtheux" of the underworld and for Hélène the sadness of "Regrettant mon amour, et vostre fier desdain." They have the power finally to inspire awe and wonder in Hélène and in her eavesdropping servant and to bring the present affair to a happy conclusion. The poet's crafted art is capable of all this and more, as long as he handles his rhetorical strategies with grace, wit, and elegance.

Sidney's *Astrophil and Stella*

Despite its reputation as the first and most "continental" English sonnet sequence, *Astrophil and Stella* (1582, printed in 1591) incorporates three important Renaissance traditions untapped by sonneteers in Europe. First is moral satire, a characteristically English tradition reaching back from the "gulling" sonnets and interludes of the late sixteenth century through Gascoigne, Turberville, and Googe to Skelton and earlier medieval forms; reference to that tradition had surfaced already in *A Defence of Poetry* (1580), where Sidney (1554–86) cited as a satiric topic the "headaches a passionate life bringeth," and it emerges fully in the headaches of his own Astrophil.[1] The second Renaissance tradition, the humorous self-deprecation frequent in such classical ironists as Socrates, Ovid, and Lucian, was a product of European humanism, especially of the Northern Renaissance in France and the Low Countries; it made its way into England early in the sixteenth century. Exemplified in the work of Erasmus, More, and their circle, this playful, witty, sly, and provocative tradition turned earlier moral satire in upon itself, so that the person or object satirized was often none other than the speaker and his own code of values. The third Renaissance tradition developed an idea of practical rhetorical persuasion, traceable to Aristotle's emphasis on the dramatic immediacy of the rhetor's relationship to his own argument.

Aspects of this last tradition are of course central to Petrarch's and Ronsard's rhetorical strategies, as I have been arguing throughout this chapter, but the earlier poets were not so self-consciously aware of it, and neither had so much direct contact with Aristotle's rhetorical theories as Sidney had. Sidney probably translated into English two books, and possibly all, of Aristotle's *Rhetoric*.[2] He could not have failed to master its emphasis on the speaker's *ethos* as a "living voice" and the importance of achieving *pathos* through the right kind of relationship between the speaker and his audience. In Sidney's practical poetics these rhetorical concerns heighten the dramatic quality evident in *Astrophil and Stella*. They render a strong sense of time and place, story and action, dialogue and conversation, and in prosody they approximate as much as possible the norm of actual speech rhythms and the language of spoken discourse.[3]

Sidney therefore accommodates his use of balanced, patterned, ornate rhetorical language to vigorous and unadorned speech in a variety of styles that contrast oddly with continental Petrarchism. For example, the style of one of the finest (and most famous) poems in the sequence, "With how sad steps, ô Moone, thou climb'st the skies" (XXXI), is formal, balanced, and precise, although the poem records an experience full of frustration, unrest, and irresolution. Here the moon is an unrequited lover whom the speaker addresses in a similar role. This speaker regards Petrarchan love with much skepticism and protest, and he conveys his attitude in the initial quatrain with its exclamatory mood, punctuated three times by the insistent *how* ("With how sad steps, ô Moone, thou climb'st the skies,/How silently, and with how wanne a face"), with its interrogative mood, given a tendentious direction by the pointed use of the subjunctive "may it be" ("What, may it be that even in heav'nly place/ That busie archer his sharpe arrowes tries?"); and in the concluding sestet with its ironic, possibly subversive questions: "Is constant *Love* deem'd there but want of wit? . . . /Do they call *Vertue* there ungratefulnesse?"[4] The poem's central irony, however, is in the speaker's projecting his own feelings onto the moon, itself a conventional figure of inconstancy and, in any case, immune to the sentiments that he imagines.

The sonnet's hermeneutic problem involves the speaker's response to an attitude allegedly projected by an outside agent, the moon. Astrophil tries to explain the meaning of the moon's silent sadness from the horizon of his own understanding, through his own "long with *Love* acquainted eyes." He finds in the moon's erratic behavior "a Lover's case": "I reade it in thy lookes, thy languisht grace,/To me that feele the like, thy state descries." Thus, the speaker's rhetorical relationship with his fictive audience, the moon, complements and extends his dramatic relationship with Stella. As so often in *Astrophil and Stella*, the problems in this poem pose the same question: How does the reading audience relate to Stella, the ultimate fictive audience of the sequence? Within such a complicated rhetorical framework, the possiblities for developing an ironic attitude at the speaker's expense are many.[5]

Though Astrophil directly addresses the beloved in twenty-five out of the 108 sonnets, and other audiences in fifty-one out of the eighty-three remaining sonnets, he often ignores the audience. His primary concern is to express his own reactions to various situations. He portrays himself as he sees himself, and to the satiric author's delight, he does very much see himself. Both speaker and audience in one, he uses rhetoric that echoes in the corridors of his own self-absorbed imagination. In "Stella oft sees the verie face of wo" (XLV), for example, he depicts his beloved as an apt audience for a fiction about unrequited lovers: "Pitie thereof gate in her breast such place/That, from that sea deriv'd, teares' spring did flow." The recollection of her tears "drawne by imag'd things" impels him to shift in the final tercet from the third person to direct address when he urges Stella to interpret the fact, not the imagined fiction, of his own unrequited love for her: "Then thinke my deare, that you in me do reed/Of Lover's ruine some sad Tragedie." With the last line of the poem, he shifts address once more as he makes himself audience of his own tragedy. Dissociating himself from his accustomed selfhood ("I am not I"), he views himself as an other with a subjective request to "pitie the tale of me." Stella, for one, is surely incapable of registering the sympathetic response he demands. In this respect, as in several others with the same ironic issue, Astrophil proves different from earlier poetic speakers in the Petrarchan tradition. Petrarch's speaker and Ronsard's managed to view themselves from a more objective perspective than Sidney's does, but then Astrophil is much younger than those others, and he is more inclined towards folly, narcissism, and naïveté.[6]

A critical sense of these qualities emerges with stunning clarity in many dramatic situations. It would be wrong to impose a false consistency on Astrophil's character, however. The virtuosity of the sonnet sequence as a genre resides in its looseness of structure, in the gaps between lucid moments of poetry when the curious reader tries to find the links that join the poems. The sonnet writer does not guarantee those links will be obvious or predictable. Nowhere in the sonnet tradition, from Petrarch through Ronsard to Sidney and afterwards, is there an attempt to portray a single, unified set of characteristics associated with the particular speaker. In *Astrophil and Stella*, moreover, the thinly veiled biographical relationship between Astrophil-Sidney and Stella-Penelope Rich frustrates the attempt to construe the sequence as pure fiction.[7]

Still, the reader will miss out on a good deal of fun by not catching the speaker in moments of certifiable folly. Thus, in "Doubt there hath bene" (LVIII) Astrophil actually discovers himself to be an audience of his own poetry, interpreting it to suit his present frame of mind. Elsewhere he willfully distorts what he sees as though he understood reality as a book that lends itself to private explication. In "And do I see some cause a hope to feede" (LXVI), for example, he no sooner admits the impossibility of Stella's returning his love than he contradicts it: "And yet amid all feares a hope there is. . . ." In the next sonnet, "Hope, art thou true, or doest thou flatter me? " (LXVII), he confesses his free choice of understanding Stella's attitude in a wholly subjective way. Here he imagines the "speech" of Stella's eyes as a foreign language that he must translate: "Her eye's-speech is translated thus by thee:/But failst thou not in phrase so heav'nly hie? " Next he imagines it as a written text that he must interpret: "Looke on againe, the faire text better trie:/What blushing notes doest thou in margine see? " In both cases the speaker has willfully misinterpreted Stella's attitude. Admitting in the poem's concluding lines that an optimistic account of the evidence is surely erroneous, he nonetheless assents to it because it satisfies his own inner need for approval:

> Well, how so thou interpret the contents,
> I am resolv'd thy errour to maintaine,
> Rather than by more truth to get more paine.

At this moment, if not indeed earlier, he has fallen prey to the rhetorical delusion that he is his own poem's best audience.[8]

One result is his inevitable fall out of favor with the object of his imagination. The tortuous syntax of such later sonnets as "Griefe find the words" (XCIV) reflects his paralysis of will in taking decisive action after Stella's displeasure with him. The dramatic apostrophe to Grief, the repetition of simple words, the trailing knots of dependent clauses increase the tension of the second quatrain, while a profusion of phrases and clauses in the sestet leads to the poem's rhetorical conclusion without any release of the dramatic tensions that have accumulated. Stasis thus marks the poem's resolution both dramatically and rhetorically, leaving the speaker on the last line just as foolish, naïve, and narcissistic as he was in the first lines.

This characterization everywhere concurs with the English penchant for overt moralization even in lyric poetry. The elegantly Mediterranean stylization of Petrarch and *savoir vivre* of Ronsard did not appeal to Sidney and his Elizabethan readers as much as the moral criticism implicit in later medieval and early Renaissance exegesis of Catullus, Propertius, and Ovid. In this respect Sidney's rhetorical strategies point back to the classical authors more completely than Petrarch's ever did—especially according to the moralizing of them as foolish, obsessed lovers used as pawns and duped by their ladies but nonetheless choosing to repeat their past errors and allowing themselves to be duped once more. Hence, among the models for his speaker, Sidney uses the sensualists of Catullus, Propertius, and Ovid to a far greater extent than Petrarch or Ronsard had.[9]

While Sidney's speaker thus plays the roles of poet and lover as Petrarch's and Ronsard's speakers do, experiences contradictory emotions as they do, and struggles to express those emotions to achieve some inner self-awareness, ultimately he follows his classical predecessors in rationalizing his own and his beloved's actions, and in resting content with the facile resolutions that unmask his own moral levity. In "Vertue alas, now let me take some rest" (IV), for example, he shows that he is no humanist moral philosopher of the Epicurean sort when he addresses Vertue as a harsh and unremitting devotion to a rigid code. Nowhere in the sequence does he ever evoke the opposing ideal of virtue as sweet and pleasurable performance that links instinct to reason, a notion that figures prominently in the writings of Petrarch, Ronsard, and other Renaissance authors. Likewise, in "Reason, in faith thou art well serv'd" (X), he argues that his audience ought to have nothing to do with affairs of the heart and other matters that pertain to the senses: "Leave sense, and those which sense's objects be:/Deale thou with powers of thoughts, leave love to will." The sophistry stems from a faulty appropriation of the scholastic distinction between reason and will, and it clearly does not hold up to the facile conclusion which subordinates reason to Stella: "Reason thou kneel'dst, and offeredst straight to prove/By reason good, good reason her to love."

In addition to poems like the preceding, where Astrophil debates with personified abstractions like Virtue and Reason, others converse with a moralizing friend whom he addresses directly and berates for having offered unsolicited advice and criticism. The model is a Roman one which later Baroque poets such as Donne in "The Canonization" would exploit for dramatic effect. In "Alas have I not paine enough my friend" (XIV), for example, he complains to a friend that his own amorous torments are not bad enough "But with your Rubarb words yow must contend/To grieve me worse." In "Your words my friend (right healthfull caustiks) blame" (XXI), he uses mocking irony to argue against his friend's accusation that he is quick to write about the proper course of action but slow to undertake it, "quicke in vaine thoughts, in vertue lame"; that he reads Plato to no avail "but if he tame/Such coltish gyres;" that he betrays the "Great expectation" of his noble birthright by squandering his talent on lesser desires. Irony emerges most strongly in the sestet. There he argues that even though his friend may have superior philosophical awareness of rightness and propriety, he has no practical experience of Stella's real attraction:

> Sure you say well, your wisdome's golden mine
>> Dig deepe with learning's spade, now tell me this,
>> Hath this world ought so faire as *Stella* is?

Even more forthrightly through direct address, in "Pardon

mine eares, both I and they do pray," (LI) the speaker urges his
friend to peddle his advice elsewhere since he himself will never
renounce Stella:

> On silly me do not the burthen lay,
>   Of all the grave conceits your braine doth breed;
>   But find some *Hercules* to beare, in steed
> Of *Atlas* tyr'd, your wisedome's heav'nly sway.

The irony here is that Astrophil, by deploring the "grave con-
ceits" of his friend's high style, chooses to reduce his own work
to a "sweet Comedie" of low style in the final tercet. He
acquiesces to the compromise of his own best aesthetic intentions and dedicates his poetry to the service of wit, pleasantry,
and sophisticated buffoonery. In other poems ("The curious
wits, seeing dull pensivenesse," XXIII, and "Because I oft in
darke abstracted guise," XXVII) evidence exists that many of
Astrophil's associates have noted his erratic behavior and are
discussing its probable causes. For his part, the speaker argues
that they "With idle paines, and missing ayme, do guesse"
(XXIII), but he himself forgets that he has retrenched to a
dangerous degree. The rhetoric of self-address functions here as
a dramatic confirmation of the speaker's own moral delusion.

Perhaps the most dramatic example in this regard occurs in
"What, have I thus betrayed my libertie? " (XLVII), a poem
modelled directly on Petrarch's "Pien d' un vago pensier, che mi
desvia" (CLXIX), where the speaker struggles to a penultimate
moment of resolution and then disintegrates, losing all in a
single splendid failure of nerve. Here the rhetorical shifts in
address reinforce the sonnet's dramatic structure with unusual
finesse. In the octave Astrophil questions himself about his loss
of will and his complete surrender to Stella. At the beginning of
the sestet, however, he turns to a radically new audience, his
own sense of virtue, which he personifies and bids to awaken:
"Vertue, awake, Beautie but beautie is." The paradoxically
negative tone emphasizes the difficulty of finding a solution.
Thus, he initiates the final tercet with an imperative addressed
to himself: "Let her go! " Hardly is the command issued, how-

ever, than he bids himself fall quiet: "Soft, but here she comes."
In a mighty surge of energy at the end of the line, he confronts
Stella and renounces her: "Go to." On the next line he addresses
her in disdain, "Unkind, I love you not," though he then qualifies his address with a private admission of the hold that Stella
has on him: "O me, that eye/Doth make my heart give to my
tongue the lie." This spectacular reversal at the very last moment
is the product of a rhetorical involvement with himself, with
virtue, with Stella, and finally again with himself, accompanied
by the recognition that he will never entirely reform his own
deepest instincts.

Very often Astrophil aims exclusively at obtaining some
witty, clever, or at least amusing effect in the sonnet's closing
lines, and the rhetorical strategies that he most frequently
employs withhold the shift, turn, and reversal until the end.
Often the effect reveals his cavalier attitude towards making
serious sense out of the conflict. For he would, he says to Cupid
in LXI, employ an "Angel's sophistrie" in order to win his
lady's favor by feigning indifference to it. Symptomatic of the
way he applies his sophistry in witty argumentation with Stella
is his attempt in "O Grammer rules, ô now your vertues show"
(LXIII) to cover up his own fallacies with a transparent manipulation of grammar rules on the one hand and a facile use of
multiple address on the other. Stella has said "No, No" to the
speaker's plea, and the speaker calls upon grammar rules to
interpret "No, No" to his own advantage as a double negative.
In the first tercet he extends his already hyperbolic apostrophe
when he bids his muse rejoice at his "high triumphing," for in
the second tercet he can construe two negatives as an affirma-
tive. He clinches his argument in the final lines by shifting his
address to Stella with tongue-in-cheek repetitions and parentheses while he gathers breath to find exactly the right words:

> For Grammer sayes (ô this deare *Stella* weighe,)
> For Grammer sayes (to Grammer who sayes nay)
> That in one speech two Negatives affirme.

Nor does the speaker employ his wit, irony, and preciosity

only to gain recognition from his beloved.[10] Even after she rewards his endeavors with a kiss, he continues to ply the same high but superficial mode of discourse as an end in itself. In "O Kisse, which doest these ruddie gemmes impart" (LXXXI), rhetorical preciosity dominates his addresses, first to the kiss and then to Stella. In the octave he apostrophizes the kiss with ineffable praise: "How faine would I paint thee to all men's eyes,/Or of thy gifts at least shade out some part." The first words of the sestet imply a new tone, however, as he registers Stella's disapproval about proclaiming their kiss to a wider public audience: "But she forbids, with blushing words, she sayes,/She builds her fame on higher seated praise." And yet he avers that he cannot neglect his desire. At the end of the first tercet he openly defies Stella's prohibitions: "But my heart burnes, I cannot silent be." In the second tercet he addresses Stella directly as a new audience, and portraying himself as "mad with delight" and wanting "wit to cease," he tells her what she can do to halt his proclamation: "Stop you my mouth with still still kissing me." Turning his wit to personal advantage, then, the speaker reveals himself as past master in making things seem what they are not, and ironically he degrades himself in the process. For though Astrophil relies upon his poetic talent to use words, still he shows himself using them only in trivial matters. In the long run the reader comes to the inevitable conclusion that Astrophil's high style is a sham.

In its implied narrative the sequence approaches its dramatic reversal in the last twenty-two sonnets.[11] Here it appears that the speaker has been separated from his beloved, ostensibly on a diplomatic mission away from home, "When I forst from *Stella* ever deere" (LXXXVII). Moreover, it appears that he has found gratification in another lady's rival attractions: "Because in brave array heere marcheth she,/That to win me, oft shewes a present pay" (LXXXCIII). Astrophil is foolish not only for permitting himself the diversion, but also for admitting to it ("They please I do confesse, they please mine eyes," XCI), and triply foolish for expressing surprise at the news of Stella's displeasure with him: "Through me, wretch me, even *Stella* vexed is" (XCIII). The poems that follow modify the Petrarchan expressions of grief, complaint, lament, and inner absorption with a *pathos* unique to the dramatic atmosphere of *Astrophil and Stella*. Modally as well as stylistically these poems belong fully to the Petrarchan tradition, with Sidney's additional touch of illustrating the speaker's folly. Thus, in "When far spent night perswades each mortall eye" (XCIX), modeled on Petrarch's "Or che 'l ciel" and on Ronsard's "Or que le ciel," the structural strategy of the octave turns on a contrast between the peacefulness of things in nature, "clos'd with their quivers in sleep's armory," and the speaker's inability to sleep during the night: "With windowes ope then most my mind doth lie." In the sestet the comparison is between the awakening of nature at dawn, "But when birds charme," and the speaker's habit of falling asleep when morning comes: "In tombe of lids then buried are mine eyes." Sidney gives the topos a witty twist, however, by allowing Astrophil on the last two lines to explain why he falls asleep when dawn comes. He is, he says, ashamed to find that external nature enjoys so much light when his own inner sense is clouded over with darkness.

The speaker's naïve but determined effort to conceive of nature as an analogue for his every action, and his confirmation at the poem's center of the "perfit harmony" between external night and his own "inward night" become telling measures of his ethical self-regard. Thus Sidney achieves the essential modal effect of Petrarchan poetry. Petrarch distances himself from the speaker in order to show the gravity of the latter's error in idolizing Laura to the exclusion of all else. But whereas in Petrarch the error is grave, in Sidney it is merely foolish.

The satiric point, however, marks Astrophil's protestations as thoroughly conventional. Throughout the sequence he alludes to and sometimes extensively comments on his role as poet, asserting his claims for holding to a consistent poetics. Its gist is his anti-Petrarchan sentiment and his innovative stress on sincerity and stylistic plainness. But just as he demonstrates himself to be naïve as a lover, he also demonstrates his naïveté as a poet. The ironic effect is especially keen when he pretends to be a cleverer, more inspired poet than he actually is. Moreover, by expressing his anti-Petrarchism and his wish to be plain, direct, and honest, Astrophil is in fact proclaiming his thorough conventionality, for by the 1580s anti-Petrarchan slogans were already shopworn in England and the quest for a relatively nonornamental style had attracted writers like Thomas Wilson, George Gascoigne, and Gabriel Harvey. In light of earlier English Renaissance aesthetics, everything that Astrophil says about his art is (though he denies it) wholly conventional to the point of being banal.[12]

In I, for example, he describes his systematic approach towards the writing of a sonnet. The description reveals that the poet has confounded the time-honored rhetorical method where the stages of composition pass from *inventio* to *distributio* and then to *elocutio*. His aim, he says, is to persuade Stella to read for pleasure, then through reading to learn of his devotion to her, and finally through her discovery to pity him and out of pity to favor him. Instead of beginning with the collection (*inventio*) and arrangement (*distributio*) of his materials, however, the speaker proceeds directly to *elocutio*, to seek "fit words to paint the blackest face of woe." True, he does turn to *inventio* in line 6, but only after he has let his first impulse lead him in a precipitous rush to find "fit words" in *elocutio*: "Studying inventions fine, her wits to entertaine." The *inventio* which he seeks, moreover, is a weak one because he assumes that other poets will furnish appropriate materials for him to express his own feelings: "Oft turning others' leaves, to see if thence would flow/Some fresh and fruitfull showers upon my sunne-burn'd braine." The result, as he confesses in the first line of the sestet, is an ultimate failure of *elocutio* because there is not enough *inventio* to contain the power of the words: "But words came halting forth, wanting Invention's stay." Even the metrical rules that others have formulated ("Others' feete") do not allow for sufficient control or flexibility. Instead of trying harder to improve his rhetorical skill, however, the speaker decides in the final tercet to abandon the attempt altogether and, in the famous words of the last line, to take the advice of the muse, who says, "looke in thy heart and write."

In this context the speaker's use of the sincerity topos and his protestation of "originality" hardly dignify his *ethos*. They amount instead to a negative action, since they evade a more traditional and useful method, as Astrophil himself knows, at least in theory. At every turn throughout the sequence, negativity in fact characterizes the speaker's announced aesthetic and determines his rhetoric. Addressing an audience of fellow poets in a hostile, reactionary tone, Astrophil decries their appraoches and states his preferences with exceptional clarity. In III, for example, he disdains the Neo-Platonic *furor poeticus* exemplified by the French Pléiade: "Let daintie wits crie on the Sisters nine,/That bravely maskt, their fancies may be told." He also scorns the imitation of the classics by those whom he calls *"Pindare's* Apes," who flaunt "in phrases fine,/. . . their thoughts of gold." He rejects also the style of classicists, who search for "problemes old" to embellish their rhetorical figures and the fashionable style of those (possibly the Euphuists) who will "with strange similies enrich each line." In the final tercet he then declares of Stella, the model for his own inspiration, "all my deed/But Copying is, what in her Nature writes."

In VI he continues to define his poetic *ethos* by extending his proscription to the conventional Petrarchan poets who complain oxymoronically "Of living deaths, deare wounds, faire stormes and freesing fires"; poets who mythologically embroider their song "in *Jove,* and *Jove's* strange tales . . ./Broadred with buls and swans, powdred with golden raine" (perhaps a direct allusion to Ronsard's famous sonnet "Je vouldroy bien richement jaunissant"); the pastoral poet who "to shepheard's pipe retires/Yet hiding royall bloud full oft in rurall vaine" (perhaps Spenser); and poets who cultivate a "sweetest stile" in order to affect "a sweetest plaint." By contrast, in the final tercet he once more asserts his own sincerity: "I can speake what I feele, and feele as much as they," but the irony is that the poetry he writes, for all its sincerity, is thoroughly conventional in its own way, right down to its skilful appropriation of Petrarchan rhetoric. All this despite his protestations that both Petrarchism and anti-Petrarchism are inadequate to express his true feeling.

Elsewhere the speaker develops his rhetoric on literary themes in similar ways. In XV he addresses an audience of poets who compose in three different modes, and he assails them all for taking "wrong waies." First, he aims at the imitators of the classics, "You that do search for everie purling spring,/Which from the ribs of old *Parnassus* flowes." Next, he touches the old-fashioned English alliterative poets, "You that do Diction-arie's methode bring/Into your rimes, running in ratling rowes." Finally he hits the Petrarchan school directly: "You that poore *Petrarch's* long deceased woes,/With new-borne sighes and denisend wit do sing." The Petrarchists' approach, he con-cludes in the sestet, is all wrong because it betrays the poet's natural creative energies, and it exposes him to the risk of being taken for a mere copier. As far as he is concerned, the only solution is to make Stella his one subject and write from his heart:

> But if (both for your love and skill) your name
> You seeke to nurse at fullest breasts of Fame,
> *Stella* behold, and then begin to endite.

The speaker uses the imperative with its direct address, there-fore, to heighten the effect of his own sincerity, as though sin-cerity itself were enough to justify his continuing composition of sonnets that honor Stella.

Astrophil never seems to question whether his audience will challenge him, but assumes instead that the authenticity of his rhetoric will resolve all questions. In XXVIII, finally, he cau-tions readers not to interpret his poetry allegorically.[13] He most objects to the allegorizers' studied habit of bastardizing the text by extracting significance that the poet never intended:

> You that with allegorie's curious frame
> Of other's children changelings use to make,
> With me those paines for God's sake do not take:

Here, though he perceives acutely the problems in public dissemination of the artist's work, all he can do is protest: "I list not dig so deep for brasen fame." Such a bare-faced response is the least effective rhetorical strategy available to any poet. Sincerity must shine through despite the speaker's protestation. True, Astrophil tries to demonstrate his sincerity through the cultivation of a simple style: "I beg no subject to use eloquence." But there are simply no styles or stylistic devices to guarantee that the audience will understand the meaning as he intends it and no norms to measure his "pure simplicitie." There are only the rhetorical strategies with which the poet must cope in presenting his poetry, and though Astrophil tries to avoid facing the fact, Sidney, the controlling poet, does face it by recognizing their importance and by exploiting them to the full.

Sidney's strategies of voice and address come thus to typify Renaissance Petrarchism. The mode derives its highest rhetorical power from the figure of the split addresser, embracing poet and speaker, and from the figure of the split addressee, embracing the fictive audience and actual reader. The development of a complicated relationship among these agents characterizes the mode's history from its inception in Petrarch's *Canzoniere* to its conclusion in the seventeenth century. This development traverses stages when irrefragable wit, strained moralization, overt and covert classicism, meditative interiority, and truculent satire dominate in their turn. In *Astrophil and Stella* each aspect plays a prominent role. Underlying their various appearances, however, are consistent norms of voice and address that identify the Petrarchan mode.

I have shown how both Ronsard's "Or que le ciel, or que la terre est pleine" and Sidney's "When far spent night perswades each mortall eye" imitate Petrarch's "Or che 'l ciel e la terra e 'l vento tace." This poem provided a model for so many Renaissance sonnets, dizains, and short lyrics that one could construct a full-length history of Petrarchism just by tracing its central topos from the Middle Ages to the Baroque. Such a history illustrates my claim that the strategies of voice and address characterize the mode better than elocutionary figures and other verbal devices do.

For a beginning we can associate the tendency to multiply

the speaker's role and the number of audiences to which he appeals with a central periodic distinction between Renaissance and Baroque. Through this distinction we can represent each period not as a succession of events so much as a concatenation of functions. These functions entail the juxtaposition, emulation, analogy, and mobility of rhetorical voice and address.[14] Already in their treatments of the motif Ronsard and Sidney exemplify an inclination towards two extremes: Ronsard towards a classical secularization of Petrarch's moral imperatives and Sidney towards a witty and satiric rendition of the speaker's folly in love. A cursory glance at the way other major poets treated the motif will illustrate the further shift from secularization and wit in the later Renaissance towards exploitation of other possibilities in the Baroque.

In the quattrocento Italian Petrarchism underwent a number of changes, epitomized in the works of three poets: Chariteo, Tebaldeo, and Serafino.[15] We cannot understand these changes, however, as mere shifts in the structure of words or diction, or transformations in the elocutionary devices and figures of speech. Indeed, the latter remain constant in the new poetry: what differ are the rhetorical conceptions of character and audience. Chariteo (1460–1506), a Spaniard attached to the court of Naples, composed a sequence of 214 sonnets and twenty canzone (*Rime*, 1506) about the love of his persona, Endimione, for "la Luna." In "Somno, d'ogni pensier placido oblio" (CXXXVII), dealing with the theme of the sleepless lover on the model of Petrarch's "Or che 'l ciel e la terra e 'l vento tace," there is not one elocutionary device that could not be found also in Petrarch. Nonetheless, Chariteo's lack of moral complications runs radically at odds with Petrarch's moral imperative. Thus, the straining tendency towards suspensive climax in the octave's word order—"Perché fuggir di me tanto ti piace" ("Why does it please you so much to flee from me?")—leads to a pronounced change of address in the final tercet. Here the speaker summons Amor in a tone of sharp accusation, even witty vituperation, such as Petrarch would never have attempted:

Amor tu 'l fai; ché chi sotto 'l governo
Vive del regno tuo, non può dormire,
Nè riposar, se non col somno eterno.[16]

[Amor, you are responsible, for whoever lives under the rule of your reign can neither sleep nor rest, unless it be in eternal sleep.]

Later forms of the mode would encourage even more witty conclusions and clever resolutions. The mid-sixteenth-century lyric, for example, would sometimes accentuate, sometimes mute the principle of symmetry and opposition in the speaker's character, while alternately contracting and expanding the distance separating the speaker from his audience. The extent to which this emphasis comes to dominate Tuscan and Neapolitan poetry can be shown by a comparison of two sonnets on the theme of the lover's sleeplessness, "O sonno, o de la queta, umida, ombrosa/notte placido figlio" by Giovanni Della Casa (1503–56), and "Orrida notte, che rinchiusa il negro/crin" by Luigi Tansillo (1510–68).[17] In the later Baroque there would be, as Della Casa's poem adumbrates, a proliferation of fictive audiences as the speaker moves from the original audience (such as sleep, "O sonno") to another one (such as the speaker's bed, "O piume"), and finally to some broader external audience (such as night, "o notti"), using multiple address to express restless agitations within himself. At other times there would be, as in Tansillo's poem, a speaker who submits his own *ethos* to a transformation in the course of the poem, or attempts such transformation, or even feigns it. Thus, Tansillo's speaker reviles night because sleep escapes him—"Orrida notte, che rinchiusa il negro/crin sotto 'l vel de l'umide tenebre" ("You horrid night who hide your dark locks under the veil of damp shadows")— while at the end he enters into a complicity with night in order to earn some sleep: "Direi ch'esci dal cielo, e ch'hai di stelle/mille corone onde fai il mondo adorno" ("I would say that you come from heaven and that you have a crown of a thousand stars whence you adorn the world"). In both cases Petrarchan clarity gives way to ironic ambiguity and the history of the Petrarchan mode is altered.

Long before the Baroque occurred in Italy, the Petrarchan mode underwent other modifications elsewhere in Europe. The publication of du Bellay's *Olive* in 1549 marks the beginning of full-fledged Petrarchism in France, though several notable experiments by the poets of Lyon preceded the work of the Pléiade.[18] In 1584 the publication of Ronsard's final version of the *Sonnets pour Hélène* marks its end, though the legacy directly modified and strongly influenced various modes of Baroque, Précieux, and even Classical poetry throughout the seventeenth century. Thus, more than a century of its evolution in the Italian lyric is telescoped into thirty-five years in the French lyric. Still, its abbreviated history is nowhere quite so simple or direct that it invariably conforms to the Italian model.

First, the Petrarchan experiments of Marot and Saint Gellais early in the century imparted to Pléiade Petrarchism a standard rhyme scheme which, it its basic difference from the Italian, dictated a radical formal difference in the structure.[19] Opposed to the conventional Italian rhyme scheme (*abba abba cde cde*) dividing the sonnet into two quatrains and two tercets with a shift or reversal in any one of its parts, Marot's rhyme scheme (*abba abba cc deed*) divides the sonnet into three quatrains with a couplet between the second and third ones. The couplet, occupying the ninth and tenth lines, encourages a shift or reversal closer to the middle of the sonnet and a denouement that unfolds more leisurely than in the Italian sonnets. The effect is a linearity quite different from the kaleidoscopic variety of Petrarch's *ethos*.

Other early works in the Petrarchan mode by poets like Louise Labé and Pernette du Guillet imparted to Pléiade Petrarchism a repertory of themes, motifs, situations, and at least a minimal stock of expressive diction and even some concrete figures to represent the themes.[20] The effect is sometimes quite close to that of the Petrarchan mode, despite the important differences that separate these French poets from their Italian counterparts. Finally there is the example provided by Maurice Scève's *Délie* (1544), a cycle of 449 dizains vaguely analogous in structure and rhyme scheme to the *strambotti* of Serafino, but otherwise rhetorically similar to Petrarch's poetry. What *Délie* imparted was a model fully in accord with the rhetoric of the Petrarchan sonnet. One of Scève's most famous dizains, for example, "Seul avec moi, elle auec sa partie" (CLXI), evokes the Petrarchan motif of the sleepless lover, and looks not only backward with creative fidelity to Petrarch's model, but also forward to one of Ronsard's best poems from the *Amours de Cassandre*, "Au plus profond de ma poytrine morte."[21]

The result is that in poetry like Pontus de Tyard's *Sonnets d'Amour* (1555) and Philippe Desportes's *Les Amours de Hippolyte* (1573) we find several Petrarchan influences operating at once. Tyard's "Sommeil fils de la nuict, faveur chere à noz yeux" and Desportes's "Sommeil, paisible fils de la Nuict solitaire" are both cast in the familiar Marotic rhyme scheme, yet both the sestets divide syntactically, thematically, and dramatically into tercet units after the Italian fashion. The chief difference is the higher dramatic intensity with which Tyard sets forth the speaker's character and his relationship with the audience.

In Tyard's sestet, for example, the poet plays with the structure of time as the speaker cries out with urgency, "Heé, Sommeil, qu'attens-tu, ne viens tu pas encore?" ("Ha, Sleep, what are you waiting for, are you not yet coming?"), and he gives a reason for his urgency in the fact that the morning star, Venus, is already on the horizon: "Ja la blanche Venus, traine aveq' soy l'Aurore" ("Already the white Venus draws away with her the dawn.")[22] At line 12 the speaker cries out with weary resignation that the sun has already risen and has chased Night and Sleep away "towards Themis-the-Titan." Here the conflation of Themis with Titan underscores the speaker's figure for an underworld that he emotionally inhabits in the torment of his frustrated love.

Desportes's sonnet by comparison is static, decorative, manifestly nonrepresentational. Whereas Tyard's speaker addressed Sommeil and recorded his own shifting emotions, Desportes's speaker does little more than apostrophize Sommeil in a series of elegantly fabricated parallelisms. The first quatrain is a string of addresses to the fictive audience. The second quatrain balances two interrogative clauses ("pourquoy m'es-tu contraire" and "Pourquoy suis-je tout seul rechargé de travaux") and two temporal clauses ("Or' que l'humide nuict guide" and "que chacun jouist").[23] In yet another series of parallel constructions, the first tercet rephrases the earlier question with no shift, turn, or evolution of the speaker's attitude: "Ton silence où est-il? ton repos et ta paix." The second tercet finally recapitulates the *pathos* of the address and the speaker's deep anguish: "O frere de la Mort que tu m'es ennemi!" In the history of the French lyric during the Baroque period, the poetry of Sponde, la Ceppède, Chassignet, Théophile de Viau, Saint Amant, and others would strive for the dramatic intensity of Tyard's style rather than Desportes's or Ronsard's, taking to heart the objections that Malherbe raised against Desportes's and Ronsard's elocutionary styles.[21]

The history of the Petrarchan sonnet in England is neither so ordered as in France nor so chaotic as in Italy. It has a clear unambiguous origin in the experiments of Wyatt and Surrey, and it reaches a full rich development in the magnificent sequences of Sidney, Spenser, Shakespeare, Drayton, Daniel, and Donne. But differences in rhetorical strategies here are more pronounced than anywhere on the continent, and the impression emerges that to a far greater extent than their peers elsewhere, the English Petrarchists reacted to the norms of the Petrarchan mode in individual, idiosyncratic ways.[25]

In all the poems that we have seen modelled on Petrarch's "Or che 'l ciel," the speaker's rhetoric heightens the sonnet's dramatic structure. The treatment of the motif by Surrey (1517-1547) in "Alas, so all things nowe doe holde their peace," however, presents a univocal point of view lacking the problematicality of the continental poems. Though the speaker feels the contarieties of joy and woe most keenly, he expresses no profound division of role and selfhood. Likewise, he conveys little sense of a complex rhetorical relationship with his audience through direct or indirect address. The sonnet's structure, moreover, employs a steady march of six rhyming couplets—*ababababababab/cc*—that effaces its structural divisions into octave and sestet and further lessens the possibilities for representing a complex sensibility. Still, Surrey does partition the sonnet into symmetrical verse units of ever diminishing length. The first, describing the peacefulness of external nature at nighttime, extends over five lines (1–5); the second, contrasting the restlessness of the speaker's inner state and evoking his *ethos*, extends over four lines (6–9); the third, rendering the speaker's *ethos* more precise in a declaration of the contrarieties that vex him, extends over three lines (10–12). Each syntactic unit, then, has a shorter metrical duration than that of its predecessor, as though it were compressing successive layers of statement and contrast until the speaker completes his own self-revelation in the last two lines: "When that I thinke what griefe it is againe/To live and lacke the thing should ridde my paine."[26]

In later English sonnets, the final couplet, decisive but mechanical in Surrey's sonnet, becomes finally organic. The rhyme schemes devised by Spenser and Shakespeare, the two greatest English sonneteers, terminate in couplets that emphasize the structural and hence rhetorical importance of the three quatrains; thus Spenser's rhyme (*abab bcbc cdcd ee*) and Shakespeare's (*abab cdcd efef gg*). In their sonnets, however, the speaker's ingenuity in accommodating his rhetoric to the structural divisions implied by the rhyme signals a clear technical advance over Surrey's mechanical application. Yet the speakers do not manipulate voice and address so much that they depart from the Petrarchan mode. In Sidney's *Astrophil and Stella*, however, one finds the playfulness, wit, and experimentation of earlier Petrarchism on the verge of assuming a new vitality. Since they are central to the moral design of Sidney's sequence, these qualities are no mere verbal strategies and are nowhere so ingenious or gratuitous as in Chariteo, Tebaldeo, or Serafino. Their elegance, formalism, and purely lyric impulse accede in Sidney to a more dramatic impulse, with a covert, though very definite moral purpose. Sidney, that is, exploited the playful witty potential of Petrarchan rhetoric without trivializing his theme's seriousness as the others had. In this respect Sidney's rhetoric is closer to Petrarch's than is theirs.

What, then, is the final result of studying the strategies of voice and address in a mode that we loosely designate "Petrarchan"? One is that we establish a rhetorical consanguinity linking several poems beyond their common usage of theme, figures of speech, elocutionary devices, and other verbal strategies. Patterns of voice and address interact with one another and with devices on the verbal surface of the poetry. Their interaction generates a system of norms governing the mode as a whole. The development of these norms gives shape to our concept of literary history. By studying changes in voice and address even when the verbal surfaces remain static, one can perceive significant workings in the process of literary history. But the norms governing this process are interlocking and interdependent. They include not only mode but also individual styles and whole genres. Just as patterns of voice and address contribute to the definition of mode, so can they also contribute to the definitions of style and genre. Hence, if we take these patterns into account, we should be able to clarify transformations in modes, styles, and genres that signal wholly new developments in literary history. The next chapter focuses on the way these strategies help to define stylistic norms.

2

The Style of Ironic Discourse

Of all questions involving literary analysis, style is the most vexing. Critics, historians, and theorists generally can agree upon historical, generic, and even modal norms, but about stylistic norms they more often dispute. Some feel that the ancient consensus on three stylistic levels—high, middle, and low—is still useful; others decry its modern application.[1] While such criteria rely upon some vague sense of a *qualitative* inner coherence, what exactly coheres? If a mere catalogue of figures, tropes, and elocutionary devices provides no answer, the study of voice and address affords another perspective. We can use them to define style by the density, coherence, and integration of not only verbal texture but also of the speaker's character and his relationship with the audience.

These rhetorical strategies play such an important part in the description of style that any judgment of the verbal surface without them necessarily falls short. Renaissance style in both neo-Latin and the vernacular literatures entails more than verbal artifice. It incorporates uses of voice and address cutting across elocutionary and even linguistic barriers, transcending Ciceronian or Attic conventions often associated with the period. It imports a panoply of effects as numerous and varied as the authors who used it.[2]

The most perceptive writers of the period shared this conviction. The first major lexicography of classical Latin, the *De Latinae linguae elegantia* of Lorenzo Valla (1444), helped to standardize Renaissance style, but it also posed a strong argument for advancing a plurality and multiplicity of styles. Its author asserts that the work of the best writers, "each in its own way, exhibits wonderful elegance of expression." The crucial phrase "each in its own way" ("pro sua vnumquodque portione") implies the lack of any single formula for good style.[3] Valla goes on to posit an effective relation between style and content when he asserts that St. Jerome expressed scruples about imitating Cicero's style, but not about appropriating Plato's philosophy. If this be so, he has rejected everything in Cicero, style and content, for the sake of one of these components alone, for style is not free from content nor is expression free from ornament.

By the end of the fifteenth century veneration of Cicero's style had hardened into idolatry. Erasmus (1469–1536) himself exalted Ciceronian abundance and syntactic elegance in his popular *De utraque verborum ac rerum copia* (1511).[4] His sensitivity to good Latin style proved more catholic, however, in his later dialogue against slavish Ciceronism, the *Ciceronianus* (1527). The spokesman for his own point of view, Bulephorus, argues that Cicero himself devised for his style particular moral situations or even particular audiences. Thus, Cicero has many styles:

> He has one when, in relaxed and quiet conversation, he teaches philosophy; another in the pleading of cases; another in letters where the language is not studied but even almost careless—very appropriate for a letter which follows the turn of familiar conversation.

Moreover, it is not only the situation or audience that determines the stylistic norm, but also the temperament of the writer himself. "There is in Cicero a certain happy, natural ease, and a native clearness. If nature has denied us this, why do we vainly torture ourselves?" In a later analogy Bulephorus develops the idea of variety as the very basis of style:

> To carry the figure further, there are as many kinds of mind as there are forms of voices and the mirror will be straightway deceptive unless it give back the real image of the mind, which is the very thing that delights the reader especially—to discover from the language the feelings, the characteris-

tics, the judgment, and the ability of the writer as well as if one had known him for years.[5]

At every turn, however, other humanists challenged these assumptions that accorded so much prestige to individual differences.[6] Basically, the humanist *ethos* offered a finite vision of the universe where everything obeys the law of concentric order. Man at its center is the measure of all things, despite limits imposed on his capacity—perhaps even because of them, since they imply a finite world with accessible limits, as opposed to a boundless infinity. Humanist rhetoric reflects this cosmos in a dual sense. The insistence on the rhetorical ordering of parts through *inventio, distributio,* and *elocutio* reflects an absolute value system. The rhetorician believes that he can obtain a perfect and desirable ordering of parts through the finiteness of their permutations: out of only so many choices, one must be superior, and if chosen well, it can provide a formula to be used over and over again. Thus, the embellishment of humanist style is less ornament than an expression of faith in the attainability of perfection that the system has made available.

The challenge to these assumptions came from Renaissance discoveries that broadened man's vision of the universe. Here are no concentric orders, only various eccentric ones, and man, subject to atomistic laws, loses his status as the measure of all things. Paradoxically, though, he finds an increased freedom to do all things because nature has dispensed with limits. No one is bound to norms that hamper or restrict one's field of activity. With regard to rhetoric, norms liberate the writer rather than restrict him. It is not so much that the options at one's disposal are infinite (they are in fact still narrowly circumscribed), but rather that they are flexible. With the multiplication of possibilities for addressing different audiences, for shifting tone and moods, for posing ingenious paradoxes, the rhetorical situation becomes exceedingly variable, if not open-ended. The author and the audience confront each other in a highly equivocal relationship that is always in the process of transformation.

The more that multiple address, rapid shifts of tone and mood, and paradox come to dominate Renaissance style, the more they approach the norms of Baroque style. Since the process begins in the Renaissance it might seem that the earlier norms are Baroque in embryo, that the later ones develop or extend them and that they differ only in frequency and intensity. To some degree the Baroque does evolve from Renaissance style, but there is still a concrete difference. The adumbrations or carryovers from the earlier period usually entail only some rhetorical strategies and exclude others. The true historical shift occurs when all the contingent rhetorical strategies have undergone changes to such a degree that the more durable structural principles of mode, style, and genre undergo changes also. Moreover, these changes in a mode, style, or genre accompany similar ones in different modes, styles and genres. Hence, what one may say about a normative period style in one genre or mode applies as well to another.

But what norms best define those styles? Once again it is not possible to determine any solely by deviation from some abstract *langue* or by the context that surrounds those deviations, since the capacity for infinite permutation marks all these forms. The norms instead must be characterized by reference to other norms, by reference to the way in which each constrains the other. The rhetorical strategies fixing relationships between speaker and audience can here suggest a system that gives coherence to a larger mode or style or genre. The interaction of these rhetorical strategies underlies all the larger systems.

How, then, can one characterize voice and address as stylistic determinants? I want to pursue this problem through an examination of two texts originally in Latin (although unconventional non-Ciceronian Latin)—Erasmus's *The Praise of Folly* and More's *Utopia*—and of one in a vernacular (although one of the strangest uses of vernacular employed in the Renaissance)—Rabelais's *Gargantua and Pantagruel*. The modal and stylistic similarities linking these works override their generic differences. Indeed, the specific genres are hard to identify. *The Praise of*

Folly begins as a parody of classical oratory and ends with an excursus on an important theological issue. *Utopia* might seem a serious dialogue, but with tongue in cheek it inclines towards jest and irony. Rabelais's *Gargantua and Pantagruel* conforms to the outlines of the folk narrative tradition represented by the *Bibliotheque bleue* and the *Grandes Chroniques*, which it then subverts in a comic way. *Tiers Livre* and *Quart Livre* evoke Lucian's *Dialogues* and *True History* respectively, while both continue to parody other literary forms. Despite differences in form and language, however, their homogeneity of mode and style makes a comparison of these works particularly efficacious.

The homogeneous mode in which they participate is seriocomic philosophic jest.[7] As I have already indicated, the classical precursor for this ironic mode is Lucian, just as Lucian's precursor was Plato. The point is worth pursuing. In the preambulatory letter of *The Praise of Folly* addressed to Thomas More, Erasmus implies that the tone is "festivus."[8] His word echoes Socrates' description in the *Phaedrus* of the writer who knows the superiority of living speech to written discourse and who yet commits his thoughts to paper "in a holiday spirit, just by way of pastime" (276b). Indeed, in the *Phaedrus* Socrates' ironic encomium of the carnal lover and his subsequent inquiry into divinely inspired love-madness which leads to wisdom suggest the shifting way in which Folly at the outset seems to be praising one thing (malevolent folly) when all along she is really praising something else (benevolent folly). The "ludus festivus" of Erasmian and ultimately Socratic discourse in turn pervades More's extension of the dialogue form in *Utopia* and Rabelais's invention of narrative forms in *Gargantua and Pantagruel*.

Erasmus, More, and Rabelais, of course, went far beyond the norms of Lucian and Plato when they formed their own unique literary discourse. Part of their transcendence of classical norms comes from their development of local stylistic effects, their propensities for puns, verbal ambiguities, paradoxes, coinages, conversions, obscurities, archaic turns of phrase, and sheer explosions of linguistic energy. In still more fundamental, though less obvious ways, their uses of voice and address that we have discussed as modal determinants become stylistic determinants. We can best approach the resulting homogeneity of styles by reference to their shared rhetorical strategies. In the course of doing so I also hope to show the aptness of analyzing style in these terms, thereby reinforcing the bonds between stylistic norms on the one hand and modal and generic norms on the other.

Erasmus's *The Praise of Folly*

An oratorical work par excellence, *The Praise of Folly* (1509) of Desiderius Erasmus sports a masterful rhetorical structure. Folly plays several roles, but her major role is as spokesman for—indeed, embodiment of—folly. A second role, paradoxically competing with the first, is as spokesman for a wisdom transcending both folly and human wisdom. Implicit in these two roles, moreover, is a third: whether a spokesman for folly or for wisdom, she is, by her own admission, a *rhetor sophisticos*: "It is my pleasure for a little while to play the rhetorician before you" (p. 8). No audience confronting her sophistry head on can emerge confident of having understood everything correctly.[1]

Early in its printed life, since Frobenius's edition of 1515, *The Praise of Folly* appeared with a running commentary by the author's friend, Girardus Listrius; Erasmus probably assisted Listrius and may even have done the writing himself.[2] In any case, aside from identifying key quotations and emblematic references, its imposition only adds to the reader's puzzlement in coming to terms with the text. Nothing is more ironic than Folly's early assurance that her audience will understand every word; for speech, she claims, is "the least deceptive mirror of the mind" (p. 10). What Folly conceals (or perhaps foolishly reveals) is its function as a possible vehicle of deceit, not to mention plain confusion. In his commentary Listrius asserts, "Above all in speech a man's frame of mind is opened up" (p. 74); and then, apparently unhappy with his own half-truth and its hazardous misapplication, he adds a marginal notation that only confirms the problematic irony: "Folly shines forth in the expression on her face" (p. 74).[3] Together with Listrius's commentary, the corruscating ironies and almost impenetrable paradoxes of Folly's monologue supply the best example of how speech can be a very deceptive mirror of the mind—especially the speech of a fool who, we come to learn, is a very special type of fool. *The Praise of Folly* testifies to the impossibility of understanding a text solely on its verbal surface alone, for Folly's audience has no way of knowing which claims she asserts as a fool and which not, indeed whether she is a fool claiming to be wise or a wise person claiming to be a fool. Folly's verbal strategies themselves supply no answer. The resolution comes only in the mind of each beholder.

Thus, the questions of which role best sums up her parts and whether folly or wisdom dominates her selfhood are ultimately unanswerable. It would be tempting to assert that Folly transforms gradually from a foolish exemplar of worldly folly to a wise exemplar of Christian folly, a metamorphosis from pagan *stultitia* which is mere foolishness to the Christian μωρία spoken of by St. Paul.[4] The problem is that Folly's transformation is not constant. It is difficult to verify a transformation at all because at the finale of her oration she is still very much the fool exhorting her audience to forget what she has just spoken. All one can say with confidence is that Folly's wisdom alternates with her madness; the truth of what she says, with the nonsense of what she says; the plainness of her speech, with the irony in her speech.

The elocutionary figure dominating her monologue's verbal surface is prosopopoeia, a figure defined in the classical rhetorical handbooks as a sudden ironic change of voice or character.[5] Thus, the speaker shifts from folly to wisdom and back with such lightning speed that she runs the risk of losing not only her reader but also her fictive audience. A good example occurs when she argues that all human affairs have contrary aspects like the sides of Alcibiades's Silenus. Indeed, even though Folly brings forth this example to emphasize the need for prudence and clear discernment, she also uses it to show her own rhetorical

character. It becomes an economical emblem for her dual roles
of folly-and-wisdom integrated within her enigmatic selfhood.[6]
With its implications of duality, division, and of rapid shifting
from one extreme to another, the comparison should warn the
reader to interpret Folly's speech with care and to accept
nothing in it at face value.

> For first of all, the fact is that all human affairs, like the
> Sileni of Alcibiades, have two aspects, each quite different
> from the other; even to the point that what at first blush
> (as the phrase goes) seems to be death may prove, if you
> look further into it, to be life. . . . In brief, you find all
> things suddenly reversed, when you open up the Silenus
> [p. 36].

The complications that this prosopopoeia engenders are enor-
mous. In her argument on prudence, Folly speaks so abstractly
that the fictive audience interrupts her. She rejoins with a
second example: "But where, one asks, does it all lead? Have
patience, and let us carry it further" (p. 37). Here she shifts her
metaphor from the Silenus to the theater and asserts that the
whole life of mortal beings is a sort of comedy. The new metaphor provides a link with the overriding notion of Folly's
speech as an oratorical performance.[7] Listrius at the beginning
of his commentary called attention to that performance as a
"declamation," indicating its relationship to a theatrical presentation: "He aptly calls it declamation so that you might know
the piece was written for entertainment and pleasure" (p. 70).
The Praise of Folly is more than a piece of oratory; it is a "live"
performance whose unfolding demands the audience's full
participation.

In addition to the roles as *rhetor*, spokesman for Folly, and
spokesman for wisdom, Folly also plays a constellation of sub-
sidiary roles or at least thinks she plays them. On the surface
these roles seem to give her a very important function in human
affairs. She sees herself, for example, as the principle of life, the
impetus which leads otherwise sane and sober men and women
to marry and raise children. Thus, she calls herself the *exordium*

(in the etymological sense of "beginning"): "And the beginning and first principle of life is owed to whom else but me?" (p. 14). She sees herself moreover as the giver of happiness to the very young and very old, as well as to the gods: "What part of life is not sad, unpleasant, graceless, flat, and burdensome, unless you have pleasure added to it, that is, a seasoning of folly?" (p. 16). And finally she sees herself as one who brings release from the ills that plague mankind, "aided in part by ignorance, and in part by inadvertence, sometimes by forgetfulness of evil" (p. 41). The irony in these passages is that Folly forgets, inter alia, that there are also other principles that lead men and women to marriage and childraising, and that human folly causes at least as much unhappiness as happiness.

Still, Folly's contentions have wider implications. Her audience of wise men will have to be on guard to find flaws in the argument, for the speaker slips from wisdom to foolishness and back at any moment, and the audience, if it is canny, will weigh everything that she says against a larger context.[8] The passage in which she describes herself as bringing relief from the world's ills, especially insofar as she teaches men to follow the intuitive bent of their own natures, provides a good example. The climax asserts: "The ones which live most happily are those which are farthest from any discipline, and which are controlled by no other master than nature" (pp. 45–46). Heightening the portentiousness of her argument, Folly peppers it with a common Virgilian refrain: "eloquarne, an sileam?" ("Shall I speak or be silent?" p. 38). In addition, she summons the Muses, the daughters of Jove, since the object of her attack is the Stoics' weighty contention that perfect wisdom must be devoid of passions. To the contrary, Folly argues, the passions contribute not only towards wisdom but virtue as well. For by any standard of measurement, the true wise man is one to whom nothing human is alien. (Here Folly paraphrases Terence: "Nihil humani a se alienum putet.") But no sooner does Folly offer this proposal than she characterizes herself as the chief deterrent to the self-destruction which wisdom counsels: "I bring relief from these ills; so that men are unwilling to relinquish their lives"

(p. 41). Surely Folly is not justified in this assertion, even if she can support her claim with a list of pagan wise men from Diogenes to Cato who counselled suicide. Here Folly mistakes the whole for the part in her argument, and she fails to make the requisite distinctions.

Even more to the point is the passage on biblical exegesis that prefaces the stunning finale of her oration. Despite the sting in her satiric barbs against ignorant editors, fanciful expositors, and extravagant interpreters of Scripture, she reveals a good deal of error, stupidity, and foolishness in her own hermeneutic approach.[9] In fact, though her interpretations are often unimpeachable, her quotations are not always accurate. One testimony from Ecclesiasticus ("whoever he was," p. 107) she prefaces with an incorrectly quoted proverb from Aristotle which she then paraphrases with an ingenuity that would rival that of her own slippery critics. But Folly's arcane interpretation of Ecclesiasticus 20:33 ("Better is the man that hideth his folly than he that hideth his wisdom") to mean that folly is more precious than wisdom since it should be hidden like gold, does not prevent her from accommodating a wiser meaning to Ecclesiasticus 10:3: "A fool walking by the way, being a fool, esteems all men as fools." Taking the fool's esteem as a compliment, Folly observes the Augustinian tenet of interpreting Scripture according to the doctrine of charity even though she is explaining the passage out of context. Unfortunately, Folly too often explains other passages out of context. Thus, she avers that the trilinguists led by Erasmus himself might disagree with her subjective interpretation of St. Paul's text "I speak as a fool; I am more" (II Corinthians 11:23). They would have St. Paul claim foolishness in order not to sound arrogant when he equals himself to the Apostles; but Folly prefers her own explanation, and thus provides a splendid example of taking the wrong turn even when she has access to the right one.

Ultimately Folly backs off from playing her role as scriptural critic with a meek "relinquo" and yields not only to the trilinguists' interpretation but indeed to anyone else's. Thus, she accredits any and all standards of critical judgment. What role is she playing now? Has she overtly joined the opposition? Or is she covertly launching an attack against it? What does she mean when she foolishly assents to follow "the great, fat, dull, and generally approved theologians, with whom the large majority of learned men choose to err" (p. 109)? The latter Folly embraces as her own because she says—and here the satire is straightforward and incisive—they are truly foolish. With flashes of critical insight revealing her wiser than before, she offers up to laughter some of the foolish exegetes ignorant of classical and Hebraic philology. Thus, Folly complains that some glean from the Bible a meaning "precisely as congruent with the spirit of Christ as fire is with water," citing an interpretation of "he that hath not a sword, let him sell his coat and buy one" (Luke 22:36) to mean that Christians should use as armor "whatever is necessary for repelling violence" (p. 112). Likewise Folly punctures holes in the nonphilological interpretation of "Haereticum devita" ("reject [*devita*] the heretic," p. 113) as "*de vita* tollendum haereticum*" ("remove the heretic from life [*de vita*]"). Folly thereby demonstrates both in theory and practice the need for interpreting Scripture with a rigorous philological exactness, an exactness which hitherto she herself has not always shown in her direct quotations.

Indeed, the ironic distance between the sometimes barbarous text from which Folly reads Scripture and the sometimes sensitive way in which she interprets it must have rhetorical significance. The author probably had several reasons for using the barbarous text: Erasmus wrote the oration on the road as a *jeu d'esprit* while traveling from Italy to England, and he may have been quoting the Bible from memory; or he may have been quoting conjectural possibilities for certain scriptural revisions that he was working on at the time.[10] Perhaps also Erasmus, the highly regarded scriptural exegete and editor, was trying to suggest a distance between himself as the controlling author and Folly as the fictive speaker. The latter reveals her own distinctive *ethos* and sometimes she misquotes and abuses Scripture, even though her creator is Erasmus himself. The rhetorical distance, then, between author and speaker becomes emblematic

of the one between speaker and audience and points to the
rhetorical strategy dominating the work's style.[11]

The question of this distance is crucial. If Folly is enigmatic
because she plays a number of sharply conflicting roles, she
heightens the enigma by controlling the audience's response
to her oratorical discourse. In rhetorical terms the relationship
between author and speaker is at issue: Erasmus has allowed
Folly to manipulate her audience to see exactly what Erasmus
wishes it to see. And to the extent that Folly manipulates her
audience, she in fact creates her own audience, a fictive audience programmed to register particular responses to her statements. Obvious examples are her frequent addresses to the
second-person plural in rhetorical questions, exclamations, and
direct statements. But other subtle devices help to create a
fictive audience and assign it a role to play. To a large extent
the rhetorical strategy in *The Praise of Folly* is to make an
implicit effect of the reading process (the creation of an audience) the explicit subject of *this* reading process.

The audience's involvement, then, both as a praiser of folly
and as a fool itself, as well as its detachment from conventional
notions of folly, are net results of the rhetorical situation.
Because Folly has flashes of wisdom, and even at times sustained wisdom, the audience may sometimes greet her speech
with straightforward acceptance. But sometimes, because Folly
is a fool, the audience must invert her words to arrive at wisdom
or truth. And sometimes, because Folly is just plain foolish, the
audience should accept what she says with nothing more than a
grain of salt. The conflict between the audience's traditional
role as privileged recipient of the author's discourse and its role
here as critical interpreter of the speaker's folly thus lends
irony to the rhetoric.

As a result the audience finds itself reading Folly's speech
with varying degrees of pathetic involvement or detachment
according to the kind of folly or wisdom that the speaker happens to be discoursing at the moment. Folly assigns her audience its dominant role at the beginning of her oration when she
calls it *Mystas* ("Devotees"). This characterization as "high

priests" is true in as many senses of the word "folly" as there are; and the whole range of meanings between the extremes of "this-worldliness" and "other-worldliness" in folly ought to warn the reader against taking the speaker blindly on her own word, for what Folly means and what the audience understands may or may not correspond with what the author intends.

In addition to its primary roles as interpreters and high priests, Folly's audience must also be prepared to play two other separate but overlapping roles. The first is the relatively wise observer of human foolishness which Folly directly assigns by pitting the audience against the world's foolish spectacle. Folly distinguishes her devotees moreover from those who call themselves "wise men" because as μωρότατοι, "most foolish," the latter truly deserve the title of μωροσόφους, "foolosophers," rather than "philosophers." Yet this procedure of aligning the audience with her own point of view is fraught with irony, since Folly herself constructs these categories and is not even sure what epithet she should use when she is addressing her *Mystas*: "You have my name, gentlemen ... gentlemen ... what shall I add by way of an epithet?" The irony might suggest that the reader should turn Folly's speech inside out to arrive at the truth. Yet even here this hermeneutic principle falters when she hesitates between addressing her audience as most wise or most foolish: "You applaud! I knew that none of you is so wise—or rather so foolish—no, I prefer to say so wise— as to err on that point" (p. 15). No designation is very secure when Folly assigns it.

The other role for the audience is partaker in the world's foolishness, a role Folly indirectly assigns by implying that she reigns everywhere. Though Folly clearly states that the whole world is foolish, she also preserves the fiction of trying to distance her audience from run-of-of-the-mill fools. No sooner has she denigrated her audience as part of mankind's foolish spectacle than she summons it to rise above the vulgar crowd and join the deities in witnessing its own movements, and a long list enumerates the follies viewed from such a perspective. She prefaces her invitation to the greater theater of fools by admit-

ting that she disdains to spend time on the common and lesser
sort of fools who are wholly hers without dispute: "They everywhere teem with so many forms . . . that a thousand Demo-
crituses would not suffice for laughing at them—and there
would be work, then, for one more Democritus to laugh at the
laughers" (p. 67). Clearly, by inviting her audience to join with
herself and the gods in viewing the spectacle of which they are
a part, Folly is maintaining an intimate but complex relationship with her audience. Listrius underlines that fact in his commentary when he explains how Erasmus's comedy allows us to
laugh at the whole human race: "The entire passage is comic,
and yet in a playful manner it depicts an image of human life"
(p. 161).

Towards the end of her oration, however, Folly qualifies
more precisely the nature of her audience's role as foolish participant. A certain confusion has inevitably resulted from Folly's
earlier refusal to partition her topic: "For it is equally unlucky to
circumscribe with a limit her whose nature extends so universally" (p. 10). It becomes clear, however, that there are two
types of madness: the malevolent type causes war, greed, pro-
miscuity, sacrilege, or any other bane that brings harm to
others; the benevolent type inflicts harm on no one and makes
the world breathe easier. Still later Folly divides this class of
benevolent fools (within which she includes herself and her
audience) into two categories: worldly fools who hanker after
things of conventionally high value, and spiritual fools who
pursue things of the spirit that the vulgar disdain: "Wherefore,
since there is so great contrariety between the pious and the
vulgar, it comes about that each appears to the other to be
mad—though in my opinion, to be sure, the word is more correctly applied to the pious than to the others" (p. 122). Listrius's note, moreover, reveals the complicity between author
and speaker, for the sentiment is fully Erasmus's, even though
it issues from the mouth of Folly: "In a festive mood she adds
'in my opinion' as if it would be proper in the opinion of
fools. For 'my' refers to the persona of Folly" (p. 240). Not
only Erasmus but even Folly has undisguised contempt for the

vulgus. Thus, by calling worldly fools *vulgus*, Folly clearly distances her audience from them; yet insofar as she deems spiritual fools worthy of her own name, Folly implies that she appeals to her audience through its capacity to be or to become spiritual fools.

Folly's ideal audience then will have in common the power to find joy in benevolent spiritual folly. Such an audience will not lament the lack of an objective yardstick to measure the wisdom or folly in the speaker's assertions. It will know that Folly is not offering a choice of wisdom *or* foolishness, truth *or* falsehood, good *or* bad, but rather of a foolishness that from different perspectives may be true and good or false and bad. Paraphrasing Plato (*Republic*, V.479d) and echoing the Stoics, Folly asserts that the happiness of man is not to be found in things as such; it resides in opinion (p. 63). On the other hand, though Folly may not be aware of it (after all she *is* Folly), one truly objective form of happiness is immune from the whirligig of opinion. It is the philosophy of Christ, available to all, not in any mere praise of Folly but in the concrete words of Scripture.

Among the members of Folly's audience there may be some at least acquainted with, if not actually trained in, methods of biblical exegesis as well as in systems of philosophy, whether of the Platonist, humanist, Stoic, or Aristotelian kind. If truly wise, these members will understand even better than Folly everything that she says and more. The ideal audience, however, would be the man to whom Erasmus addressed the *praefatio* of Folly's oration, Thomas More. Directly addressing this audience, Erasmus praises More for being accustomed to enjoy jokes that are somewhat learned—such a joke as *The Praise of Folly* will be. Erasmus praises him for being accustomed to dissent from the crowd that lives by the vulgar norms which Folly satirizes. And he praises him for being able to play the role of Democritus, a Democritus who can distance himself from all the vulgar norms that rule the world without distancing himself so much that he loses the power to relate to others, the power to be, as Folly says, a man for all seasons: "At the same time because of your incredibly affable and easy ways you can play the man of all hours with all men, and enjoy doing so." But admittedly this combination is too much to ask for in every member of the audience. Folly is content with a little learned sympathy on the part of her devotees and exegetes, and not much more.

The Praise of Folly, then, is a work whose style is determined not so much by the quality of its verbal surface—although witticisms, puns, slips of the tongue, prosopopoeia, and other elocutionary figures give the style a distinctive texture that enhances its ironic mode—as by its rhetorical strategies governing the characterization of the speaker and her relationship to the audience. The alternations between folly and wisdom, traversing all the grades between the two and confirming the complexity of her roles and selfhood, together with her drawing of the audience into her speech and manipulating it to uncover the ironies and ambiguities concealed there, define the style of *The Praise of Folly*. In a similar way these strategies become rhetorical determinants for the style of More's *Utopia* and Rabelais's *Gargantua and Pantagruel*.

More's *Utopia*

The *Utopia* (1516) of Thomas More (1477–1535) is more complex than *The Praise of Folly*. It has two speakers rather than the single one of Erasmus's work, and both of them are variously reliable and unreliable at random times. A single interlocutor like Folly causes problems, but two more than double them. One is Raphael Hythlodaeus, the traveller who describes Utopia's institutions; the other is "Thomas More," a fictive author who conveys the description and is quite distinct from Thomas More, the real author who controls the dialogue. (Hereafter I will use quotation marks to distinguish the former from the latter.) In addition, the rhetoric of *Utopia* involves more than one audience. Just as it has two main speakers, so it has two different audiences, a fictive one inside the text ("More" and Giles as hearers of Hythlodaeus's speech, and Hythlodaeus as hearer of "More's" and Giles objections) and a larger collective one outside the text (including both the empirical reader to whom "More" relates his account and the whole society that it indicts).[1] The use of the second-person pronoun in *Utopia* is therefore ambiguous. Sometimes *you* refers solely to the fictive audience limited in time, place, and performance, and sometimes it refers to the heterogeneous collective audience in the real world, the European society that Utopian society exceeds in perfection.

The rhetorical complexity of *Utopia* thus originates in its ethical complexity. The least problematic character in this complex is Peter Giles. Though More introduces him in an elaborate preamble, he hardly asserts himself as a speaker in the dialogue: once to sketch Hythlodaeus's background for "Thomas More"; again to initiate the conversation among themselves in book I by asking Hythlodaeus why he never attached himself to a king; after that to banter with him over a mistake in Latin diction when the latter protests about entering *in seruitium* ("into servitude") to kings, rather than *in servitudinem* ("into service"); and finally to oppose Hythlodaeus's assertion that the Utopians are the world's best ordered people by defending the Europeans' excellent minds and their long experience of good government.[2] These few intrusions hardly give Peter Giles an important dramatic role in the dialogue. They serve instead another function. They set him forth as the standard against which to measure the virtues and vices of other men, including the Utopians themselves and their advocate, Raphael Hythlodaeus. In fact, Peter Giles supplies the model for the audience—both fictive ("More" and Hythlodaeus) and real (the empirical reader)—to emulate: "For he is most virtuous and most cultured, to all most courteous, but to his friends so open-hearted, affectionate, loyal, and sincere that you can hardly find one or two anywhere to compare with him as the perfect friend on every score" (p. 48). If people like him ran the world, it would have no need for Utopian institutions; or, rather, Utopia would be everywhere, here and now.

The characterization of Raphael Hythlodaeus, Utopia's principal spokesman, moves almost counter to Peter Giles's.[3] The

rhetorical complexity of book I assigns its most reliable character, Peter Giles, the least dialogue and its least reliable character,
Raphael Hythlodaeus, the most. The latter's lack of reliability
emerges only very slowly through his manner of speaking. The
first indication (as "More" reveals in his "letter" to Giles) is
stylistic: he was "not so well acquainted with Latin as with
Greek" (p. 38), and Hythlodaeus' infelicitous use of Latin confirms the remark.

The reason for this stylistic eccentricity, as Peter Giles later
explains, is that Hythlodaeus "had devoted himself unreservedly
to philosophy, and in that subject had found that there is
nothing valuable in Latin except certain treatises of Seneca and
Cicero" (p. 50). That he speaks in Latin, and certainly not in
the elegant Latin of either Seneca or Cicero, makes for several
puns (the above-mentioned use of *in seruitium*), inaccuracies
(for example, the barbarous use of a reflexive *suis* for the personal pronoun *eorum*, p. 136), and even ambiguities (for example, a confusion between the genitive meaning or the dative
meaning in the case of *naturae*, p. 166).[4] Not only is Hythlodaeus given to "careless simplicity" in his "hurried and im-
promptu" prose style, as More writes to Giles (p. 38), but he is
also careless in his physical appearance as well (p. 48). More
first sees him as a man "of advanced years, with sunburnt
countenance and long beard and cloak hanging carelessly from
his shoulder". He wears the uniform of a traveler, indeed of a
pilgrim, one who has seen the best and worst of human society
and is able to speak about it, one who envisions a better society
towards which men can journey in this world.

Beyond his role as traveler, however, his role as philosopher
best defines him. As an eclectic he refuses to take for granted
any one philosophical system rather than another. He voices
more than a little skepticism on many matters, as the humorless
judgment on Utopian manners and morals interspersed throughout his account shows. He thinks, for example, that the Utopians are "somewhat too inclined" towards *voluptatem*, owing
to the pleasure that they take in supper, dessert, music, spices,
and perfumes (p. 144). As though austerity itself were a virtue,

he repeats his opinion that the Utopians "lean more than they should" towards the principle of *voluptas* in their philosophy (p. 160). And he finds *ridiculum* the practice of exposing suitors naked to each other before marriage (p. 188). True, he can accept the political norms of the Utopian people, but not their social norms. Perhaps for this reason he has never taken the final step of becoming a permanent citizen. He prefers instead the role of peregrinating expositor, painter in words rather than doer in deeds. The vision of Utopia obsesses him, not the experience, and this obsession colors the rhetorical strategy of his account of life in Utopia.

But skepticism and lack of humor are not all; there is much that is admirable in his style. For one thing, despite his own inflexibility, he concurs with "Thomas More" that their mutual friend, Cardinal Morton, was the best of men, "as much for his prudence and virtue as for his authority," (p. 58), and he commends the cardinal's willingness to try out new ideas: "No danger can come of the experiment" (referring of course to proposals that Hythlodaeus himself made about social reform). In considering the causes of social and political ills, he reveals a freedom from superstition and habit far ahead of his contemporaries' attitudes. He assumes, for example, that social ills (crime, poverty) derive not from original sin (as the disputatious lawyer suggests) but from man-made systems and institutions (war, capitalist economy, separation of classes) (p. 60), and that a ruler earns authority from the people, who should choose him (*deligere*) for their own sake and not for his (p. 94).

Still, despite his glowing praise of the spirit of rebellion—"generosos rebellandi spiritus" (p. 94)—Raphael Hythlodaeus seldom lets his style inflame the audience to open revolt. He cultivates instead an abrupt, almost rigidly doctrinaire manner of speaking that strikes at least one listener as insolent. To the suggestion of "Thomas More" that he suit his advice to political needs, he stoutly complains: "By this approach . . . I should accomplish nothing else than to share the madness of others as I tried to cure their lunacy," and he adds that his own principles require a blunt abrasive style (p. 100). Hythlodaeus then offers a "sermo tam insolens" (p. 98), as "Thomas More" earlier calls it, operating poles apart from the openness and flexibility which he praises so highly in Cardinal Morton and the Utopians.

"Thomas More," the third member of the rhetorical complex, whose central role is to report the substance of the conversation, also professes an eclectic philosophy. Unlike Hythlodaeus's, however, his proceeds less from cynicism than from a kind of *gai savoir* that accords with his own temperament and turns his style into a freewheeling play of ideas.[5] "More" is, for example, a Platonist up to the point where he can urge the dignity and virtue of serving as the king's advisor for the public good (p. 54), but he stops far short of Platonism in his rejection of communistic ideas. He eventually resembles those whom Hythlodaeus condemns for accepting only part of Christ's law: "The greater part of His teaching is far more different from the morals of mankind than was my discourse" (p. 100). Often "Thomas More" is so blind to Hythlodaeus's position that he seems something of the "Tom Fool" which Erasmus's playful etymology in the dedicatory letter of *The Praise of Folly* suggests (More=*Moria*=folly). Thus, he refutes communism at once with a puerile cliché: he repeats the old Aristotelian assertion that the removal of capital incentive is conducive to sloth, sloth to want, want to civil insurrection. By an unwarranted distortion of Hythlodaeus's argument, he assumes that Hythlodaeus has been speaking about not only economic but also political communism, or, more accurately, anarchy. He does not always have the last word, nor is he the perfect spokesman for either the book or its historical author, the real Thomas More.[6] Still, by comparison with Hythlodaeus's in book I, his style emerges as generally more humane.

A case in point is his ironic defense of "philosophia ciuilior" as opposed to Hythlodaeus's impractical, pedantic "philosophia scholastica" (p. 98). He knows that Hythlodaeus's arrogant style rather than his ideas will insure their defeat, that tolerance and good-will reap a better harvest than aggressive revisionism. Nonetheless, "More" does not really win his own argument either. The metaphor of the theater does not exactly reinforce his point about "philosophia ciuilior." One must, he says, respect the play without interfering in the performance, but he ignores a fundamental difference between theater and court. Actors play preassigned roles whose outcomes are guaranteed from the start. Courtiers however play various roles, none of them preassigned, and their outcomes are not guaranteed; politics involves endless experiment and readjustment in which the participants play not so much a part as a game. And yet, aware of human complexities, "More" knows that the style of "obliquus ductus" achieves more tangible practical results than the straightforward one.

"More's" disagreement with Hythlodaeus becomes incontrovertible when he asserts that human politics are complex primarily because human nature is complex. This reasoning explains why he has little of Hythlodaeus's confidence in the ability of Utopian institutional norms to reform society: "For it is impossible that all should be well unless all men were good, a situation which I do not expect for a great many years to come" (p. 100). The final modifying clause crowns "More's" style, revealing less the skepticism of the cynic than the caution of the realist. For him the reform of institutional norms may improve social relations, but it will never cure the real problem, which is the flaws in human nature. Hence the insistent irony of "More's" style and hence the ironic detachment with which he plays the role of audience to Hythlodaeus's oration. As a man of practical affairs he distances himself from what he considers a bloodless and impractical vision, but too much a gentleman to violate the norm of *courtesia* by arguing against a tired speaker, he poses his objections only obliquely and problematically. His reticence thus becomes a rhetorical device stimulating the audience to consider its own reactions to Hythlodaeus's vision, to carry on its own interior dialogue after closing the book. Like *The Praise of Folly*, the *Utopia* is above all a performance that invites active participation in interpretation.

Actually, the ambiguity of "More's" responses has a stylistic preparation early in the dialogue. Hythlodaeus himself establishes

the author's attitude when at the end of part I he narrates how
the good Cardinal Morton, for all his wisdom and sympathy, did
not wholeheartedly or unconditionally accept his own witty
proposals for eliminating theft in England. The cardinal knows
better than Hythlodaeus that his audience ought to weigh and
consider every shred of evidence for its substantial rather than
surface wisdom, and that it ought to distinguish between jest
and earnest when wit plays its trump. We know that Thomas
More composed this portrait of Cardinal Morton after he had
completed part II, containing Hythlodaeus's account of Utopia.[7] Whether or not his motive was to exemplify in Morton the
proper role for the audience to play in interpreting what follows, the author certainly raised the question of the audience's
relationships to the performer, and he implies an answer close
to Morton's.

This question leads directly to the problem of rhetorical
strategies. On every page Hythlodaeus attempts to manipulate
his audience's responses, and one of his favored techniques is
liberal use of first-person and second-person forms of verbs and
pronouns. They appear quite suddenly, for example, when he
explains the Utopian norms governing a maximum work load of
six hours per day. Lest you be mistaken, he warns, it is necessary to examine this point more closely (p. 128). You might
think that such brief work-loads lead to some scarcity of
necessities. But the reverse is true. You will understand this
paradox if you consider the way in which so many idle rich in
Europe exempt themselves from labor. Add to all the women
and clergy all the rich who don't work in Europe, include with
them their retainers, add the beggars, and you will find a work-
force of fewer than you thought (pp. 128–30). But for his
crowning point Hythlodaeus reserves the first-person plural
form of the verb, urging his audience to estimate ("Expende")
how many workers are involved in nonessential trades according
to the way we measure ("metimur") everything by the standard
of money. The return to "you" is all the more forceful when he
concludes that you would easily see ("facile animaduertis")

how small an allowance of time should be enough if Europeans redistributed the force of labor (p. 130).

The passage with the most extended and skillful use of direct address occurs in his account of the Utopian's philosophy of pleasure in book II. Here the speaker refers to his own private opinions in the first-person plural "editorial" form of the verb: "Quippe qui narranda eorum instituta, non etiam tuenda suscepimus" ("We have taken upon ourselves only to describe their principles, and not also to defend them"). At other times he uses the first-person plural to effect a rapprochement with his audience on arguments that the latter might consider questionable or at least odd. Thus, he shows how Utopian philosophical traditions resemble European ones. "In ea philosophiae parte qua de moribus agitur, eadem illis disputantur quae nobis" (p. 160), he says, with particular emphasis on *nobis* ("In that part of philosophy which deals with morals, they carry on the same debates as we do"). Using the conventional first-person plural of moralists and theologians, he rationalizes the Utopians' philosophy of pleasure by arguing that to good and decent pleasure our nature is drawn by virtue itself (p. 162). And he affirms that virtue, in the Utopian system, is living according to nature as we were created by God (p. 162).[8]

For all its critical edge directed against European institutions, Hythlodaeus's rhetoric does not completely flatter Utopian institutions.[9] Thomas More has used irony in the styles of both his interlocutors so that it is difficult, if not impossible, to determine whether the problems stem from the obtuseness of the speaker, Raphael Hythlodaeus, or from the obfuscations of the fictive transmitter, "Thomas More," or "Tom Fool." In some cases the author allows the speaker to approve of Utopian views that he himself could hardly condone. Hythlodaeus's persona allows for the ironic possibility that he is sometimes unaware of strong objections that others could bring against his argument. With a semblance of objectivity, Hythlodaeus introduces such questionable Utopian practices as the complete turnover of all farmworkers every two years, the exchange of their homes by lot every ten years, and the practice of transferring by adoption to other families children who wish to pursue trades different from their fathers'; but he never asks about their moral legitimacy. Thus, he exonerates practices which, whether or not they can be condemned out of hand, need at least some measure of defence or explanation.

On balance then, irony weighs against irony in Hythlodaeus's account of Utopian institutions, sometimes to the detriment of Europe, sometimes to the detriment of Utopia, sometimes to the detriment of both.[10] Utopian values are not overwhelmingly absolute, though they come off better than their European counterparts. True, the Utopians cannot prevent war, but their motives for waging war are sounder than the Europeans. True, the Utopians try to win battles without bloodshed, yet they do so by playing on the depravity of others, though such depravity is endemic to Europeans. True, the Utopians hire mercenaries and even delight in their killing of one another; still, they do not conscript citizens involuntarily as the Europeans do. As for religion, it is true that Utopian pluralism can lead to dissension among sects, but in practice there is little dissension and certainly no intolerance of the sort found in Europe. It is also true that the Utopians have not embraced what Catholic Europe regards as the one, holy, apostolic religion, but in practice the Utopians observe the ideals of Christianity more faithfully than many European Christians do.

The stylistic problem of multiple irony only underscores the central hermeneutic problem. If the chief interlocutors are unreliable guides, then what (if any) stylistic point of reference exists to control the audience's response? To what degree does the author operate behind the fiction so that he allows his audience to view the ironic event in full perspective, so that he motivates his audience to understand the truth as neither Hythlodaeus nor the Utopians might see it, nor as "Thomas More" or Europe might have it, but rather as all can see it simultaneously, now with greater, now with lesser clarity?

We have little to go on here, but perhaps the audience confronting the ambiguity is enjoined not to await solutions but rather to explore possibilities. The call to interpretation signals the audience's role in the text. The way to read *Utopia* is as an intellectual exercise which demands every last bit of mental agility, sensitivity to nuance, and readiness to meet challenging thrusts at accepted opinion. Thus, the final gesture of manipulation occurs in "Thomas More's" concluding assertion: "I first said, nevertheless, that there would be another chance to think about these matters more deeply and to talk them over with him more fully. If only this were someday possible!" (p. 244). "Thomas More" may be speaking entirely in his fictive persona as "Tom Fool," insofar as his failure to confront the problematic issues reflects his foolish, purblind, conservative selfhood. On the other hand, Thomas More might be speaking *in propria persona* as an author encouraging his audience to extend the debate pro and con beyond the text's limits. "Thomas More" and Raphael Hythlodaeus, the fictive characters, are too tired to continue. But Thomas More the real author has set the stage for further discussion by implying a need to resume somewhere else. In effect the author passes the responsibility onto the reader, since the reader alone can go beyond the end of the book.

The conclusion is tentative, reflecting the dialogue's overall attitude, both in style and in meaning. Perhaps in recognition of the ultimately unproductive effect that this tentativeness could have, Thomas More made one last effort to secure his relationship with the audience through a late insertion, the prefatory letter to Peter Giles.[11] There he analyzes in some detail his own fictive role as writer and mere "transmitter" of the dialogue as well as of his real-life role as member of society with attachments to clients, family, king, and friends. An implicit comparison with Hythlodaeus, who has no family, no king, and (for lack of mentioning them) no friends, suggests that it may be preferable in the long run to suffer the real Thomas More's responsibilities, upon which societies grow and develop, than to evade those responsibilities with Hythlodaeus's self-indulgent freedom. The latter travels, experiments, and engages in a speculative philosophy, but ultimately renders no concrete practical good to society. Thomas More may welcome the interlude of a conversation with him and perhaps even enjoy a vicarious share in his adventures, but after leaving the conversation in the garden of his temporary lodgings in Antwerp he returns to real society, where he undertakes the practical work of maintaining the commonwealth. Similarly with the reader of Utopia: he may welcome the book as an interlude, an escape, in many ways a joke or satire, but after he finishes it he too must return to society.

Thomas More once and for all drops his ironic mask in his letter to Giles. The precise moment occurs when he lashes out against audiences who fail to appreciate jokes, wit, and satire, suggesting by implication the audience's need to enjoy the jocular, witty, and satiric style of his own fiction. The kind of fictive audience he encourages must be attentive to the comic nuances of the work. The warning is important because comedy prevails throughout the book. Once the audience has grappled with the ironies, it may be wiser about accepting or rejecting possibilities for reform, though it is not necessarily enjoined to carry out Utopian reform in its own society. Here More's awareness of human limitations enunciated at the beginning of his letter to Giles comes full circle to the resigned awareness that in absolute terms one can never fully accomplish what one wants. The numerous roles that one plays make claims on one's time as well as on one's location in space and, in unexpected and sometimes unproductive ways, tax one's ability to sail clear and easy. But one doesn't for that reason abandon ship. Perhaps the only real joke is on those who do abandon ship, and who find to their dismay that the Utopia they sought is really no-where.

The style of *Utopia* is deliberately oblique and problematic. It does not allow either the fictive audience listening to the speakers' accounts or the empirical reader trying to cope with them to rest secure in their interpretations. Its verbal surface lacks the complication of ornamental diction, tropes, figures of speech, and other elocutionary devices. Its other rhetorical strategies, however, are highly complex, and they shape the style in their own distinctive ways. No less than *The Praise of*

Folly, therefore, More's *Utopia* testifies to the impossibility of understanding a text through its verbal strategies alone and shows the need for coming to terms with the characterization of the speaker and his relationship with the audience.

Rabelais's *Gargantua and Pantagruel*

Though the work of Rabelais (1494–1553) more clearly belongs to the narrative genre than either *The Praise of Folly* or *Utopia* do, it participates in the mode of comic, ironic, and philosophic jest that the others share, and it evinces a style whose rhetorical strategies compare in every way with theirs. Rabelais, that is, absorbs the rhetoric of Erasmus's oratory and More's dialogue in his own characters' monologues and conversational exchanges and in his sometimes lengthy prologues and editorial intrusions. He also uses the characterization, style, and world-view of the speaker—named Alcofribas Nasier in *Pantagruel* and *Gargantua*—to mediate the characterizations, styles, and world-views of other personages throughout the book.[1]

As a result, the speaker's characterization comes to dominate the book. It begins with his conception of the individual as one whose public roles complement, supplement, or otherwise coincide with the individual's inner private life in a one-to-one relationship. Rarely does he express or imply a conflict between any character's selfhood and the roles that he plays, conflicts such as epic poets, dramatists, and modern novelists usually develop. He emphasizes instead correspondences between the character's inner world and his role playing in the outer world; correspondences, that is, between mannerisms betokening the character's selfhood, and the external *visibilia* the character displays—his size, clothes, gestures, appearances—often betokening his role.[2]

Early in *Pantagruel* (1532), for example, the pedantic Limousin scholar speaks in a style associated with the Parisian school, full of extended periods, quasi-metrical cadences, and latinate elocutionary devices. When Pantagruel lays hands on him, however, he expresses himself spontaneously in his native language: "Vée dicou, gentilastre! Ho, sainct Marsault, adjouda my! Hau,

hau, laissas à quau, au nom de Dious, et ne me touquas grou!"
(p. 34) ("Haw, guid master! Haw, lordie! Help me, St. Marshaw.
Ho, let me alane, for Gaud's sake, and dinna hairm me!" p.
185).[3] Even the clothes that he wears, alternately shabby, eccentric, and just plain foolish, along with his subsequent loss of
bowel control, confirm the crude, ridiculous nature of the
hollow role that he is playing: "But the poor Limousin beshat
all his breeches, which were cut codtail fashion and not full-
bottomed" (p. 185). The number of minor characters whose
voices and *visibilia* confirm the bond between their inner and
outer worlds extends across the breadth of Rabelais's book,
from the sophistic scholar Maistre Janotus de Bragmardo in
Gargantua (1534) to the gallery of fools, scoundrels, and
pedantic authorities in the *Tiers Livre* (1546) and *Quart Livre*
(1552). The confrontation between these characters and the
major ones—Gargantua, Pantagruel, Panurge—results in a clash
of styles which provides the chief impetus for the narrative
action.[4]

With the major characters the speaker's technique of differ-
entiation is more complex. Because they play a limited number of fixed roles—father, son, student, military leader, and
chatelain—the speaker develops subtle stylistic and rhetorical
contrasts to differentiate them more precisely. Between Pantagruel and Panurge the speaker emphasizes differences in voice
and selfhood as well as in the roles and *visibilia* dominating each
character's style and *ethos*. On the surface no two characters
could play more dissimilar roles, Pantagruel as serious soldier-
scholar, Panurge as carefree knave; even their outward appearances clash, the one a giant, the other of average size. Yet they
share a mutual talent for accommodating their natural spon-
taneity to normative discipline for creative purposes. Through
the principle of comparison and contrast the speaker brings
them together in ironic juxtapositions so that one's characterization and style best reflects the other's.[5]

In the *Tiers Livre* the speaker shows them in league against
the world (in this case the numerous "authorities" from whom
they seek an answer to Panurge's question about being cuck-

olded), even though the speaker emphasizes their very pronounced idiosyncracies. Pantagruel urges his friend to halt his
ironic praise of debtors with an astonishingly curt "Let us leave
this subject. This is the second time I have suggested it," p.
303). A few sentences later he lapses into the *tu* form of address,
implying a measure of contempt for his audience.[6] His petu-
lance and irascibility stem partly from a superior awareness of
the subtleties of language and the subjective biases that hamper
interpretation of another's speech. In chapter 19 when Pantagruel speaks in praise of dumb men's counsel, he warns of
"ambiguities, equivocations, and obscurities in the words,"
owing to the fact that "words, as the dialecticians say, have
meanings not by nature, but at choice" (p. 339). Pantagruel
always acknowledges the subjective significance that choice
confers on the speech act. For Panurge, however, words have
objective significations which admit only of univocal meanings,
no matter how complex the mode of expression or underlying
intent. He assumes an identity between what one says and what
one means, and between what one is thought to have meant and
what one is thought to be. Thus, in chapter 22 Panurge rejects
the advice of Raminagrobis the poet because he suspects him of
heresy without having understood his argument. Panurge never
knows how style complicates meaning, while Pantagruel always
does. Throughout the *Tiers Livre*, therefore, the speaker accentuates their roles as two different types of audience responding
to the authorities' answers. While Pantagruel characteristically
receives each answer with a skeptical detachment, weighing its
folly and wisdom, Panurge receives each as absolute, definitive,
and unqualified.

In the *Tiers Livre* the speaker shows how certain stylistic
peculiarities evoke the *ethos* of whole professional classes which
they typify.[7] In the *Quart Livre* he shows how the stylistic
peculiarities of other individuals are rooted in public idiosyncrasies on a larger social scale. Thus, the language of the Ennasés,
Andouilles, Papefigues, Papimanes, and Gastrolatres—exclamations and apostrophes, hyperboles and paradoxes, parentheses
and sententiae, immoderate language lacking rhetorical focus—

betokens the character of immoderate speakers who lack moral restraint and the character of whole societies that lack all containment.

Once more Panurge emerges as a fool. In chapters 20 and 22, for example, during the great storm at sea, the stylistic control of the sea captain conveys a sense of skill and expertise which manages to save the day, while Panurge's flood of words confirms the character of the fool. Even on the last page of the *Quart Livre* when he moves his bowels so untimely out of fear, he pours forth words in arguing to the contrary. Here the malodorous excrement that covers him is a tactile, visual, and olefactory confirmation of his lack of containment, but Panurge still thinks his logorrhea can explain away what his audience perceives so plainly. His obstinacy in refusing to admit his loss of control parallels his obstinacy in coming to terms with himself as a fool. As though to exorcise himself from the excrement that covers him, itself a burlesque reduction of the spirit of the inner man to the matter of the inner man, Panurge constructs a litany of synonyms for his feces and concludes by calling it another name: "It's saffron from Ireland, that's what I think it is. Ho, ho, ho! Saffron from Ireland! It is indeed. Let's have a drink!" (p. 597).

Pantagruel, for his part, assumes a more and more complex style which signals his role as the moral center of the book. Rabelais's hero has become magisterial in his gestures of approval and disapproval, gestures that often seem strangely motivated in the context of his former style. His new style is difficult not because any mannerisms, tics, or peculiar inflections of voice render it opaque, but because its ethical intention remains so open-ended. In the *Quart Livre* his account of the children of Physis and Antiphysis implies that men have within themselves powers of reason and will which can both transform nature and deform it. It also implies that natural man ought to accept himself as he is, somewhat less than perfect, perhaps, but only because it is natural for him to be so. Antiphysis's children (Amodunt, "Without Measure," and Discordance) are "prettier and more attractive than Physis's" (p. 521), but they are monsters.[8] The norms which men in the strange societies of the *Quart Livre* have wilfully devised for themselves illustrate both implications. By no accident Pantagruel's speech on Physis and nature's norms comes at both the mechanical and the moral center of the book, and its style reflects the enigmatic character of the hero who delivers it. It also points to the central rhetorical problem of coming to terms with the *Quart Livre*, a problem arising from the book's emphasis on fantasy, which everywhere challenges not only the imagination but also the interpretive faculty of the audience.

By posing this last problem Rabelais may be suggesting that the interpretation of his fiction can provide some sort of testing ground for experience itself, that reading it can sharpen one's ability to confront the ironies and enigmas of life. Thus, Rabelais's *oeuvre* presents a constant challenge, a constant puzzle, a constant call to interpret the manifold levels of irony implicit in it.[9] In the long run its irony makes the reader more aware of the problematic nature of even everyday occurrences. But here the conspiracy of reader and author goes beyond the problem of fictional characterization presented by the book and raises the problem of other rhetorical relationships.

The complex relationship between the speaker and the audience needs careful study. In *The Praise of Folly* we have seen that when the speaker mediates between author and audience by expressing her own point of view but not necessarily that of Erasmus, she complicates the reader's understanding. In *Utopia* we have seen how the speaker ("Thomas More") mediates between author and audience, and also between them and other fictive characters (Raphael Hythlodaeus and Peter Giles) who in turn comment on reality from their own subjective stances. In Rabelais not only does the narrator allow his characters to interpose and complicate the relationships between the reader and the author, but he also creates a fictive audience—generally typified as "bon beveurs"—to interpose between the reader and the speaker on the one hand and between the reader and the author on the other.

Thus, from the start the reader must be aware of the role the narrator assigns to him or her. The role, especially if it is low and repulsive, can have a decisive effect on the reception of the text.[10] If it is very specific, it can alienate from the text every nonmember of the class that it specifies. But paradoxically the role can also involve the reader more closely by its challenge to play the role regardless of inclination. The author does not so much have to convince the reader of the role's appropriateness as he has to promise the reader profit and enjoyment in seeing the role worked out. His purpose is to wean the audience from its own prejudices and to help it perceive the world in a new way. If the fictive role proves difficult to interpret, it is so because life itself is even more difficult to interpret; and the interpretation of fiction in the final analysis affords good testing ground for the interpretation of life.

In the Prologue of *Pantagruel* the fictive audience consists of "Trèsillustres et trèschevaleureux champions, gentilz hommes et aultres, qui voluntiers vous adonnez à toutes gentilesses et honnestez" ("most illustrious and most valorous champions, noblemen, and others, who gladly devote yourselves to all gentle and honest pursuits"), especially readers who amuse ladies by recounting episodes from the *Gargantuan Chronicles*. This audience is literate, sophisticated, and urbane, acquainted with some philosophy, literature, ideas, general culture. The speaker, Alcofribas Nasier, assigns it a very specific role: "I would have every man put aside his proper business, take no care for his trade, and forget his own affairs, in order to devote himself entirely to this book" (p. 167). In turn he implies his attitude towards the *Gargantuan Chronicles* by urging that it should be passed from hand to hand, generation to generation, "like some religious Caballa." The profit in the *Chronicles* is literally a therapeutic one, as Alcofribas asserts when he describes its curative effects for sufferers of chill, toothache, and pox. So convinced is he of its value that he offers a reward of tripe to anyone who finds another book as good.[11]

Alcofribas delivers a less tolerant challenge to the audience that does not share his attitude towards the book, ranking them with deceivers, predestination men, impostors, and seducers. The radical shift in tone from mild banter to outright abuse signals the speaker's tendency to swing between extremes of tone and attitude. It should alert the audience to the fundamental irony that till now Alcofribas has been according praise to another book, the *Gargantuan Chronicles*, at the very moment when the audience would expect him to be touting his own. But this topos of modesty works two ways, since the speaker soon appropriates for himself the very claims which he has lavished on the *Chronicles.* Not only is his own book, as he later declares, as good as the *Chronicles*, but it is even "ung peu plus équitable et digne de foy" ("a little more reasonable and credible," p. 168). Still he tries hard to retreat behind a double veil of modesty and buffoonery, characterizing himself as the humble slave of his audience and a thoroughly reliable narrative reporter.

The motif of a telepathic confidence becomes important, governing the reader's response to the text. At the close of the first chapter, attempting a more intimate relationship with his audience, Alcofribas admits that he anticipates its honest doubts about the survival of Pantagruel's ancestors from Noah's flood. Here the telepathy works two ways. Just as the audience is obliged to give itself wholly to the speaker, so the speaker responds by giving himself wholly to the audience. He not only appreciates the audience's problems in wrestling with the text, but perhaps even shares some of them. By raising the issue of doubt, the speaker may be exorcising his own incertitude, but as a byproduct he evokes in the audience the very reaction that he pretends to allay. At the same time, however, he encourages the audience to renew its ties with him who so confidently "reads" its attitude.

Throughout the rest of *Pantagruel* Alcofribas relates to his audience on levels that reinforce his central intention. In his role as historian he encourages his audience to share his attitude even at the expense of reporting the fiction itself. Indeed, he takes more care to affirm the rapport with his audience than he does to describe the action. Thus, in chapter 2 on the birth of Pantagruel he mediates between the audience and the account with casual remarks like "You will note . . . you would have seen . . . you might have seen . . .," despite the anything but casual and ordinary nature of the action.

He also plays the role of his protagonists' contemporary and associate. When he tells of a book composed by Panurge on *The Utility of Long Codpieces* he radically foreshortens his narrative's pastness and historicity with the aside "It is not printed yet, so far as I know" (p. 222). And in chapter 17 he enters the fiction directly as participant with Panurge in a tour of churches to buy pardons. From this moment on Alcofribas becomes an eyewitness of the events he relates: "One day I found Panurge somewhat woe-begone and taciturn." Henceforth he emphasizes his temporal and physical proximity to his subject in every respect, culminating in an episode where he undertakes a private journey through the world that he discovers in Pantagruel's mouth (chapter 32).

Finally, as a literary artist who dominates the narrative, Alcofribas plays one last controlling role as writer, reporter, and on occasion parodist of certain well-known literary themes, archetypes, and stylistic conventions. Early in *Pantagruel* he establishes his talent to reproduce others' speech and styles in episodes such as the encounter with the Limousin student (chapter 6) and the catalogue of books in the Library of St. Victor (chapter 7). Later he recalls from a model so august as Virgil's *Aeneid* several parallels such as the relationship between Pantagruel and Panurge "such . . . as Aeneas and Achates" (p. 201) and the departure of Pantagruel from the Lady of Paris in a haste that reminds Epistemon of "Aeneas's conduct towards Dido" (p. 247). Above all, in his treatment of King Anarch's war he becomes an overt epic parodist who shifts into high style from the invocation to the muses at the end of chapter 28 through the description of Pantagruel's battle with Loupgarrou in chapter 29, to Epistemon's account of his descent to the Underworld in chapter 30.

The purpose of this elaborate rhetorical strategy in *Pantagruel*, however, remains limited. Here in the first book Rabelais forged a magnificent parodic, satiric, and comic narrative, but out of it he seldom fashions any really substantial vision of life or human activity.[12] In *Gargantua*, however, he transcends this limitation by lending substance to what he says through an appropriate rhetoric. The point of Rabelais's skillful rhetoric becomes evident in *Gargantua* as the author draws his audience into an ever expanding conspiracy against the customs, conventions, and accepted mores of the day.

In the Prologue Alcofribas addresses two fictive audiences: his drinking companions ("Beuveurs tresillustres") and his medical patients, victims of syphilis ("Verolés tresprecieux"). The drinkers thirst for the truth that his book can bring, while the syphilitics seek a cure for the ills that human flesh is heir to.[13] The speaker assures them of a cure in his book, which he compares to the ancient Silenus, a gaily ornamented medicine box, named after the old satyr who taught Bacchus. Upon opening it one would have found "une celeste et impreciable drogue" that Alcofribas identifies with the therapeutic value of his text. To strengthen his claim, he points out that the ancients regarded Socrates in his enigmatic duality as a Silenus. In the next paragraph he extends this duality to his audience as good disciples and fools of leisure, "quelques aultres folz de sejour" to whom he will nonetheless reveal truths deeper rather than mockery, fooling, and pleasant fictions. Dual audiences, dual meanings, dual attitudes toward both will animate the entire text.

Two examples follow. Asking whether his audience has ever picked a lock to steal a bottle, Alcofribas comments that just as it might have devoted all its energies to the task, now it must break the lock of this book. With the more elaborate example of a dog who guards the marrow of a bone, he exhorts his audience to seek the *substantifique mouelle* nourishing the substance beneath the fictional surface. At the same time he undermines this example by ridiculing the allegorizations of texts like Homer's *Iliad* and *Odyssey*: "But do you faithfully believe that Homer, in writing his *Iliad* and *Odyssey*, ever had in mind the allegories squeezed out of him by Plutarch?" (p. 38). The attentive audience will find here a sophisticated awareness of the hermeneutic process that he would have each of its members share. Far from denying the value of polysemous reading, the speaker is affirming it by urging his audience to engage all its faculties in that task and by debunking the attempts of others (such as Homer's allegorizers) to reduce complex texts to straightforward statements. Like the dog looking for the marrow, the audience must never give up its active quest for meaning, just as it must never take the pat formulations of allegorizing monks for the last word in literary interpretation.

Throughout the balance of *Gargantua* the fictive audience's role undergoes several transformations from prominence in the early chapters dealing with Gargantua's birth and youth, to a lesser prominence in later ones involving his education and the war with Picrochole. In chapter 3, for example, dealing with Gargamelle's eleven-month pregnancy, Alcofribas addresses the fictive audience of out-and-out lechers when he cites a law legitimizing a widow's child born up to eleven months after her husband's death: "So I beg of you, all my fine lechers, if you find any of these same widows worth the trouble of untying your codpiece, mount them and bring them to me" (p. 47). The vulgarity, which may shock some, serves to remind others of one's proper distance from the fiction. Alcofribas enforces this distance when he recounts the marvelous birth of Gargantua: "Si ne le croiez, le fondement vous escappe!" ("If you don't believe it, may your fundament fall out!" p. 47). Later he dismisses unbelievers in his midst with a flippant appeal to written authority, even though he challenges such authority throughout the book: "But an honest man, a man of good sense, always believes what he is told and what he finds written down" (p. 52). And still further on, with a skillful, though crude rebuff, he calls his audience clods from the flatlands if any finds his account of Gargantua's mare hard to believe (p. 73).

The speaker's purpose in these and other episodes is comic intimidation. His account of Gargantua's clothes, colors, and livery exemplifies the technique. As he takes on the part of the "vieil beuveur" which he originally assigned to his audience in the Prologue, the audience takes on the role of medieval authority earlier parodied in chapter 1: "I quite realize that on reading these words you will laugh at the old boozer, and consider his interpretation of colours most ungentlemanly and infelicitous" (p. 57). Still, he intimidates it into rejecting the authors of explicatory works like *Le Blazon des couleurs* as tyrants "who would have their will take the place of reason" (p. 58). Right reason aims toward understanding the significance of things in their own true nature. In chapter 10, therefore, he affirms that white stands for "joy," "as you may verify if you will set aside your prejudices and listen to what I am now about to explain." The audience must conclude not just that colors have natural significance transcending the authorities' normative interpretations, but also that the very concept of authority exercises unjust tyranny over the life of reason and ought to be usurped.

In the final episode of *Gangantua*, the description of the Abbaye de Thélème, the speaker once more asserts his presence as a stabilizing force. He does so prominently in his consistent use of the past tense: "The building was hexagonal in shape" (p. 151); "The said building was a hundred times more magnificent" (p. 152); and "So it was that Gargantua had established it. In their rules there was only one clause: DO WHAT YOU WILL" (p. 159). The rhetorical strategy of using the past tense, as though the monastery no longer exists, distances the audience from the world of Thélème, and it also raises the question of Thélème's power to survive in the present world: the question, that is, of its relevance, it actuality, its status as an illusion. Indeed, its essential fragility endangers the whole project. Only one other mention of the abbaye occurs in Rabelais's work. When Panurge on the Island of Medamothi ("Nowhere") in the *Quart Livre* buys a painting depicting the myth of Philomele, the speaker comments, "Vous la pourrez veoir en Theleme, à main guausche, entrans en la haulte guallerie" (p. 39) ("You can see it at Thélème, on the left-hand wall, as you enter the high gallery," p. 454). But Medamothi is literally "nowhere," a fiction, a utopia, a place where Pantagruel buys three unicorns and a tarand, and his friend buys a work of art for an imaginary monastery. Like any fabulation, however, Thélème has its own rhetorical function, not the least of which may be enjoining the audience to consider its own Thélème, not as a physical structure in time or space, but as a spiritual structure governing one's relationships with other human beings.[14]

The speaker's relationship to his audience in the *Tiers Livre* is considerably different. To begin with, the speaker identifies himself as "Rabelais" and not as "Alcofribas Nasier." Large portions of this book, moreover, present straightforward dialogue, with few expository links other than the Prologue and some intrusions by the author scattered throughout. Still, the speaker's skepticism makes his relationship with the audience more complex than before, culminating in his violent denunciation of certain types of fictive audience. In the Prologue he correlates from the Prologue to *Pantagruel* the "Bonnes gens" who devote themselves to higher pursuits, and from the Prologue to *Gargantua* the "Beuveurs tresillustres, et vous Goutteaux tresprecieux" with whom he enjoys a telepathic confidence. Their conflation points to the unique concern of the *Tiers Livre*. The speaker's declarations and his imperatives to drink and listen echo the earlier books with a difference: that the story of Diogenes which he now offers may touch upon his and his audience's own concerns in very intimate ways, for just as Diogenes had certain human imperfections, so has he, and so has his audience, "for none but God is perfect" (p. 281).

Whatever the audience's relationship to Diogenes, the speaker clarifies his own in a single brilliant anecdote. As Diogenes during the war needed to engage in some militant activity, so does the speaker. He holds little love for those who in such time stand idly by watching the *tragicque comedie* and through their silence approve the grotesque *prosopopée* (p. 14). Thus, he portrays Diogenes as a philosopher who cynically refused allegiance to either side, but hardly preserved his neutrality. He acted instead with a purpose, not in the substance of what he did—for rolling his earthen tub and twirling it and whirling it ad infinitum was merely foolish—but rather in the process of what he did, for by representing his attitude obliquely and enigmatically he impelled bystanders and onlookers to question their own feelings.[15] The process resembles the search for the *substantifique mouelle* in the Prologue to *Gargantua.* The audience's proper response, whether to Diogenes' politics or to the speaker's fiction, consists in a replication of the quest, the active involvement that it finds in perpetual motion and that the speaker reinforces in his own verbal effusion as an apt stylistic equivalent of what Diogenes did.

The speaker now voices his fears that audiences will not receive him as he hopes they will. He illustrates the conflict with the anecdote of Ptolemy, who wished to please the Egyptians by giving them a black Bactrian camel and a particolored mulatto, but who found himself attacked by his audience instead. Here Ptolemy's "error of nature" ("monstre infame, créé par erreur de nature," p. 17) is emblematic of the speaker's own work of art, which itself thrives on ironic combinations of disparate materials. The artist's ability to use irony, to present the same situation from two or more perspectives simultaneously, to dramatize antithetical attitudes as equally valid, to say both Yes and No at the same time meaningfully, as the poet Raminagrobis does, will comprise the subject of this very book, forcing the audience to share in the difficult process of interpreting the truth.

And yet just when the audience acquires a clearer sense of its fictive role in the *Tiers Livre*, it begins to lose its sense of the speaker's role. The dominant form of the book is dialogue, with only a minimum of connecting narration, so that the voice of the speaker as controlling agent practically drops out of the fiction. The diminution of the speaker's role becomes particularly apparent in his confusions about time, place, and narrative continuity. In chapter 13, for example, at the end of the long conversation between Pantagruel and Panurge on the subject of divination by dreams, Frere Jan unaccountably begins to speak, without any prior indication of his presence. And throughout the book Frere Jan (chapter 20) and other characters like Epistemon (chapter 21), Carpalim (chapter 33), Ponocrates (chapter 34), and Gymnaste and Rhizotome (chapter 38) reemerge as participants in scenes where the speaker had not specified their presences earlier. Above all, Gargantua, whose death the speaker had indicated in chapter 23 of *Pantagruel*, suddenly enters the action in chapter 35 of the *Tiers Livre* and exits just as precipitously after he denounces modern philosophy in chapter 36.

The effect is a challenge to the speaker's credibility. An audience that has pledged unqualified support has already learned to accept his caveats about placing faith in the appearance of things. It knows that explanations of reality derive their truth content from words, but words, to respect what Pantagruel tells Panurge in chapter 19, have meaning not by nature but by choice. Inevitably then, both speakers and audiences share their understanding of each other's discourse in highly personal, highly subjective ways. The action of the *Tiers Livre* deals explicitly with Pantagruel's and Panurge's reception of the words of others, though implicitly it also deals with the audience's reception of the narrative about Pantagruel and Panurge. Just as the latter confront the problem of interpretation without any recourse to external aids, so the audience sets out to interpret the narrative without the aid of the speaker's exposition or commentary.

The rhetorical strategy giving such independence to the audience's reception of the *Tiers Livre* becomes problematic in the context of humanist philosophy animating the narrative. Such an enterprise, posited on the notion that each word has an absolute meaning which can be established with philological rigor, falls to pieces if each audience construes meaning subjectively and differently. Because public and private affairs mediate between the speaker and his choice of words and between those words and the audience's understanding of them, it would seem that humanism, viewed strictly as a philological endeavor, has little chance for success. The popular folktale tradition of the *Bibliotheque bleue*, so scoffed at by the schoolmen, becomes thus the perfect vehicle, exploited so brilliantly by the speaker in *Gargantua* and *Pantagruel*, to express his distrust of dreary academic wordplay. The vehicle of the *Tiers Livre* is different. Of all the books in the Rabelaisian *oeuvre*, this is least indebted to the fabulous events of the folktale tradition. Not once does it refer to Pantagruel's gigantic stature or prowess, and not once does it recount an action which could be called fantastic or grotesque or in any way extraordinary. Instead it, and later the *Quart Livre*, derive their narrative traditions from Lucian. The latter's dialogues and philosophic parodies inform the dramatic exchanges of the *Tiers Livre*, and his *True History* inspires the fantastic voyage of the *Quart Livre*.

The form of Rabelais's *Quart Livre* thus marks a return to conventional narrative. The narrator also reenters as the hero's companion on his journey to Bottleland, "l'oracle de la dive Bouteille Bacbuc," and hence as an eyewitness reporter. These numerous references to his role in the *Quart Livre* have a resonance not heard earlier. First, the speaker's attitude towards his audience is considerably milder, even conciliatory. In the prologue to the *Quart Livre* he addresses its members as "Gens de bien," not as boozers or syphilitics, and he compliments their willingness to find rapport with him as sharers in the secrets of Pantagruelism: "I am, thanks to a little Pantagruelism—which, as you know, means a certain lightness of spirit compounded of contempt for the chances of fate—I am, as I said, sound and supple, and ready to drink, if you will" (p. 439).

Second, the speaker's attitude towards himself is more open and vulnerable. In the prologues to both the *Tiers Livre* and the *Quart Livre* he accords himself his proper name, François Rabelais, and plays upon his own professional status as physician in a confessional manner. In the latter prologue he weaves this role into the fictional fabric itself. He relies, he says, on the will of God expressed in Luke, where the physician who neglects his own health is told "Physician, heal thyself." The implication that as a physician-author he means to heal himself through his medicine-book goes deep, for just as he may achieve bodily health through the one, so through the other he may achieve spiritiual health, an integrated and harmonious sense of selfhood.

A third effect quickly follows upon these. Turning from Scripture to secular history, the speaker cites the example of Galen, who preserved his own health for a singularly different motive: "out of fear of exposing himself to vulgar and satirical jibes." The speaker's sense of the precariousness of his public role is stronger here than anywhere else in Rabelais's work, and it gives the *Quart Livre* a new and distinct tone. For in the context of Rabelais's development, the rhetoric of the *Quart Livre* aims less at didactic edification (as in *Gargantua*) and more at justifying the author's role as artist and privileged manipulator of the audience's sensibilities.[16] Moreover, the speaker himself justifies this role not by arguing theory but by demonstrating his practice. He narrates, for example, his tale of Couillatris's request for a new hatchet, enfolding within it not only another tale, that of the trials and tribulations of Jove in granting the requests of Ramus and Galland, but also one more narrative, that of Jove's petrification of the fox and the dog. The manipulation of a tale-within-the-tale-within-a-tale advances the narrator's narrative and rhetorical mastery and forewarns the audience to expect a most subtle control of fictive and rhetorical structures.

And, indeed, throughout the *Quart Livre* the author demonstrates the most sustained development of craft yet offered in his work. In small matters, such as telling the audience what books Gargantua sent Pantagruel on his voyage (chapter 4), or in more complex ones, such as comparing the customs of Renaissance Europe with those of the Ennasés regarding marriage, family relationships, and language (chapter 9), the speaker is equally adept at establishing his presence, his reliability, and the authenticity of what he says.[17] In the episode concerning the Gastrolatres, for example, the speaker seeks to prove that Maistre Gaster was the first master of arts in the world by disclaiming arguments in favor of other origins. Directly addressing the audience, he asserts the error of believing that fire is the prime mover of the arts, as Cicero wrote, and further of taking the matter so seriously, since Cicero himself did not believe it (p. 570). In the episode on the ambush of the Andouilles, the speaker uses the entire chapter to affirm his own credibility. By addressing his audience as *beuveurs*, he reestablishes his collegiality with it while calling into question its powers of discrimination. By asserting that he reads its members' minds ("You do not believe that what I tell you is really true," p. 531), he skillfully preempts any objection to the veracity of his tale. By concluding, "I don't know what to do about you," he heightens his own allegedly subjective dilemma. Actually, the choice that he allows—"Believe me if you like; and if you don't, go and see for yourselves"—amounts to a nonchoice, for no audience can ever verify the speaker's claims about sheer fiction; its only choices are either to "believe" and read on, or to disclaim and close the book.

The subsequent claim that "nothing is truer than my tale, except the Gospel" raises the issue of veracity. Owing to greater emphasis on the purely fantastic and improbable in the *Quart Livre*, the need to defend the fiction has become greater, and not just from the perspective of interpreting the action, as in *Gargantua*, but more radically from that of questioning the ontological status of fiction itself. Thus, the speaker's defences reflect a growing interest in defining and delimiting the parameters of fictional possibility.

The subtlety with which the speaker manipulates his audience to accept the fictional validity of Pantagruel's purchase of three young unicorns and a tarand on the Island of Medamothi is exemplary.[18] In order to persuade the audience of the animals' very existence, he first points out that Democritus had written about chameleons (and, by implication, if they exist, why shouldn't tarands also exist?) and second, he stresses his own eyewitness account of the tarand's change of color ("what we found most remarkable about this tarand," p. 455). The speaker maneuvers such a rhetorical strategy in order to defend the fabulous animal against an even unformulated attack because the tarand itself typifies the ontological status of fiction: it does not exist of and by itself, but an author creates and confers existence upon it.

If the tarand acts as one figure for the fiction, there are other figures as well, and ones whose validity the speaker no less subtly attempts to authenticate. Bringuenarilles, for example, whose customary diet consists of windmills, kettles, and cauldrons, dies choking on a lump of butter. The speaker feels that this unlikely manner of death suggests others recorded in history, such as the deaths of Aeschylus, Anacreon, Fabius, and Philemon. Ironically, Bringuenarilles is not even Rabelais's own creation. The strange creature first appeared in one of the many anonymous imitations of Rabelais's work during the 1530s, *Panurge avec les prouesses du mervieuleux Bringuenarilles*. By incorporating another author's character into his own fiction, Rabelais emphasizes its own independent existence. The nature of fiction is such that it can appropriate materials from anywhere, from real life, history, imagination, other works of fiction, but once they become part of a given text, they exist only for its purposes. The Bringuenarilles of the *Quart Livre* work is like no other Bringuenarilles; he is *Rabelais's* Bringuenarilles, an organic part of his work no more and no less real than any other part of it, a fiction for which the speaker is responsible.

A similar figure dominates the chapter on thawed words (chapter 56). Pantagruel tries to liberate them because it is "folly to store up things which one is never short of" (p. 569). Just as they remain frozen chunks until the heat melts them and they emit sound, so the text remains but a printed page until some reader reads it and allows it to emit meaning. Yet just as the words truly exist in the ice whether or not they eventually melt, so the text may be said truly to exist even though it finds no readers. It exists precisely because it contains within itself its own audience, its "fictive" audience, regardless of whether it encounters an actual reader. The parodic separation of Platonic form (words) from content (meaning) comes to epitomize the essential relationship between text and audience. The effort finally to preserve the text or verbal form for its own sake, divorced from its audience, is futile, because for each text the audience supplies the content and ultimate meaning. The artistic manipulation of diction, tropes, schemes, and other figures is no longer the sole determinant of meaning in Rabelais's work. The inordinate pains that he takes to involve the audience within his own fiction prove that the author regards other rhetorical strategies as at least equally important determinants of style.

Thus, Rabelais's attitude toward style, embodied in the shifting relations between speaker and audience throughout the book, challenges language's potential to reveal absolute truth or to communicate straightforward objective content. More particularly, it challenges the assumptions of a philological humanism which posits faith in linguistic transparency and in its own scholarly capacity to arrive at a full and accurate understanding of others' words.[19] Rabelais's choice of popular materials from the *Bibliotheque bleue* reinforces this attitude. What better vehicle to challenge the sage and serious sagacity of a self-styled intellectual elite, and thus to deride the academic humanists' faith in a narrowly construed empirical philology, than the vehicle of popular tales couched in the vernacular of an anti-intellectual marketplace?

Paradoxically, Rabelais's questioning of humanist assumptions became possible only after the humanist movement had achieved some measure of success. On the one hand, the humanists' philological competence brought to light certain ironies and ambiguities latent in ancient texts and pointed to their function in modern ones as well. On the other, it allowed these ironies and ambiguities to gnaw on humanism's own intent. Rabelais, and to a lesser extent Erasmus and More before him, came to recognize how language conspires against experience by mythologizing reality into phonemic, morphemic, and syntactic units. Any change in those categories will motivate a corresponding change in the culture that supports them. Thus, the stylistic evidence of the texts suggests that Rabelais, with others, participated in just such a transformation within their own culture. The ways in which Erasmus and More in an academic language and Rabelais in an emerging vernacular exploited their linguistic media for such distinctive expression and such varied effects are emblematic of the civilization we call "Renaissance."

This style, furthermore, amounts to much more than a mere tissue of favored elocutionary devices. Instead, it derives its norms from adjacent and complementary strategies of voice and address that animate the texts and give them an unmistakable identity and integrity. An order of devious coherence links the speaker's production to the audience's: "devious" because each style subtly but effectively challenges the audience's expectations about its own norms; "coherence" because it assimilates intention and reception, manipulation and response, formulation and affect.[20] The strategies of voice and address function at the very heart of style, and their coherence concretizes each particular style in its own way. Such stylistic affinities among particular authors, then, lend weight to the definition of period or movement that I intimated above. As in my previous comments on the development of the Petrarchan mode, one can see in the history of a prose style such as Erasmus's, More's, and Rabelais's the development of a system of resemblances with discernible limits that distinguish the Renaissance from the earlier medieval and later Baroque periods.

The prose styles of other contemporaries confirm those limits. In his *Memoires*, Philippe de Commynes (1445–1511) attempts to implicate his audience through interrogatives, exclamations, and hyperboles. The purpose is avowedly moralistic, yet frequently the speaker confronts his audience with a proposition, often political or pragmatic in nature, that violates the logic of his own moral argument. Thus, he punctuates his account of Louis XI's last days with interjections on the aptness of his dying in psychological uncertainty about his heirs' loyalty. "Or regardez, s'il avoit faict vivre beaucoup de gens en suspicion et craincte soubz luy, s'il en estoit bien payé" ("Now see, if he had forced many people to live under him in suspicion and fear, whether he was well paid for it").[21] The effect is to impel the audience toward a closer critical reading of the weight of his assertions. It demands the audience's full cooperation.

A few years later in *Les Illustrations de Gaule et Singularitez de Troye* (1510) Jean Lemaire de Belges attempted a chastened, more elegant style with latinate vocabulary and hypotactic syntax, but the strategies of voice and address remain similar to Commynes's. Throughout the work the writer appeals to his audience as guide and master, helper and authority, enlisting his audience's participation in reconstructing the ancient history: "Mais à fin que lhistoire soit mieux entendue, nous declairerons icy la situation dudit fleuue, et de la montaigne Ida, et demonstrerons à locil, lassictte de la gran cité de Troye" ("But so that the history may be better understood we will here clarify the situation of the previously mentioned river and Mount Ida and we will show to the eye the position of the great city of Troy").[22] The audience's task is to concretize that map.

I have called the diction and syntax of Jean Lemaire de Belge's style latinate, even though the vogue for approximating the latter in French did not crest until several decades later. The rigid distinction between written and spoken French, maintained more strictly at the beginning of the Renaissance than at the end, allowed for a greater degree of latinization with impunity in the written language, though as the latter approached spoken form, it lost its antiquarian license.[23] Symptomatic of older attitudes is the view of Henri Estienne in 1579 on the analogy of French to Greek and its superiority to other vernaculars, couched in a hypotactic order which emulates the canonized conventions of academic classicism: "Et pource que j'estimerois avoir trop bon marché de la comparaison qu'il me faut faire, si je la faisois avec le langage Italien, je ne craindray point de la faire avec le Grec, lequel est à bon droit estimé riche pardessus tous les riches" ("Since I would deem it too cheap to have made the comparison which I must make if I did it with the Italian language, I would not at all shrink from doing it with Greek, which rightly is thought to be richest above all").[24] And symptomatic of the change in form is the style of Montaigne in his *Essais*.

The *Essais* (1580–88) present a wholly new style of voice and address. One has clearly come far enough from the norms of an earlier Renaissance to have reached those of a new period. In "Au Lecteur" the author is fully aware of the distance between the *je* who endeavors to present "ma façon simple, naturelle et ordinaire, sans contention et artifice: car c'est moy que je peins" and the *tu* who may view the work as "un subject si frivole et si vain."[25] Throughout the work he takes infinite pains to resolve this distance. In the later essays, for example, he adopts highly complex, even tortuously convoluted strategies of voice and address as he attempts to manipulate the rhetorical situation to his best advantage. In "Du repentir" he uses them to achieve a gradual—very gradual—alignment of his sympathies with his audience's, and then, at the conclusion, a final distancing of his feelings from theirs. In the famous opening sentence he unequivocally distinguishes himself from others and accentuates his own individuality: "Les autres forment l'homme; je le recite et en represente un particulier bien mal formé" ("Others form man; I tell of him, and portray a particular one, very ill-formed"). A few pages later he begins to involve the *vous* in a complicity with himself by pitting *vous* against "les autres": "Others do not see you; they guess at you by uncertain conjectures" (p. 613).

As norms of prose style these techniques have affinities with those characterizing the Petrarchan mode of lyric poetry. They involve strategies of voice, whereby the speaker registers changes of tone, mood, and attitude by accommodating them to the roles that he plays and to his selfhood, and strategies of address, whereby he creates his fictive audience and endows it with attributes that clarify and complicate its relationship to an empirical reader. One sees, furthermore, in the evolution of prose style from Commynes and Jean Lemaire de Belges through Erasmus, More, Rabelais, and Henri Estienne finally to Montaigne the same movement as in the evolution of the Petrarchan mode from Petrarch through the Petrarchisti, the Pléiade, and the Elizabethan sonneteers to the metaphysical and Baroque poets—the movement, that is, from a fairly straightforward employment of these complex strategies to an ever more oblique and problematic exploitation of them in new and different contexts.

With reference to historical period, then, one could speak of a shift from Renaissance to Baroque, with the understanding, of course, that it is never entirely constant, progressive, or irreversible unless adjacent changes in voice and address affect larger structural principles of modes, styles, and genres. Certainly the structural principles of mode vary from one period to the other, as we have seen in our examination of the Petrarchan mode in chapter 1. Those of style also vary, as we could see in the stylistic norms of other prose works from the Baroque period, such as those of Brantome and Sorel, Burton and Bacon, Cervantes and Quevedo. The structural principles of genre which style and mode both modify also vary over the course of time. The question of degree is the topic of the next chapter. Suffice it to conclude here that the concept of rhetorical analysis liberated from the linguistic model, extending beyond the analysis of mere elocutionary figures, measuring its norms not by deviation or by context, but by other norms that take into account the characterization of the speaker and his relationship with the audience can be used in the description of larger systems of mode, style, and genre and ultimately in tracing the literary history of those systems.

3

The Epic Genre and Varieties of Form

Like Rabelais, the Renaissance epic poet inherited a rhetorical tradition whose immense resources offered almost infinite subtlety and diversity. Whereas Rabelais, however, provided his interlocutors with roles that almost always correspond to their selfhoods, the Renaissance epic poet provides his interlocutors with quite different ones that almost always chafe against their selfhoods. The result is a much more dramatic use of rhetorical situation. Regardless of the styles or modes that distinguish particular works, therefore, the epic poet's rhetorical strategies have as a common denominator a conflict between the speaker's roles and his selfhood, modifying the further relationships among poet, speaker, character, and audience. One of the chief differences between the epic and Rabelais's narrative, which resemble each other in many superficial and incidental ways, stems from the generic nature of the rhetorical situation particular to each.

Here however we are comparing one work (Rabelais's) to an entire genre whose history spans the centuries from what the Renaissance knew as the first great epic of Europe, Homer's *Iliad*, to what Europe came to know as the last great epic of the Renaissance, Milton's *Paradise Lost*. Between these terminal points the variations and permutations of epic mode and style, to say nothing of its central formal classification as either oral or literary, make it hopeless to specify a limited set of fixed norms for the genre. In the Renaissance alone one can distinguish several major modalities, from chivalric and romance epic to heroic and historical epic, and from sacred and allegorical epic to mythic and even burlesque epic. The various styles within these modalities further complicate the genre. How does one compare the style of the *Orlando Furioso* with that of *Les*

Tragiques, or *Gerusalemme Liberata* with *The Faerie Queene*, *Paradise Lost*, or Marino's *Adone*? Even when they treat of the same cycle of events, a chivalric epic like the *Orlando Furioso* differs from an epic-romance like Boiardo's *Orlando Innamorato* in its qualitative appropriation of romance devices, while both in turn differ from a burlesque epic like Pulci's *Morgante Maggiore*, which reduces those same devices to parody.

Fortunately we have in Thomas M. Greene's *The Descent From Heaven* an excellent starting point. Greene calls particular attention to the epic's expansive imagery, the awe engendered by the extraordinary actions of the limited human hero, the alternation between "executive" and "deliberative" structures of narrative, and the uncommon energy of epic language, and he warns that "the student should not be disposed to quarrel either over the classification of individual works within or without the genre; he knows that works may *participate* in the mode to varying degrees."[1] From this perspective the problem with genre theory lies not in what to designate as norms, but rather in how we construe the norms designated. In the past, before Croce repudiated generic distinctions, genre theory tended to be prescriptive and absolute, ascribing to all works within a given class a necessary conformity to the chosen model in every respect. Nowadays genre theory sanctions critical descriptions from a variety of perspectives that usually deal with only part of the whole: linguistic, structuralist, formalist, archetypal.

The need for a comprehensive theory of genre is more pressing than ever. In his provocative study of *Validity in Interpretation*, E.D. Hirsch argues persuasively about the "genre-bound character of understanding,"[2] and others, like Claudio Guillen in his study of the picaresque and Rosalie Colie in her study of Renaissance genre theory, support Hirsch's claim at least implicitly.[3] But whether in structuralist criticism, where myopic attention to the woof and warp of poetic texture often obscures the relationship of the individual work to larger groups of works, or in archetypal criticism, where the relationship of the individual work to the genre often obscures the more variable idiosyncrasies of individual works, or in the aging offspring of formalism and Anglo-American New Criticism, where the study of idiosyncrasy reigns supreme, the debilitating excesses of modern critical methods reflect the lack of a properly stabilizing notion of genre.[4]

If instability and relativism are vices in critical theory, however, flexibility can be a virtue. Thus, Paul Hernadi finds that "the best twentieth-century critics look for partial resemblances between unique individuals. . . . They present 'ideal types' . . . to which literary works correspond in varying degree"; their formulations are "descriptive" rather than "prescriptive."[5] The central question is then how modern genre theory can preserve its flexibility without risking instability or relativism. One way may be to describe the various genres as fully as possible through their rhetorical strategies of voice and address.

For the epic, both ancient and modern theorists have proposed definitions usually predicated on such verbal strategies as epithets, allusions, conventional formulas, elocutionary figures of speech, and other linguistic constructions.[6] In moving toward questions of characterization, action, and world-view, however, they have all too often evaded more difficult questions about modality and style. Since these distinctions should be an integral part of genre theory, and since greater precision results from an analysis of how the speaker manipulates his audience, it follows that genre theory can profit from a clearer awareness of rhetorical functions that go beyond the mere use of verbal figures and tropes. Perhaps in this way genre theory may even discover a missing link between the purely structural analysis of form and the more subjective analysis of the ways in which the audience understands form. At the very least it may contribute to a more comprehensive theory of genres than what we have now.

This chapter, then, explores how the rhetorical strategies of voice and address can be used to describe the norms of the epic. It focuses on three epics representing the chivalric, historical, and mythic-dramatic modes: the *Orlando Furioso*, *Les Tragiques*, and *Paradise Lost*. They each encompass a wide variety of styles, profiting alternately from classical, early Renaissance, and contemporaneous influences which greatly expand their horizons. Indeed, each poem has a noble classical pedigree. If Ariosto's chief model was Ovid, d'Aubigné's was Lucan, and Milton's was Virgil.[7]

Such a reduction of epic mode and style to the example of these three Roman models of course distorts the originality of each as well as the intractability of literary history, but it does serve to emphasize that the norms of Renaissance epic were not so exclusively Virgilian as fifteenth-century and sixteenth-century critical theory might lead one to expect. Even though every Renaissance poet paid lip service to the idea of the Virgilian epic, none succeeded in writing a truly Virgilian epic. The chivalric epics of Ariosto and Tasso and, to a greater degree, those of Pulci and Boiardo were suffused with the matter and form of romance narrative, while Milton's sacred epic, by the author's own admission, sought to pursue a "more heroic" argument (IX.14) and concomitant "answerable style" (IX.20) than any poem before his, including Virgil's. In *Les Tragiques, The Faerie Queene*, and *Adone*, the dominant forms are non-Virgilian, despite occasional passages that clearly evoke the *Aeneid*.

Not even the most important neo-Latin epics are constant in their allegiance to Virgilian norms. The fidelity of Petrarch's *Africa* to history and its avoidance of mythological action and supernatural machinery derive from the example of Lucan rather than Virgil, while its lack of complicated diction and syntax evoke Ovid, Catullus, or Propertius more often than Virgil. The latter, for example, would never have interrupted his narrative action for a gratuitous description of the heroine's beauty as Petrarch does during Sophonisba's first encounter with Masinissa (V.12–73), nor would Virgil have concluded with an emphasis on paradox in such oxymoronic language as Petrarch does:

> liquitur ille tuens, captiva captus ab hoste,
> victaque victorem potuit domuisse superbum.
> Quid non frangit amor?
>
> [V.73–75][8]

> [He melts as he beholds her, captured by his captive
> enemy, and she, the vanquished one, was able to have
> tamed her proud vanquisher. What doesn't love
> overcome?]

In later neo-Latin epics Virgilian norms are similarly muted. The philosophical model for Pontano's exploration of the starry sphere, the *Urania*, is Lucretius's *De Rerum Natura*, while his structural model for interweaving brief accounts of mythic figures as he traverses the heavens is Ovid's *Metamorphoses*. And though Sannazaro's *De Partu Virginis* (1526) and Vida's *Christiados* (1525) replicate Virgilian elocution, they hardly approach the *Aeneid* in range, tone, subject matter, or narrative structure. Their central rhetorical strategies, moreover, are far from Virgil's. The rhetoric of *De Partu Virginis* belongs to the category of divine praise, as a succession of speakers (Fame, King David, St. Joseph, the angels, shepherds, the tutelary deity of the River Jordan) present various accounts of the action and offer tribute in elegantly formed hymns. The rhetoric of the *Christiados* centers on the narrative retelling of Christ's life by several personages directed towards several audiences. In books II and IV, St. Joseph and St. John give Pontius Pilate detailed summaries of Christ's life, teaching, and miracles; elsewhere the speeches of angels, apostles, and Mary tend toward monologic exposition rather than dialogue or dramatic exchange in the Virgilian manner.[9]

Notwithstanding his failure to recreate the Virgilian epic, Vida still remains one of Virgil's most self-conscious champions in the Renaissance. In his *De Arte Poetica* (1527) he credited Virgil with a triumph of polish and elegance, grace and discipline: "Vocem, animumque deo similis" (I.168) ("godlike in voice and spirit").[10] Vida wrote the *De Arte Poetica* when Homer and other Greek epic poets were still imperfectly understood and only a few short yet decisive years before the publication of Aristotle's *Poetics* (1536), which commended Homer's epic scale and grandeur of effect.[11] Thus, among his rules for invention and disposition Vida urges, contra the Greeks, the elaboration of a small though always richly appointed design: "Exiguum meditator, ubi sint omnia culta,/Et visenda novis iterumque, iterumque figuris" (III.340–341) ("lay plans . . . for a short work, one in which everything is highly polished and ornamented consistently with new figures"). Even after the Aristotelian revival Julius Caesar Scaliger, in his posthumously published *Poetics Libri Septem* (1561), stabilized a comparison between Homer and Virgil to the latter's benefit in terms that Tasso and Spenser, Boileau and Milton would later echo. For Scaliger as for Vida and most of their generation, the master of epic poetry is Virgil, not Homer.

Before the sixteenth century the most notable commendation of Roman technical skill was the *Institutio Oratoria*, but Quintilian had gone on to denigrate the "diligence and exactness in the work of Virgil" by comparison with "the immortal and superhuman genius of Homer," before which "we must needs bow" (X.i. 86). In his estimation, Homer succeeded through his astonishing virtuosity: "He is like his own conception of Ocean, which he describes as the source of every stream and river; for he has given us a model and an inspiration for every department of eloquence" (X.i. 46). Though Quintilian's judgment had been known since Poggio rediscovered the *Institutio Oratoria* in 1416, and especially since Cardinal Campano edited the complete text in 1470, it took the sixteenth-century deepening of interest in Hellenic culture to reassert the importance of the *Iliad* and the *Odyssey* as models for the epic.[12] Particularly in France, where Hellenism had a greater hold on the creative imagination than in Italy, the Homeric norms earned high praise from Sibilet, du Bellay, and Jacques Peletier du Mans, while Ronsard in his preface to the *Franciade* deferred at least as much to the amplitude of the Homeric epic as he did to the polish of the Virgilian epic: "A genous Franciade/Adore l'Aeneiade, adore l'Illiade."

In Italian literary theory the dichotomy between Homeric amplitude and Virgilian polish actually promulated great freedom in the interpretation of epic norms. Writing his *Discorso intorno al comporre dei romanzi* (1549), Giraldi Cinthio char-

acterized Ariosto as an epic poet who had mastered both qualities in his *Orlando Furioso*, while regarding neither Homer's
epics nor the rules which Aristotle deduced from them as
prescriptive for all ages: "It would be a great error now to follow
Homer in those things which, though suitable to his time, . . .
are unsuitable in our times."[13] Thus Cinthio upheld his plea
for literary freedom by pointing even among the ancients to the
example of Ovid: "Delivering himself with admirable skill from
Aristotle's laws of art, he began [the *Metamorphoses*] with the
beginning of the world and with astonishingly good sequence
treated a great variety of things" (Gilbert, p. 263). Minturno,
who found his own taste for Virgilian polish no impediment to
his enjoyment of Homeric amplitude, admired both and chided
lesser poets in *L'Arte poetica* (1564) for not observing "the
form and the rule that Homer and Vergil follow, and that Aristotle and Horace command as appropriate."[14] Even Tasso,
despite his pathological obsession with Aristotelean rules and
the authority of ancient poets, hesitated to establish exclusive
and prescriptive norms for the epic. Thus, in his *Discorsi dell'
arte poetica* (1564? pub. 1587), he censured Trissino for slavish
adherence to classical norms while complimenting Ariosto for
violating them to give pleasure and delight: "In the *Furioso* one
can read of loves, knighthood, adventure, and incantations, and
in short, inventions more delightful and better suited to our
ears than those of Trissino."[15]

Pluralities of mode and style thus dominate the Renaissance
epic. Virgil was only one among many classical poets whose
example shaped the concept of epic; Apollonius and Hesiod,
Varro and Lucretius, Ovid and Lucan, Valerius Flaccus and
Silius Italicus, Statius and Claudian were others. The *Orlando
Furioso*, *Les Tragiques*, and *Paradise Lost* betray evidence of
these influences, though the authors of each shaped their bor-
rowings to harmonize with their chosen mode and style. Thus,
Milton, and to a lesser extent d'Aubigné, learned much from
Ovid, and even Ariosto learned from Lucan, while all three
appropriated for their own poems what they took to be central
Virgilian norms.[16] Beyond the diversity of their modes and

styles, however, they share a generic form that links these poems and confers upon each the name of epic. To describe this generic form, literary theorists frequently cite the repeated use of such surface conventions as summaries, lists, invocations, and catalogues, or of such basic narrative motifs as battles, storms, and prophecies, or of structural principles involving cyclic organization, encyclopedic scope, length and diffusiveness of action, and beginning *in medias res*, or of such elocutionary strategies as formulaic epithet, elevated diction, extended simile, and stately rhythms. On the other hand, the interplay of rhetorical strategies associated with the speaker and his audience modifies both the style of epic poetry and its tone, affecting the material structure and the substantive meaning of individual works. They better describe the form of epic and account for its permanence amidst incalculable varieties of mode and style. Following the classical paradigm afforded by Ovid, Lucan, and above all Virgil, one can discern in each Renaissance epic the presence of a controlling speaker noted for his own subjective intrusions, for his powers of inspired synthesis and authoritative mediation, for his ability to be equally at home in specific scenic description and in the representation of speech and ample formal dialogue, and for his conferral of a focused world-view on a vast amount of material, one that is not so much personal as it is public and collective, expressive of the values of a certain class, society, culture, or religion whose members constitute the poem's original fictive audience. And between this audience and the speaker one can also discern a relationship bounded by a sense of formal convention, alternately detached from and involved with the action, alternately hortatory, when urging the contemplation and acceptance of certain values, and demonstrative, when showing the consequences of heroic performance patterned on them. These norms characterize the Renaissance epic and contribute to its generic definition.

Ariosto's *Orlando Furioso*

One of the few widely accepted norms of epic calls attention to the speaker's and audience's distance from the heroic action.

Mindful of his role as bard, the speaker invokes his muse's aid to recount past deeds. In certain older poems like the *Iliad*, the *Odyssey*, the *Chanson de Roland*, and *Beowulf*, he stands apart from his characters and at times even effaces his own temporal authority as inspired mediator. In the late Roman and later Renaissance epics, however, he fashions for himself and his audience specific roles that imply a very active involvement with at least the main hero. What remains constant, and hence generically normative, in all these epics is the speaker's implicit rhetorical identification with the audience by himself playing an audience to the action that he recounts as transmitter or mediator.

Among Renaissance epics the *Orlando Furioso* (1532) illustrates fully the consequences of the speaker's heightened involvement. The model for Ariosto (1474–1533) at least in part may have been Virgil, who relates to the action that he reports with sympathy and compassion, but maintains rhetorical distance. Ariosto develops on the other hand not just a compassionate relationship between speaker and material, but a completely personal involvement between them, splintering the action and allowing his intentions to change in midcourse. Unlike Virgil, furthermore, who sought to represent the public and private life of one heroic individual within the compass of a single action, Ariosto's speaker represents many characters: Charlemagne, Orlando, Ruggiero, and Bradamante, and in a minor way, Rinaldo, Astolfo, Angelica, and Rodomonte, among others. Finally, unlike Virgil, who in nearly every line confronts a homogeneous Augustan audience with a programmatic and propagandistic aim, Ariosto's speaker confronts a fully diverse audience which he attempts at once to please, appease, entertain, flatter, cajole, enlighten, and uplift.[1]

Ariosto achieves his varied effects through the mastery of several forms that he integrates superbly while yet retaining the flavor and quality of each: epic sweep and romance imagination, lyrical set pieces and novella-like subplots, all with a Virgilian and ultimately Ovidian overlay. More often than not the Ovidian influence looms larger than the Virgilian. Ovid's *Meta-*

morphoses in fact supplies the chief structural model for the *Orlando Furioso* with its episodic interlaced action, its penchant for detail and descriptive embroidery, and its mercurial alternation of tone and mood, which most often depend upon the speaker's own characterization. Like Ovid, Ariosto masters small forms first. The tale, the isolated dramatic incident, juxtaposed variations or elaborations of action or motif all find a haven within the amplitude of the *Orlando Furioso*. Unit after unit of the *ottava rima* verse form weaves them into one long continuous whole.[2]

Reconciling such diversity lends a special character to the speaker's role and locates it at the very center of Ariosto's epic. The splintering of narrative and action, in fact, reflects his world-view. Out of the fullness of his rhetoric emerges a profound sense of the discrepancy between man's wish to control his universe and his practical ability to do so. The first hint comes in his petition that his patron kindly receive what he, a humble servant, wishes to give and alone is able to give: "questo che vuole/e darvi sol può l'umil servo vostro" (I.3).[3] The separation of powers between wishing and being able to, *volere* and *potere*, initiates a theme that comes to dominate the rhetoric.

This separation in turn conditions his relationship to both poem and audience. Ariosto's predecessors in the chivalric mode, Pulci and Boiardo, evinced an almost wholly objective interest in character and action. Such objectivity typifies the romance, with its emphasis on intricate plot construction, extreme circumstantiality, and myriad detail, all contributing to a sense of the story's autonomous existence from its creator. In Ariosto, however, the fictive world often seems inseparable from its creator's imagination. A vital part of his rhetorical strategy is to refract everything that he sees through the focus of his own single vision, even to the extent of flattening out the rest of the plot, character, and action in order to express that vision.[4]

Thus he demonstrates his control over every aspect of the poem in ways that Pulci's and Boiardo's speakers never did.

He turns a technical feat like the Ovidian interlacing of episodes into a functional reflex of his *ethos* and *pathos*. Through the ironic juxtaposition of sometimes similar, sometimes dissimilar actions the speaker expresses his sense of a substantial order underlying the seeming chaos and confusion of events, and he makes explicit the unexpected ironies that he perceives there. In revealing heroic characters from these unexpected perspectives, the speaker carries to an extreme the subjectivity of both Virgilian and Ovidian rhetoric, and he turns the objective action of his epic into a parable of his own dramatic life.

As in Virgil's poem, the chief source of drama in the *Orlando Furioso* is the discrepancy between role and selfhood.[5] Angelica becomes the central symbol of this frustration, the beloved whom so many of the heroes wish to possess (will, *volere*) but cannot (ability, *potere*) subdue. Orlando's madness provides the most powerful example of what happens when an individual's will conflicts with his ability. The furious assertion of his will in madness amounts to his denial of limits. In one luminous simile at the start of Orlando's search for Angelica, the speaker says that if Orlando had been equal to the goddess Ceres in power (*poter*) as he was in desire (*desio*) he would have left no stone unturned in his quest for Angelica: "S'in poter fosse stato Orlando pare/all'Eleusina dea, come in disio . . ." (XII.3). Deep within himself he knows he is not adequate to the task. I am not what my face makes me seem, Orlando cries on the brink of insanity: "Non son, non sono io quel che paio in viso" (XXIII.128), indicating the profound division between his concept of himself and what he is in reality.

Nearly every episode dramatizes the discrepancy between the role and the self, between wish and frustration, including some episodes that seem to be merely ornamental digressions about minor characters. The story of Olimpia, for example, which Ariosto added as an almost self-contained unit to the final edition of the poem, sums up all the issues of *volere* and *potere* developed throughout the poem.[6] Even if she had the power to fail Bireno in the faith that she has given him, Amor would not let her wish that she could, much less be ungrateful.

> Io ch'all'amante mio di quella fede
> mancar non posso, che gli aveva data;
> e ancor ch'io possa, Amor non mi conciede
> che poter voglia, e ch'io sia tanto ingrata.
>
> [IX.26]

Later abandoned, she can only lament that she has served up her will to a traitor and cannot do anything to save herself: "What ought I to do? What can I do here alone?" (X.27).

In the poem's major episode the speaker depicts the conflict between role and selfhood, *volere* and *potere*, in Ruggiero and Bradamante. Few episodes are more typical than the one on Alcina's Isle in which Ruggiero, warned of the dangers by Astolfo, no sooner sets off with determination to resist Alcina than he too falls prey to her charms. His very will is proof against his ability, for within a few octaves the speaker depicts him intending one course of action yet performing another despite himself. Like everyone else who has ever visited Alcina's garden, Ruggiero too falls to the blandishments of the false enchantress.[7]

Even after Ruggiero has extricated himself from Alcina with the aid of Melissa, the speaker shows how he falls to other temptations directed against his will. Though halfway through the poem he renews his will (*voler*, XXV.89) to convert to Christianity before he marries Bradamante, he adds in the very next stanza that he also wishes to disrupt the siege from around the Saracen lord who long ago conferred on him his role as knight. The conflict between satisfying Bradamante and satisfying Agramante involves Ruggiero's very ability to achieve what he wills, for he cannot forsake his master without incurring the name of traitor, and branded with that name, he can never deserve the hand of his lady. The double use of *poter* in one of the speaker's comments emphasizes the dilemma:

> Ruggier potrà alla donna satisfare
> a un altro tempo, s'or non satisfece:
> ma all'onor, che gli manca d'un momento,
> non può in cento anni satisfar né in cento.
>
> [XXXVIII.6]

[Ruggiero can satisfy his lady at some future time, if he did not satisfy her now, but he who lacks honor for a moment cannot give satisfaction for it in a hundred years or in a hundred more.]

The speaker shows how Bradamante, too, must face the test of desire. Borrowing the conventional rhetoric of Petrarchan complaints, she portrays herself as a woman driven by mad, unreasonable longing for the impossible, not able to sustain her wish: "poi non potendo sostener, mi lassa/dal ciel cader" (XXXII.21). Blaming her desperate *desir*, she laments that all her power fell to it: "It carries me from bad to worse, and I am not able to bridle it, for it does not have a bridle." (XXXII.22). Yet however much she wishes to blame herself, she—and the narrator as well—know that she cannot refrain from loving Ruggiero:

> se fu inganno il consiglio che mi diede
> Merlin, posso di lui ben lamentarmi,
> ma non d'amar Ruggier posso ritrarmi.
>
> [XXXII.24]

[If the counsel Merlin gave me was a deception, I can lament over him, but I cannot draw back from loving Ruggiero.]

At the climax of the poem Bradamante finds herself affianced to Leone, son of the Holy Roman Emperor, by her parents' command. Once again the conflict between *potere* and *volere* dominates the speaker's rhetoric as he presents Bradamante's struggle to reconcile herself to the roles that she must play, not by choice but by necessity. As Beatrice's daughter she cannot think of disobeying her mother, but she is not willing to forsake Ruggiero because she cannot forsake him; love has taken from her all power to dispose of herself (XLIV.39). The solution to this conflict—Leone's voluntary renunciation of his claim—lies outside her power. For all its intensity, the rhetorical outcome depends upon chance.

The speaker's apotheosis of Ruggiero and Bradamante at the end of the poem (XLVI.73-100) evokes other rhetorical problems. When the hero and heroine emerge in full command of themselves and of their newly acquired roles as husband and wife, founders of the d'Este line, and renowned warriors in their own right, their identities begin to merge with those of the principal fictive audience whom the speaker has been addressing throughout the poem, members of the d'Este family itself. The reader sensitive to the ironic twists that the speaker has given Ruggiero's and Bradamante's careers will no doubt feel the oblique edge which he puts on their relationship to the d'Este, whether intentional and veiled or potential and problematic. They are hardly perfect models for the d'Estes, and their performance imparts a dim luster to the flattery and blandishment that one might have expected the speaker to accord his chief fictive audience.

Moreover, especially when couched in prophecies uttered by Merlin and Melissa in praise of the d'Este family (III.16–63; XIII.57–63), the speaker's tribute belongs to a fictive context which attentuates it.[8] Even in the more straightforward direct addresses to the d'Este family in preambles of individual cantos, the speaker's tribute shows a speculative awareness of his patrons' foibles and limitations. In the preamble to canto XIV, for example, the speaker celebrates Alfonso d'Este's victory over the Spanish at Ravenna (11 April, 1512); he seems to go out of his way to call ironic attention to the probability that the victory cost his patron more than it was worth:

> Quella vittoria fu più di conforto
> che d'allegrezza; perché troppo pesa
> contra la gioia nostra il veder morto
> il capitan di Francia e de l'impresa:
>
> [XIV.6]

[That victory had more of consolation than of gladness, because against our joy weighs too heavily our seeing the captain of France and of the enterprise dead.]

Similarly in three separate addresses to Ippolito d'Este on the siege of Polesella (22 December, 1509), the speaker quietly suggests the possibility that his victory may have been a mere stroke of luck (XV.1), in any case qualified by wicked deeds performed on both sides (XXXVI.2), and verified by only the lamest reports from secondhand sources (XL.3-4). The reader may begin to doubt whether the speaker's fictive audience achieved any victory at all.

If the speaker's relationship with the d'Este family is oblique, so too are his relationships with other historical personages.[9] Some of them he addresses in a wry and playful way, as in his aside to Federico Fregoso, refuting the claim that it would have been impossible for six knights to engage in equestrian combat on the rocky plains of Biserta (XLII.20-22). Others he addresses effusively, as in the final canto when he thanks his friends and well-wishers who receive his bark into harbor, including among them such literary giants as Berni, Vida, Navagero, Aretino, Bembo, Fracastoro, Sannazaro, Bernardo Tasso, and Victoria Colonna. This speaker readily acknowledges other practitioners of his art, even if he deems their talent less than his.

Thus, the speaker's sincerity in adapting his private selfhood to his role as an epic poet poses a rhetorical problem. On the one hand, his official function is to offer praise and even blandishment to his patrons and colleagues; on the other, his wish is to limit that praise through ironic ambiguity and the undercutting of his own intentions. Some of his addresses to fictive audiences are doubtless sincere, as in his celebrated tirades against firearms (XI.26-28) and against foreign harpies feeding upon Italy in her time of troubles (XXXIV.1-3), or in his earlier plea for the armies of Spain, France, Switzerland, and Germany to redirect their engines of war to a crusade against the Turks in the Holy Land (XVII.74-79). But in the last case, despite the apparent urgency of his multiple address (Europe in stanzas 74-75, Italy in 76, and Pope Leo X in 79), the speaker stops far short of convincing his audience, which might ascribe his intentions to form rather than substance.

The nature of its fictive audience is thus an especially important determinant of the epic quality of the *Orlando Furioso*. On the whole the poem implicates five central but separate fictive audiences: the speaker's patron, the patron's princely colleagues, women in general, the speaker's own beloved in particular, and a final, unaffiliated kind of audience who is neither patron nor prince, not necessarily a woman or even in love with women, but a type of impartial observer who construes the relationships among these audiences and assigns each its proper place. Nowhere do they come together with such significance as in the episode of Astolfo's journey to the moon and his recovery of Orlando's wits, and nowhere does the speaker specify their relationships with such clarity. Women, for example, he appeals to when Astolfo reaches the Limbo of Vanities on the moon, reminding his audience that feminine charms ensnare men's wits like birdlime (XXXIV.81). He addresses his own beloved in the opening of the next canto with the implication that her feminine charms have driven him mad. His patron, meanwhile, who seems immune from the follies that afflict the rest of the human race, enters the poem when Astolfo's guide, St. John the Evangelist, points out that the richest thread on the spinning wheel of the Fates belongs to Ippolito d'Este; his name will be rescued from oblivion by "two swans only, as white, My Lord, as is your flag" (XXXV.14). The speaker, moreover, insures Ippolito's superiority in the company of his own peers, the princes of Europe, when he reminds the latter that their fame will vanish altogether unless they follow Ippolito's example in patronizing poets and artists who confer immortality:

> Oh bene accorti principi e discreti,
> che seguite di Cesare l'esempio,
> e gli scrittor vi fate amici, donde
> non avete a temer di Lete l'onde.
>
> [XXXV.22]

[O princes indeed wise and discreet, you who follow the example of Caesar and make the writers your friends, so that you do not have to fear the waves of Lethe.]

Throughout the episode, however, the speaker accords the richest epic status to a more general audience, one that he represents as triumphant in its impartial observation of the manners and mores of the speaker's other fictive audiences. This palm goes to the reader or listener who can adjust his or her perspective and look at the earth from the vantage point of the moon (XXXIV.71), who can make intrinsic connections within the poem and keep its many threads separately in view (XXXIV.91, XXXV.11), and who ultimately synthesizes the poet's work with the right attitude and just evaluation. In the scope of its endeavors this fictive audience emerges as a fully epic one and reinforces the generic epic quality of the poem.

The address to such a fictive audience would have been thoroughly familiar to Ariosto's reader after the examples in Pulci's and Boiardo's chivalric poems. Neither the *Morgante* nor the *Orlando Innamorato*, however, encompass such a variety of audiences as the *Orlando Furioso*, nor does either sustain such a complicated relationship among speaker, reader, and audience. In Pulci's *Morgante* the speaker tries to dignify his subject matter with a series of quasi-religious moral preambles and divine invocations in the opening stanzas of individual cantos:

> In principio era el Verbo a presso a Dio, . . .
> Però, giusto Signor, benigno e pio,
> Mandami solo un degli angel tui,
> Che m'acompagni e rechimi a memoria
> Una famosa, antica e degna storia.
>
> [I.1] [10]

[In the beginning was the Word with God; . . . therefore, just Lord, mild and holy, send me one of your angels to accompany me and recall to mind a famous, old, worthy history.]

Beginning with this opening address to God as his fictive audience, Pulci's exaggerated parody of biblical, Dantesque, and Petrarchan styles exploits the norms of the epic in ways which even Ariosto, for all his irreverence, would not have dared.[11]

In Boiardo's *Orlando Innamorato* the speaker poses as a transmitter of Archbishop Turpin's tales about Charlemagne's

times, and he addresses them to a courtly audience, predomi-
nantly male, "Segnori e cavallieri," with a pronounced interest
in past history: "La bella istoria che 'l mio canto muove"
(I.i.1). By I.xix, however, he turns his attention to tales of love
and amorous intrigue, signaling the shift by using the adjective
inamorati and by including women as members of his audience:

> Segnori e cavallieri inamorati,
> Cortese damiselle e grazïose,
> Venitene davanti ed ascoltati
> L'alte venture e le guerre amorose.
>
> [I.xix.1] [12]

[Lords and knights in love, courteous and gracious young
ladies, come forth and listen to high adventures and amorous combats.]

He actually summons an audience with firsthand amorous experience to judge his celebrated hero:

> Chi provato non ha che cosa è amore,
> Biasmar potrebbe e due baron pregiati . . . .
> Ma chi cognosce amore e sua possanza,
> Farà le scusa di quel cavalliero.
>
> [I.xxviii.1–2]

[Whoever has not experienced what love is, could blame
the two barons. But whoever knows love and its power will
excuse the knight.]

Finally, the speaker invokes his own beloved Antonia Caprara in
II.iv.1, as well as women whom other worthy men love. Women
now function as audiences for his own epic performance:

> Dame legiadre e cavallier pregiati,
> Che onorati la corte e gentilezza,
> Tiratevi davanti ed ascoltati
> Delli antiqui baron l'alta prodezza.
>
> [II.viii.2]

[Beautiful women and worthy knights whom court and courtesy honor, step forward and listen to the high exploits of the old barons.]

Ariosto extended Boiardo's precedent along with his mastery of the *ottava rima* verse form.[13] Throughout the *Orlando Furioso* the speaker addresses a much larger number of fictive audiences. He is much more aware of his own role as audience of Turpin's "source." Boiardo's speaker paid his respects to this role, too, but never so self-consciously. For Ariosto's speaker, Turpin becomes a secular "muse," a nod, however playful, to epic convention. But on the whole his attitude proves highly variable, ranging from skepticism to utter naïveté about the authority of his source, and as a result the response of his audience to the changes is bound to be highly complex.

Especially keen to secure the reactions of his volatile audience in the most apparently innocuous of situations, the speaker beguiles it with intimate asides expressing confidence in its ability to follow his fiction. In canto XII, for example, he interrupts a heated exchange between Orlando and Ferrau to remind the audience that Ferrau is enchanted: "Ch'abbiate, Signor mio, già inteso estimo/che Ferraù per tutto era fatato" (XII.48). Similarly he reminds it in XIII.2 how Orlando saved Isabella from bandits; in XIII.80 how Bradamante, even though imprisoned in Atlante's castle, is destined for a great future; in XX.117 how Zerbino pursued his prey through the woods; in XXII.25 how the hippogriff returned to Atlante after Ruggiero abandoned it; in XXVIII.96 how Isabella accompanied the corpse of her beloved Zerbino. These facile asides become almost a necessity in a poem whose plot admits such length and complication as the *Orlando Furioso*, but what is distinctive about Ariosto's handling of them as rhetorical devices is the way he personalizes his audience in order to secure better contact with it.

The rub is that the speaker does not always trust his audience to the limit of its capacity. In fact, he gently mocks it for following current fashion and priding itself on its own alleged cleverness and sophistication. In canto VII.2, for example, he disingenuously shames it into acknowledging the credibility of his story: "I am certain it will not appear false to you who have the clear light of reason." There is obvious irony in his distinction between those who will consider his fiction a tall tale and others who will interpret it correctly. Quite naturally everyone will esteem himself or herself in the latter category, but the speaker deflates those expectations by revealing his own inability to come to terms with the truth of his fiction concerning Ruggiero's encounter with Erifilla: not only does he draw himself into the action ("I don't believe that there is one so huge in Apulia," VII.4), but he also goes on to express wide-eyed wonder at what ensues, flagrantly mistaking the appearances of things for their reality and leading his audience down a blind alley.

Even earlier when Ruggiero first approaches the walls of Alcina's palace, walls the audience may assume to be artifice and illusion, the speaker sides with his hero in mistaking them for pure gold. Some may dissent from his opinion, he says, and call it alchemy; perhaps the dissenter is wrong, and perhaps also he knows better; but to him it appears gold since it shines like gold (VI.59). Soon afterwards he rationalizes Ruggiero's attempt to secure the favors of Angelica after saving her from the orc, for though Ruggiero does not remember his fiancée as he did before, he is mad if he does not also value and esteem the damsel in his presence (XI.2). And even much later he defends Ruggiero's prolonged absence from Bradamante because in saving his honor he deserves not only to be excused but even to be praised (XXXVIII.3).

As the poem progresses and the speaker shows himself less and less reliable, the audience should become more and more aware of the lack of any firm narrative base to make judgments about the fictional action. Certainly the speaker himself, with all his rhetorical command, provides no such base. Throughout the poem he resolutely defends people and causes that he later discovers—and admits—to be wrong. He mitigates, for example, the blame of Bireno's falling out of love with

with Olimpia by describing the new object of the hero's affections with obvious sympathy: she was such a delicacy that he would have deemed it foolish courtesy to take her from his own mouth and give her to another (X.10). He defends Griffone's love for the unworthy Origilla with the excuse that everyone distressed in love knows whether its arrows are well tempered (XV.103). He approves of Doralice's ready shift of allegiance when her Mandricardo meets his death; he was good for her while alive, but what could he do for her afterwards? (XXX.73).

Such defenses become necessary in a poem where the speaker's vision of the world—and of his characters' aspirations—points to ironic discrepancies between reality and illusion, intention and execution, will and ability. The doubt generated by the speaker's naïveté serves to situate the audience at a critical distance from the narrative with the subversive effect of involving its members more fully in the business of interpreting the action. Ariosto's chief literary model here is Ovid, whose dramatized speaker in the *Metamorphoses* quite regularly warns his fictive audience that it is foolish and futile to believe the stories that ensue. The result in Ovid, as later in Ariosto, is often the opposite of what the speaker seems to have intended; instead of deterring, it impels the audience onwards not only to read the controversial sequence but also to make a judgment.[14]

Throughout the *Orlando Furioso* this Ovidian effect takes precedence, especially when the speaker addresses an audience composed of members of the d'Este family, of their cultured and sophisticated peers, of women in general, and of lovers in particular. Moreover, he often addresses these fictive audiences with a good awareness of his own limitations. This rhetorical strategy secures the audience's involvement with him on his quest for self-discovery and heightens confidence in his narrative ability. Thus, by the poem's end the audience finds him actively reasserting his claim to control over himself and the poem that he has produced.

The poem, as the audience who has carefully followed it

learns, is not just a random collection of episodes and events narrated without a concern for order and causality, but an elaborately structured network of interrelated motifs that all achieve resolution.[15] In fact all along the speaker has been concerned to plot his stories with careful calculation, as he indicates when he claims that he needs to lay out various threads like a weaver: "Ma perché varie fila a varie tele/uopo mi son, che tutte ordire intendo" (II.30); or that he will vary his story so as to avoid boring his audience, "Just as changing food reawakens the taste." (XIII.80).[16] The key to his ultimate control, however, as both he and his audience know, is his talent for judicious selection: "It will be a mad act to promise to recount to you one by one Orlando's mad acts" (XXIX.50).

Personal experience has taught him this lesson. As narrator he confesses in the final preamble to have undergone some difficult moments and near-failures, with the fear of wandering forever. Still, he has managed to produce not only a whole poem but one that merits his friends' congratulations: "It seems all of them are happy that I have come to the end of so long a voyage" (XLVI.2). The admission is not so much self-congratulation as a climactic statement of the poem's epic theme. It entails a subtle manipulation of the rhetorical situation so that the speaker brings together the diverse interests of his audience. Certainly he is not claiming univocal success. But through his open-ended relationship with his audience, he is encouraging every reader, every listener who confronts his poem to seek some meaning in the poem's action.

In the final analysis this problematic rhetorical situation distinguishes the *Orlando Furoso* in the epic tradition. True, the poem is not so solemn or tragic as most epics in Western literature, though even in this regard it has significant classical precedent in Ovid's *Metamorphoses*. Like Ovid, and to a lesser extent like Apollonius in his *Argonautica*, Ariosto prefers to direct his irony, ambiguity, and skepticism through a comic route which, however much it sometimes borders on the tragic, ultimately issues in a serene acceptance of the ways things are. It results in an awareness as profound as the awareness of other epics.

The epic quality of the *Orlando Furioso* thus derives from the rhetorical strategy that characterizes the figure of the speaker and his relationship to the audience. To be sure, Ariosto employs conventional epic motifs such as catalogues, invocations, prophecies, and panoramic battle scenes, among others, and he employs conventional elocutionary devices associated with the epic, such as the formulaic epithet, extended simile, and elevated diction. The mere use of these motifs and elocutionary devices, however, fails to ensure epic stature, especially since Ariosto's predecessors in the mode of chivalric romance, Pulci and Boiardo, employed similar motifs and elocutionary devices and yet rarely achieved his epic dimension. Their poems, like all romances, play on the surface and unfold in relatively straightforward rhetorical ways. Ariosto's poem, on the other hand, tries to explore the depths and heights, and it achieves an epic dimension through the use of rhetorical strategies essential to the genre, ones developed to their fullest in poems like the *Aeneid* and the *Metamorphoses*, the *Gerusalemme Liberata* and *Paradise Lost*. Despite the dazzling array of modes and styles that link passages of the *Orlando Furioso* to the chivalric romance, the moralistic tale, the fantastic voyage, satiric caricature, Petrarchan lyric, and numerous other forms, the *Orlando Furioso* is fully and completely epic.

There are generic resemblances, then, between Ariosto's rhetorical strategies and those of other epic poets, especially in the heroic conception of division between the public role and one's deepest personal instincts, between what one wants to achieve and what one is able to achieve. Like Ovid, Ariosto fashions a speaker whose rhetoric cannot always be taken at face value even—perhaps especially—when it asserts its own truthfulness; a speaker whose imperfect control over his own perception of others belies a very perfect control over narrative interlacement. And like Ovid, Ariosto relates his speaker to an audience that does not quite believe in his incredible and anachronistic fiction, that alternately judges him adversely and yet allows him to manipulate it quite consciously as long as he tells a good story. Neither Ovid nor Ariosto seems to exhibit many pretensions to elevation, moral commitment, and the mythic continuity of epic, at least on the surface. Both have cultivated a rhetorical art beneath the surface, however, that transforms their seeming naïveté into genuine sophistication. The *Orlando Furioso*, then, must rank with the *Metamorphoses* as proof of the epic genre's durable vitality.

D'Aubigné's *Les Tragiques*

To turn from the elegant Ovidian interlacement of the *Orlando Furioso* to the linear chronicle and straightforward diatribe of *Les Tragiques* (1616, but written for the most part in the 1570s) is more than to turn from the sophisticated polish of a highly self-conscious art form to the coarser texture of topical satire and polemical invective; it is to turn to a unique but very important mode of the epic genre. Neither Ovidian nor Virgilian, the long poem of d'Aubigné (1552–1630) incorporates many diverse poetic traditions. Above all it absorbs the model of the Roman satirists, especially Juvenal, whose example proved convenient for many of d'Aubigné's special purposes. Still, the scope, control, panoramic continuity, and rhetorical conviction of *Les Tragiques* are epic, and for these effects the single model most attractive to the Huguenot poet was Lucan.[1]

Superficially, d'Aubigné's style shares many eccentricities associated with Lucan's: excesses of detail, a profusion of lists and enumerations, strained emphases, forced antitheses, involuted expressions, and occasional monotony. It is unfair to dwell on these superficial comparisons, however, for *Les Tragiques* shares more profoundly a number of structural, thematic, and above all rhetorical qualities associated with *De Bello civili*, qualities which confirm the poems as major achievements in epic form.[2] Both d'Aubigné and Lucan fashion discontinuous narrative assemblages of scenes that in their sheer mass and weight convey an epic vision. Both focus not on outdated myth or legend or romance but rather on recent, even contemporary history. Both finally manage to evoke a tone (implicit in Lucan, explicit in d'Aubigné) heavy with polemical invective against its alleged audience, the current regime. In both, finally, a heightened rhetorical emphasis on voice and address deepens the epic impact.

The figure of the speaker dominates *Les Tragiques* more than his counterpart in Lucan's poem does.[3] From the beginning he presents himself in roles associated with the historical author, d'Aubigné; he is a Christian soldier, scholar, and one-time courtier privy to people and events shaping his nation's history in the later sixteenth century; above all, he is a poet who records God's inspired message through his own experiences on the battlefield and at court. His role as poet, moreover, generates a tension with his other roles as active participant in the history of his times and as passive intermediary between God and man. Part of the tension is reflected in the various modes and styles that he integrates into his epic despite their discrepancies, as in his attempted reconciliation of the biblical, satiric, and historical modes with lyric, dramatic, oratorical, and allegorical styles.[4]

Despite his variety, however, the poet maintains an ostensible loyalty to certain fixed principles. In diction and syntax, for example, he shares the Pléiade's preferences for native French words and constructions rather than experimental or neologistic ones: in "Au lecteur" he compares those who would do otherwise to Rabelais's Limousin student.[5] In poetic inspiration he holds to Ronsard's and du Bellay's doctrine of *furor poeticus*, but he explicitly rejects their amatory subject matter and sugared style. He turns instead to his own "Subject, stylle inconnu" (II.21) because he has other, more urgent matters to deal with. Here d'Aubigné, like Lucan, cultivates a deliberately harsh style in order to represent the injustice that he feels in the world around him. D'Aubigné's most direct homage to Lucan, recorded in his unedited Latin verses, states the preference clearly: "We have the same spirit, same tastes. Lucan's pen is tough; mine is tougher."[6]

The title, *Les Tragiques*, conveys the speaker's other preference for visual, dramatic representations. It suggests both the standard devices of the Renaissance stage, especially pageantry, spectacle, and pictorial tableaux, the "general discours/De mon tableau public" (I.367–68) and also a concept of dramatic tragedy that represents a struggle between good and evil in the rise and lamentable fall of princes, nobles, and magistrates. It also insists that its audience is not just a spectator of these tragic events but an actor in them (I.170).[7] Above all the speaker is aware of his own involvement in these "tragiques." With verbal reminiscences drawn from Lucan's *De Bello civili* and Livy's *Annales* in the poem's first lines, he depicts himself as a Protestant Hannibal invading the Rome of pagan Caesars and Catholic popes, penetrating through Alpine crags with infusions of hot gall: "Mon courage de feu, mon humeur aigre & forte/Au travers des sept monts faict breche au lieu de porte" (I.5–6) ("My fiery courage, my strong vinegary humor makes a full breach rather than a tiny portal through the seven hills of Rome"). The analogy, a strained one even though founded on historical fact, slights one important aspect of the speaker's role that goes well beyond Hannibal's situation: God has ordained him a chosen member of His church, a defender of the true faith, and an instrument of His will. These roles he will embrace with all his strength, so that he becomes through his poetry an inspired intermediary between God and man.[8]

But he cannot achieve these ends by writing as a poet according to norms fashionable in his day. Instead he must exchange Petrarchan and classical fashion for idiosyncratic, fully expressive ones. Rather than wear the cothurnus of an actor performing tragic drama, he will wear the boot of a soldier engaged in military combat. He will summon the muse of historical narrative, not from any literary ideals of the past, but from the war-torn horrors of the present (I.78–79). A participant in the events of his time, he has been an audience to the action performed on the stage of history. Hence, he can dispense with representing the ills of the age figuratively through metaphors, symbols, allegories, and myths and can aim instead at representing them directly and with scenic accuracy, "Car mes yeux sont tesmoins du subjet de mes vers" (I.371) ("for my eyes are witnesses of the subject of my poetry"). As Christian poet, however, he must avoid representing the fall of princes in a

merely personal or satiric or confessional manner and direct his
rhetorical talent instead to moral account. He must activate
language beyond satire and confession to a form where it pro-
duces a concrete effect on an audience here and now.[9]

The speaker is honest in admitting that he has not always
been faithful to the demands of his poetic mission. In a moment
of curious introspection at the opening of *Princes* he questions
his own past performance: "Subject, stylle inconnu: combien
de fois fermee/Ai-je à la verité la lumiere allumee?" (II.21–22)
("Unfamiliar subject, unfamiliar style: how often have I extinguished the lamp which I originally kindled for the sake of
truth").[10] The self-accusation centers on his cowardice in
refraining from attack on powerful and important personages at
court. To some extent his cowardice is understandable, for the
poet's rhetorical art is always subject to interpretation and misinterpretation. Not only is his audience free to understand the
poem from its own point of view; it can in turn articulate its
understanding in language no less convincing than the poet's.
The explicator has the power both to distort the poet's deepest
intention with a malice that jeopardizes his whole enterprise
and also to uncover damaging meanings only half-intended or
wholly unsuspected by him:

> Lasche jusques ici, je n'avois entrepris
> D'attaquer les grandeurs, craignant d'estre surpris
> Sur l'ambiguité d'une glose estrangere.
>
> [II.27–29]

> [Cowardly until now, I had not ventured to attack their
> majesties, fearing to be caught unprepared on the ambiguity
> of an alien interpretation.]

No wonder the speaker recoils in self-consciousness at the mercy
of a potentially hostile audience.

The poet's lack of control over the way others receive his
work is one explanation. Another is his failure to match his own
moral aspirations to his rhetorical ability. He is very conscious
of this failure, for he wills to uphold his honor in the fight

against evil, yet he knows that the forces of evil are powerful and apt to discredit him entirely. "Je voi ce que je veux, & non ce que je puis,/Je voi mon entreprise, & non ce que je suis" (II.43–44) ("I see what I wish to do, and not what I can do; I see my attempt and not what I am"). Paradoxically, the humility gained from this self-appreciation enables him to deal with the effect of his poetry on others. To the audience who reproaches him for fleshing out his lines in bitter, tortured verse, he responds that the time's customs demand it: "Ce siecle, autre en ses moeurs, demande un autre style" (II.77). If a more ingratiating style could not shield him from the misinterpretation—and none really can when the audience willfully misinterprets—then the harshness that d'Aubigné found in Lucan might prove effective.

The style is especially appropriate to the epic when it enlists the satiric and historical modes as vehicles of aggression.[11] The speaker can use them to exorcise demons not only from himself but also from those in the outside world who threaten God's order. The major problem is to determine the object of the poet's aggression. The speaker does not hesitate to turn his rhetorical engines on those whom he feels to be demonstrably wicked: Catherine de Medici and her royal sons, the Cardinal de Loraine, Philip II of Spain, the Jesuits, all the Roman popes, and the list is very much longer. But more than once he expresses uneasiness:

> Au fil de ces fureurs ma fureur se consume,
> Je laisse ce sujet, ma main quitte ma plume,
> Mon coeur s'estonne en soy; mon sourcil refrongné,
> L'esprit de son suject se retire esloigné.
>
> [II.1099–1102]

[In the current of these furors my furor is consumed; I leave this subject, my hand drops the pen, my heart is shaken; my eyebrow frowning, the spirit retreats from its subject.]

He articulates his fundamental dislike of the abrasive style (III.926–27) and of the terrifying theme (VI.925–26). Above

all, he nearly despairs about his rhetorical ability to communicate them to a proper audience: "I'm afraid, reader, that your
spirits, weary from my tragic discourse, have said: Enough"
(VI.1103–1104). He realizes that no amount of verbal aggression will convert the "serfs de la vanité" (VI.1107); at best he
can hope to persuade the "enfans de verité" (VI.1108) that
their own witness to history is worthwhile. Condemned to being
misunderstood, he must endure his opponents' falsification of
every statement he makes. Such is the poet's fate, and yet he
will never slacken the rhetorical reins on his performance, for he
remains honor-bound to acknowledge it as proof of his election
to salvation. Accepting this fate, he exemplifies the tragedy of
the Huguenot: he lives on earth not to enjoy life, but to serve,
to witness, and to stand up against the attacks of those who see
in his enterprise a threat to their own independence.

This personal dilemma becomes a miniature reenactment of a
much larger Calvinist problem concerning damnation and election, fate and free will, freedom and history. History records
God's providence and each man's destiny; every event, seen in
its total context, affords indisputable proof that God has his
finger on man. The problem for the individual is to know
whether or not he belongs to God's elect. Living an upright life
in the just community may constitute a merely outward mark
of election, but accepting it in faith lessens the intolerable burden of total doubt.[12]

The speaker is keenly aware of the limitations of this accommodation. As both a poet and the historian mediating between
God's external plan for human history and man's temporal
enactment of it, he feels constrained in selecting and interpreting historical material for his poetry. In the opening lines of
Les Feux conscience accuses him of arbitrariness in assigning
praise to only some of the Huguenot martyrs and not to others,
and likewise in meting out shame to their persecutors. Worse,
conscience implies that as poet he has allowed art to claim his
attention more than truth, that he has shaped his account of
history only to conform with the stylistic norms of his poetry:
"I'm afraid that the band of martyrs chosen by you serves only

the style of the century and the rules of poetry" (IV.33–34). In defense of his stylistic choices the speaker cites the pressures of composition. Granted leisure, he will produce in the future a more detailed, more circumstantial account of the persecutions; right now, however, he will conflate his style with the subject to achieve a richer texture:

> Je m'advance au labeur avec cette asseurance
> Que, plus riche & moins beau, j'escris fidellement
> D'un style qui ne peut enrichir l'argument.
>
> [IV.50–52]

[I advance to my work with this assurance, that I am writing in a richer but less beautiful style which cannot enrich or distort the argument.]

By so renouncing the merely technically adept and structurally pleasing, the speaker best responds to the distinctive grace God has granted him. He thereby reconciles public performance to private desire, action and event to reason and will, role to selfhood, rhetoric to morality.

Acceptance of selfhood and renunciation of inadequate roles thus bespeak the true Christian's confidence in his election. They are the surest marks of his salvation. But the act of witnessing has no meaning without a sympathetic audience to confirm it. For a Huguenot, especially a Huguenot poet fashioning a weighty poem, the audience is very important. Thus, the speaker of this Calvinist epic attempts to address many audiences and to implicate them in the act of making his own witness meaningful.

The first audience the speaker must address is himself. Before he can report his witness to others, he needs to know himself and his response to things outside himself. He needs also to establish his and his informants' authority as messengers of truth. Recipient of God's grace and divine inspiration, he enjoys privileged access to the history of his time, and he endeavors to communicate it to his audience. Thus, he achieves the central epic effect of distance from the action and of communal affinity to the audience whom he inspires, and whose relationship to the action he mediates, as inspired bard.

The speaker has an intense awareness of his effect on others. No other major epic in Western literature is so full of vocatives, and no other is so directed towards its audience. A comparison of its essential rhetorical strategies with those of Lucan's *De Bello civili* is particularly apt. Quintilian had characterized Lucan as an orator more than as a poet (10.1.90), implying Lucan's success in making persuasive contact with his audience.[13] The characterization applies equally well to d'Aubigné. Many passages in *Les Tragiques* pulsate with vibrant oratorical appeal; speeches, for example, where Fortune and Virtue vie for the dedication of a young courtier (*Princes*, 1193–1318, 1335–1486); where David admonishes his councilors (*Chambre dorée*, 1011–54, in imitation of Psalm 58); where Protestant martyrs like Anne du Bourg (*Feux*, 591–602) and Richard Gastine (*Feux*, 739–914) exhort their brethren to remain committed to the just cause. Each of these speakers addresses a concrete fictive audience or a series of such audiences. Employing all the strategies of rhetoric at a classical rhetor's disposal, he implicates the reader of the poem in the complex rhetorical situation. Anne du Bourg, for example, in fewer than ten lines of his declamation, addresses three separate and distinct audiences. To the magistrates who have condemned him to death, he urges that each should profit from the example of courage which he himself offers: "Cessez, ô senateurs! tirez de mes tourmens/Ce profit" (IV.592–93). To the crowd awaiting his execution he protests his innocence: "Amis, meurtrier je ne suis point;/C'est pour Dieu l'immortel que je meurs en ce poinct" (IV.595–96). And finally to God himself he offers his last prayer: "Mon Dieu, vray juge & pere, au milieu du trespas/Je ne t'ay point laissé, ne m'abandonne pas" (IV.599–600). The reader, caught up in the play of these multiple rhetorical addresses, enters imaginatively into the poem as a spectator and participant, evaluating the speaker's performance and situating it in the context of the episode's meaning as a whole.

Vocatives abound not only in the characters' reported speech, but also in the speaker's continuing commentary. Each implies a distinct fictive audience, ranging from religious and political enemies whom he attacks overtly to others towards whom he maintains a sometimes ambiguous, frequently ambivalent attitude. When he addresses a hostile audience he often applies pure vitriol to cleanse the gangrenous wounds of hatred and intolerance. He may on occasion let pass a mocking double entendre or mordant play on words, as in the pun on *vers* in his address to the dying Philip II of Spain: "Espagnol triomphant, Dieu vengeur à sa gloire/Peindra de vers ton corps, de mes vers ta memoire" (VI.865–866) ("Triumphant Spaniard, God venger in his glory will afflict your body with worms, your memory with my verses").

In general, however, he addresses three types of enemies with unrelieved antagonism. First, he assaults whole classes of people in a fit of rage: the Jesuits ("vermine espagnolle," I.1245); hostile princes ("Vous qui avez donné ce subject à ma plume," II.9); flatterers ("Serpents qui retirez de mortelles froidures," II.105); and false judges and hypocritical clergy ("Et vous qui le faux nom de l'Eglise prenez," III.595). Then there are particular individuals whom he vilifies, ranging from the enemies of the old church, such as Herod (VI.455), Nero (VI.519), and Maximian (VI.627), to the enemies of the new, such as Catherine de Medici (I.747), Henry III (II.983), Archibishop Arondel (VI.769), Philip II of Spain (VI.863), and Marechal de Retz (VI.991). There are finally, especially in the *Chambre dorée*, abstractions of evil whom the speaker addresses directly and describes in full allegorical dress, such as Jalousie (III.333) and Pauvreté (III.353). In each case the speaker's attitude towards his audience is direct and uncomplicated, and often strangely unimpassioned.

Some of the fictive audiences evoke a more finely calibrated response. One is d'Aubigné's former patron and political leader, Henri de Navarre, who in the years following the fictive date of the poem's composition (1578–79) would betray his allegiance to the Protestants. Already sensing the power that Henri would inherit as presumptive heir of the crown in 1584, "when the scepter of lillies will join that of Navarre" (I.596), the speaker offers gratuitous advice: "Remember some day how ignorant they are who in order to be kings wish to be tyrants." Nor does he stifle his unrest on other occasions, as in his account of the St. Bartholemew's Day massacres, for example. There he thanks Henri for reporting the atrocities that he later witnessed as a prisoner in the Louvre. Nonetheless, two lines later he warns his benefactor that God will exact vengeance on him if he dismisses his own memory of the past so abruptly: "If one day you are forgetful and lose the memory of it, God will remember it well, to your shame, to his glory" (V.1029–30).

In another passage, written after 1610 as an apophetic forecast of Henri's assassination in that year, an angel functions as the speaker's spokesman by revealing future events according to the heavenly pattern (V.1245–1430). The rhetorical use of the angel to express the speaker's skepticism allows the poet to manipulate several different fictive audiences at once, including among others the speaker himself. First, the angel addresses Henri as victor of battles at Arques (September 1589) and Ivry (March 1590) and immediately judges him as betrayer of his own—and God's—cause: "Tout ploye sous ton heur, mais il est predit comme/Ce qu'on devoit à Dieu fut pour le Dieu de Rome" (V.1369–70) ("Everything yields to your luck, but it is predicted that what we owe to God will be ceded to the god of Rome"). Next he addresses the city of Paris, where Henry IV's ensuing offensive wrought havoc and famine in May of 1590: "Paris, tu es reduite à digerer l'humain" (V.1371) ("Paris, you are reduced to digesting human bodies"). He then turns to the speaker, "Si tu pouvois conoistre, ainsi que je conois" (V.1375) ("If you would know as I know") and afterwards to a still larger external audience, the great national states of Europe: Sweden, Moscow, Poland, and Austria (V.1379). His aim is to depict further sources of trouble: "Que te diray-je plus? Ces estoiles obscures/Escrivent à regret les choses plus impures" (V.1381–82) ("What more will I say to you? These obscure stars regretfully write the most impure things"). Referring to Henry IV's later partial successes at Savoy (August–December

1600) and Geneva (December 1602), and to his failure with Venetian diplomacy (1606), the angel implicates his audience in a negative judgment on the elusive gains: "Que te profitera, mon enfant, que tu voye/Quelque peu de fumee au fond de la Savoye" (V.1385–86), ("What will it profit you my child, that you see a little smoke at the foothills of Savoy?"). In cold indifference to his achievements, the angel finally proceeds to limn his assassination (14 May 1610) darkly, verblessly, as an act of divine retribution in payment for the former's defection from the Protestants' cause:

> Quoy plus? la main de Dieu douce, docte, & puis rude
> A parfaire trente ans l'entiere ingratitude,
> Et puis à la punir: ô funestes apprests!
> Flambeau luisant esteint!
>
> [V.1389–92]

[What more? hand of God, sweet, wise, and then stern in bringing to perfection complete ingratitude for thirty years and then in punishing it: Oh murderous preparation! shining torch extinguished!]

Only at the very end does the angel show the slightest compassion for the fallen king by averting the eyes of his audience—the speaker himself—from further consideration of the horrible event: "Ne voy rien de plus prés" (V.1392).

The reservations implicit in the speaker's treatment of Henri de Navarre are all the more conspicuous against the praise accorded to Queen Elizabeth of England. *La Chambre dorée* concludes with an *éloge* in honor of the most enlightened Protestant monarch in Europe. The exhortation to multiple audiences, including the Swiss, the Grisons, the English, and the Dutch (III.945), to hearken to just praise for a just ruler, provides a dazzling conclusion to the third book, for the speaker uses the queen's glorified reputation as a foil to his subsequent attack on France's own Catholic persecutors and false judges. He couches his judgment, moreover, in a vision of change and mutability that applauds her steadfastness and tenacity on the one hand, and her earthly mission and eternal destiny on the other: "Heureuse Elizabeth, la justice rendant,/Et qui n'as point vendu tes droicts en la vendant!" (III.953–954) ("Happy Elizabeth, rendering justice, you who have bartered away none of your rights in selling it"). So successful was she in holding true to her ideals that she has boldly inspired her subjects to hold true to theirs: "Tes guerriers hazardeux perdent, joyeux, pour toy/Ce que tu n'eus regret de perdre pour la foy" (III.985–86) ("Your warriors, prepared to take risks, lose joyously for you what you have no qualms in losing for the faith").

The speaker's rhetorical involvement with the reading audience is just as complicated and even more variable. He knows that readers come to the poem from diverse backgrounds with different skills and capacities. Some may embrace his cause wholly and without reservation, even to the extent of martyrdom for their convictions. Others may not be able to share his vision or have rejected it in favor of worse ends. Still others, apparently the majority, occupy a vast middle ground, inclined towards good but subject to occasional distraction, and constantly must be reminded of their possible destiny; the speaker knows that he can never convert them if God does not will him to, but he can take special pains to heighten his poem's rhetorical relevance as a permanent witness of the truth.[14]

To those who already embrace his cause the speaker assigns several roles. One is as his trusted confidant, especially when he has incriminating material to present. Early in the poem, for example, he rages against the currently fashionable practice of settling arguments by dueling, a practice which he himself had adopted a few years earlier. Now he appeals to his audience to believe in his change of heart: "Do not think, reader, that I narrate this deed for my own glory; I write of it to my own shame" (I.1073–74). Significantly he does not ask exoneration for past sins, but focuses instead on the marks of his own election into the community of the saved.

Nor does the speaker expect his audience to be flattering or congratulatory. If he asks the audience to judge him, he does so only in his role as poet and messenger of God's word. He urges it to accept the harsh and strident tone, the lurid and offensive imagery, and the frightful, ugly action of his poem, since only by these devices can he portray the reality of the situation with uncompromising artistic integrity:[15] "Friend, the words which you criticize supply apt diction for the project which I undertake" (II.63–64). By playing these roles, listeners can become willing pupils whom the speaker instructs in the art of renouncing and abandoning the ills of his age: "Flee, Lots, from burning Sodom and Gomorah; don't bury your innocent souls with these reprobates" (II.1503–05). Here, if God has chosen them to do so, those who hearken to the speaker's advice find themselves complying with grace in a most unexpected way. Both speaker and audience will be fulfilling their destinies in the drama of salvation.

The members of the audience whom the speaker cannot persuade, those obdurate sinners whom God has marked for destruction, enact other roles. No less than the elect, they play their parts according to God's preordained plan, and as the speaker says to financiers and legal authorities starving France with unjust laws, they are not merely passive onlookers but active performers (I.169–70). To those fallen members who enjoy power or prestige over the elect, the speaker addresses his harshest rebuke. He scorns poets who advance other religious persuasions by composing divine verse in the styles of *grands rhétoriqueurs*, Petrarchan sonneteers, and mere academic classicists: "In vain you display harangue after harangue unless you use the language of Canaan" (II.441–42). On the other hand, no members of his audience are so irredeemable that they cannot effect some good if God chooses. Even foreign armies, potential invaders and destroyers of France, can use their immense power and might to attack French corruption and decadence:

> Estrangers irrités, à qui sont les François
> Abomination, pour Dieu! faictes le choix
> De celui qu'on trahit & et de celui qui tue.
> [V.1539–41]

[Angry foreigners to whom the French are an abomination, for God's sake, choose between him whom one betrays and him who kills.]

Forcible aggression is not the only way in which the enemy fulfill God's plan. Sometimes the adversary's mere presence can provide a stimulating force for good. When in the last book the speaker discourses on the resurrection of the body and the immortality of body and soul, he fortifies his proofs with arguments from the pagan philosopher Hermes Trismegistus that are ultimately irreconcilable with Calvinist doctrine and Christian orthodoxy. He addresses "Atheistes vaincus," "Sadduciens pervers," "Enfans de vanité," and "Payens," but he clearly intends the faithful to follow his argument as one more confirmation of their already established belief.[16] The rhetorical point is less to convert unbelievers, who in any case can never mend their ways unless God grants and they accept divine grace, than it is to reinforce and validate the sense of God's word revealed elsewhere. That God has already condemned his enemies once and for all lends the speaker no real strength in his arguments against unbelievers—only powers of retaliation. His rhetorical strategy thus becomes once and for all a prop and support for those who already enjoy the marks of election.

In the end, all possible audiences of the poem will be ranged either on the right or on the left hand of God. On the right will be the saved, whose triumph the speaker proclaims in a series of paradoxes and inversions, "A vous la vie, à vous qui pour Christ la perdez" (VII.27) ("Life is yours, you who lose it for Christ"). On the left will be the damned, whom the speaker addresses and taunts with hyperbolic irony: "Je retourne à la gauche, ô esclaves tondus" (VII.81) ("I return to the left, o tonsured slaves"). Into one or the other camp will fall all the indeterminate members of his present audience, shown as yet no special marks of either salvation or damnation, the vast majority of mankind who will have to work out in patience and humility their own human destinies without knowing what God has established for them. No amount of persuasion can move the audience to redemption unless God wills it, but through such appeal the speaker can nonetheless dispose his audience to receive God's grace. Thus, he never gives up on his addresses to the audience. Even if his exhortations depend upon God's will for their efficacy, the speaker can at least console himself that he has tried his best. Poetic rhetoric, and in particular the rhetoric of epic poetry, can do no more.

The speaker's heroic resolve to play the role at all costs, against all odds; his hortatory relationship with a multifarious audience, some of whose members, having grace, accept what he urges, while others who lack grace reject his message; and the panoramic sweep and dramatic detail of a vision keen to advance the specific values of his own religious cause, all mark the epic dimensions of *Les Tragiques*. The poem is certainly not an epic in the sense that the *Orlando Furioso* or *Paradise Lost* are; it develops no continuous narrative or dramatic action as they do, nor does it hold up to view the conventional diction, rhythms, tropes, and elocutionary devices of the "high style" associated with the epic since antiquity; it moreover incorporates other modes and styles not usually found in the epic: personal, political, and polemical invective; topical satire; and strained, elliptical, deeply enigmatic verbal expression. Still, *Les Tragiques* does sustain a complicated interplay of rhetorical strategies characterizing the speaker and his collective audience in much the same way that other epic poems do. In this manner it adheres to norms which are both more intrinsic and more essential to the genre. If d'Aubigné transmutes for his own purposes the conventional epic motifs and elocutionary devices, he still preserves the fundamental norms of epic in his treatment of the complex rhetorical situation.

As a result d'Aubigné adapts to the generic demands of his epic various aspects of biblical, satiric, and historical modes and lyric, dramatic, oratorical, and allegorical styles. By comparison with *Les Tragiques*, the earlier epics of d'Aubigné's own countrymen seem much smaller accomplishments. Peletier du Mans's *L'Amour des Amours* (1547), Ronsard's *Franciade* (1572), du Bartas's *La Semaine* (1578), and even Scève's

Microcosme (1562) all respect the conventional norms of the genre, but none accommodates itself to divergent modal and stylistic demands. In that regard *Les Tragiques* approaches the achievement of the very best epics, those works of Ariosto, Tasso, Spenser, and Milton that wed conventional epic norms to the demands of the chivalric, historical, allegorical, and dramatic modes and the ironic, poetic, lyric, and classicistic styles. In their distinguished company, *Les Tragiques* is a worthy peer.

Milton's *Paradise Lost*

The conjunction of historical drama and mythic significance in the Virgilian epic—indeed in all the classical epics with the partial exception of Lucan's—was a challenge that the Renaissance poet rarely met successfully. Francesco Filelfo in the *Sphortias* (1461, unfinished), Giangiorgio Trissino in *Italia liberata dai Goti* (1547–48), and Ronsard in *Franciade* (1572), for example, took their subjects as much from legend as from alleged history, but they strained ineffectually to make them meaningful as either history or legend. Maffeo Veggio (d. 1458) in *Vellus Aureum*, Giovanni Pontano (d. 1503) in *Urania*, and Giraldi Cinthio in *Ercole* (1557) took their subjects from classical myth, but they assimilated them to history only through the weakest appeals to their patrons' careers. And Jacopo Sannazaro in *De Partu Virginis* (1526), Marco Girolamo Vida in *Christiados* (1525), du Bartas in *La Semaine* (1578), and Marino in *Strage degli innocenti* (1632, published posthumously), took their mythic and historical subjects from the Bible, but they used them neither to figure nor to foreshadow the course of events that stretched beyond them as the writers of the Bible and their Judaeo-Christian interpreters did.

The most talented and ambitious epic poets of the Renaissance, however, fashioned their subjects, whether mythic, historical, or legendary, in ways that could point to a pattern in the past, suggest a meaning for the present, and signify a direction that the future might take. Thus, with varying success Pulci, Boiardo, and Ariosto romanticized the distant history of Charlemagne's epoch and related it to certain events (the wars in Italy,

voyages of exploration, the Protestant Reformation) that trans-
cended the merely local interests of their patrons. In *The Faerie
Queene* (1590–96) Spenser figured forth his "profitable and
gracious . . . doctrine by ensample," as well as the entire history
of Britain, in an elaborate allegory that sustains at least as much
interest on its literal dramatic level as it does on the didactic
moral level.[1] Still other Renaissance poets fashioned their epics
around more recent heroic exploits. Thus, Camoens invested *Os
Lusiades* (1572) with encomia on the kingdom of Portugal and
the explorations of Vasco da Gama, and Tasso inserted into his
Gerusalemme Liberata (1575) allusions to contemporary events,
but both failed in the long run to capture the truly problematic
moral, dramatic, and rhetorical subtleties implicit in the Virgilian norm.

It remained for Milton (1608–74) to find for his own audience the historical and mythic equivalent of Virgil's subject and
through the rhetorical strategies we have been discussing exploit
their potentials to the full. Just as in Virgil's poem, where the
whole history of the Roman Empire is the consequence of
Aeneas's expedition, so in *Paradise Lost* (1667–74) the whole
history of mankind is the consequence of the heroes' fall. At
every turn a sense of future destiny conditions both epics.
Milton, however, uses his rhetoric to qualify this sense of future
destiny differently from Virgil. By focusing on only three major
characters—Adam, Eve, and Satan—he assigns each a unique
rhetorical *ethos* entailing conflicts emblematic of all that mankind in later history could experience. His speaker, moreover,
interests himself in the characters' action out of a profound
sense of its continuing relevance in the present scheme of things.
The rhetorical strategy reflects this emphasis. It also engenders
a new and special problem: the speaker's commitment to
Christian orthodoxy prevents him from registering discontent or
disillusion with his theme of the fall as Virgil did with his theme
of Roman destiny. Instead, the speaker manipulates his audience to interpret human history with an awareness of its complexity.

One result is a complication of both the speaker's and the

reader's attitudes towards the poem. Consider their responses to
Satan's rhetoric. Not only have many modern readers found
Satan convincing in his speeches about rebellion, but some have
even regarded him as the hero of the poem. Yet nothing could
be further from the Miltonic speaker's intent.[2] Rather, he
frames Satan's discourse so as to show a conflict between the
character's roles and his selfhood. This conflict reveals the
fallacies hidden in Satan's rationale, diminishing his stature with
dramatic and rhetorical point. By no coincidence, for example,
Satan's incredulous first words in the poem ("If thou beest hee;
But O how fall'n! how chang'd/From him . . ." I.84-85) recall
the speaker's own exclamation at the sight of the fallen angel
nine lines earlier ("O how unlike the place from whence they
fell!" I.75).[3] Besides confirming the speaker's prior authority as
the standard against which to measure Satan's debased exclamation, the echo confirms Satan's damnation to an existence as
agent of the words of others, a thrall to their intentions, nothing,
ultimately, but a tool for God and man.

The polarities of failure and accomplishment become infi-
nitely subtle in the speaker's own rhetoric. He, no less than his
characters, suffers consequences of the primal fall. They emerge
in the complications, qualifications, and vacillations that mark
his syntax. The audience, in turn, whether more or less flawed
than the speaker, comprehends the poem's action only through
these syntactic obscurities.

In the first twenty-six lines of book I, for example, the
speaker manages a single period that radically upsets the audience's expectations about the poem.[4] Full of statement and
revision it shows how he will allow the rest of the poem to start
and stop, backtrack, modify, and clarify its discourse in ex-
tremely self-conscious ways. He seems, in fact, to be moving
towards clarity away from the unclarity that his own syntax
begets. The sentence, however, which appears to end with the
word "*Chaos*" on line 10 ("who first taught the chosen Seed,/
In the Beginning how the Heav'ns and Earth/Rose out of
Chaos", I.8-10), continues for another six lines when the
speaker adds (with an unexpected allusion to Ariosto!) that he

invokes the muses' aid to pursue "Things unattempted yet in Prose or Rhyme." Nor does he rest content within those lines. Purposively sharpening the Homeric and Virgilian "aut . . . aut" formula to suggest an epistemological confusion that goes well beyond the intent of the classical convention, he elaborates several possible alternatives ("or . . . or") for key statements, representing Moses "on the secret top/Of *Oreb*, or of *Sinai*" and bargaining with Urania: "Or if *Sion* Hill/Delight thee more" (I.6–11). The collective will of both speaker and audience to grapple with these difficulties requires more than just patience: it requires a commitment to the work of encoding and decoding the poem to achieve the maximum insight and illumination from the task.

No less difficult than the speaker's epistemological problem is his private moral dilemma. It emerges in the address to "holy Light" at the beginning of book III. Here the crisis of his blindness generates a quest into the meaning of physical affliction as another justification of God's ways to man.[5] The repetitions "Thee I revisit now" and "thee I revisit safe" culminate in the opposing statement of God's refusal to reciprocate: "but thou/ Revisit'st not these eyes." Despite God's denial, however, the speaker says that he has not ceased to look for inspiration. Thus, in a strikingly delayed use of direct address, while he credits the classical pagan muses with the power of supplementing divine inspiration, he confirms the priority of Mt. Sion as the chief abode of his muse: "but chief/Thee *Sion* and the flow'ry Brooks beneath/That wash thy hallow'd feet, and warbling flow,/Nightly I visit." Still, he is prone to a dejection that even the strongest faith cannot allay. At the finale comes the renewed address to God with the plea for inner vision to compensate for his blindness: "So much the rather thou Celestial Light/Shine inward" (III.51–52). It is not clear whether the speaker sees his own suffering as one more consequence of the fall; what is clear is his supplication that despite physical blindness he "may see and tell/Of things invisible to mortal sight." But the rhetorical poise and control belie an accommodated solution to the continuing dilemma. The speaker has no real guarantee that God will answer his plea, nor that he himself can attain a sharpened inner vision. The questions have no answer and the dilemmas no resolution, even if the speaker acts as though they do.

While the invocation of book I reveals the epistemological complexities and that of book III reveals the moral ones, the beginning of book VII states the rhetorical problems of finding an apt audience for the poem. Addressing his muse, Urania, the speaker fears lest his poetic career take a turn suffered by Bellerophon, whom the gods once favored but afterwards hated and condemned to the Aleian field, "Erroneous there to wander and forlorn." True, he feels more confident in dealing with the temptation and fall of Adam and Eve during the poem's second half in marked contrast to his hesitancy in dealing with the revolt of Satan during its first half. Still, he ironically qualifies his statement "More safe I Sing" with the admission that he has "fall'n on evil days." Suffering from blindness, political oppression, and solitude, he is confident that he can continue his poem if only his muse hears his plea, "fit audience find, though few." The fitness of that audience and his rhetorical relationship to it the speaker defines best in a convoluted allusion to the Orpheus myth:

> But drive far off the barbarous dissonance
> Of *Bacchus* and his Revellers, the Race
> Of that wild Rout that tore the *Thracian* Bard
> In *Rhodope*, where Woods and Rocks had Ears
> To rapture, till the savage clamor drown'd
> Both Harp and Voice.
>
> [VII.32–37]

He would seem to divide the audience into three groups: the "fit audience," however few in number, who would participate with him in his attempt to write the epic; the "barbarous" crew, perhaps larger in number, who oppose his attempt by threatening to silence the poem; and a middle audience, indeterminate in number, who, like the "Woods and Rocks" of Rhodope that had "Ears/To rapture" but were ultimately incapable of defending the bard or of hearing him out, passively accept the poem's substance without fully experiencing it at its deepest levels of meaning. According to Puritan theology, the speaker would be seeking an audience of the preelect who can journey with him every step of the difficult way toward clarifying the nature of sin in Adam and Eve and all mankind.[6] Such an audience can see through the veil of the speaker's blindness, too; it will judge and evaluate his performance no less than Adam's and Eve's, Satan's and God's; it will appreciate his inadequacies and correct if possible his unintentional distortions; and finally it will join him in admitting his inability to unravel the mysteries quite whole and quite clear. This rhetorical strategy, however, radically forecloses the possibility that the great intermediate class of mankind will ever come to understand the ways of God to man. Though they may profit from the poem, they will never discover all that the mystery implies.

In the invocation of book IX the speaker represents himself finally in quest of poetic inspiration. Here he brings together the concerns of his earlier invocations and resolves them by postulating his "answerable style." His choice of subject matter—the origin of sin, death, and misery—he defends as "Not less but more Heroic" (IX.14) than the Homeric theme of wrath or the Virgilian theme of rage, to say nothing of the "long and tedious havoc" of "fabl'd Knights" in the chivalric epics. His claim to visionary insight in book III he now defends as the divine inspiration that his "Celestial Patroness" visits on him nightly, while his selection of a "fit audience" in book VII he implicitly defends against the possibility that "an age too late," a reading public which has grown tired of the epic, may "damp my intended wing" (IX.45). But inspiration above all has enabled him to choose his subject, assert his insight, and select his audience. The problem now is to draw an analogy between that inspiration and the gift of grace bestowed by God on chosen members of fallen mankind:

> If answerable style I can obtain
> Of my Celestial Patroness, who deigns

Her nightly visitation unimplor'd,
And dictates to me slumbr'ing, or inspires
Easy my unpremeditated Verse. . . .

[IX. 20–24]

The recipient of inspiration must turn it to good account in a
style "answerable" to the poem's subject matter. Answerability
of course implies much more than mere competence. The more
complex the argument of the poem, the more complex its style
will have to be. In this sense poetic inspiration resembles the
Trinitarian spiration that proceeds from the answerability of
Son to Father and results in the perfection of the Holy Spirit.
The inspired poem proceeds from the answerability of the
poet's style to his transcendent subject matter and results in a
perfection of "simple, sensuous, and passionate" language
capable of moving its audience to greater contact with God the
Father, Son, and Holy Spirit.[7] On this count the speaker of
Paradise Lost asks the audience to judge his work.

The relationship of Milton's speaker both with his subject
matter and with his audience is thus subjective, but with a
difference. In Virgil a conflict between the official political
point of view and the subjective human point of view results in
the assertion of a balance between the two.[8] No victory remains
unqualified for either side, nor does any defeat. For Milton to
have dramatized a comparable tension between ideology and
feeling, however, would have been tantamount to questioning
the principles of Christian orthodoxy, which would have been
impossible. Hence, the speaker's attack on the enemies of God
is unremittingly harsh. On the other hand, as an epic poet,
Milton did recognize the value of a dramatic *pathos*, and he
ultimately fashioned a speaker with a highly subjective point of
view. In this regard Milton inherited the Italian tradition that
carried to an extreme the subjectivity of the Virgilian speaker.
In the Italian epic, especially in Ariosto, the speaker maintains
an attitude towards his material as ironic as in Virgil, but not
because he feels a conflict between abstraction and human
feelings. Irony springs instead from the speaker's compliant

urbanity, from his sympathies with the characters' all too human failings and foibles, hesitations and tergiversations, weaknesses and inconsistencies. In Milton, however, it springs from an involvement with his characters that is fully tragic.

The speaker accomplishes this by playing several different roles which intersect throughout the poem. In the introductions to books I, III, VII, and IX he embraces a staple conventional role of the classical epic: the poet who invokes the inspiration of the muses. Indeed, at the beginning of book I he calls for the aid of not just one "Heav'nly Muse, that on the secret top/of *Oreb*, or of *Sinai*, didst inspire/That Shepherd" but of another: "And chiefly Thou O Spirit, that dost prefer/Before all Temples th' upright heart and pure" (I.17–18). In the opening lines of book III he invokes "holy Light, offspring of Heav'n first-born,/Or of th' Eternal Coeternal beam" and promises not to foresake the classical muses either (III.26–29). Elsewhere he invokes Urania (VII.1) whom he designates in the poem's final invocation as his "Celestial Patroness," (IX.21), prime mover of his "unpremeditated Verse" (IX.24).[9] Significantly, while the speaker embraces his role as recipient of the muses' aid, he also embraces it as an audience who gives full witness to the events vouchsafed him by the muses. Here he functions as something more than a mere agent who records the narrative action. He becomes interpreter of the action that he portrays and mediator between it and the audience.

This mediation charges his rhetoric with a difficult problem, especially when it affects his characters' own speech. In his fabrication of dramatic dialogue, monologue, or soliloquy, for example, the speaker attributes words to characters who are either spirits (God, His angels, the fallen angels) and hence use no language, or else humans (Adam and Eve) who lived at the dawn of time and spoke a language different from our modern one.[10] Here the rhetorical problem parallels the difficulty enunciated by Raphael at the beginning of his account of the war in heaven: how to describe superhuman action, how to condition oneself and one's audience against the wrong response to it, and how to elaborate the bare sketch with meaningful insight into the nature of things. As Raphael complains:

> High matter thou injoin'st me, O prime of men,
> Sad task and hard, for how shall I relate
> To human sense th' invisible exploits
> Of warring Spirits; how without remorse
> The ruin of so many glorious once
> And perfet while they stood; how last unfold
> The secrets of another World, perhaps
> Not lawful to reveal?
>
>   [V.563-570]

But whereas Raphael functions as the translator of divine and angelic languages, the speaker functions as the translator of diabolic and primal languages as well, and like all translators he needs to begin by interpreting the original utterance.

The speaker attempts to solve this problem by finding the right style for each speaking character, an effort that in turn compels him to establish for each a rhetorical *ethos* commensurate with his role and selfhood. For the persons of God the speaker assigns a plain style that reflects the unfragmented unity and *simplicitas* of God's nature. Free from conflict between roles and self and addressing an audience made receptive by his own grace, God speaks with a singular clarity and directness. God's word is His will and His will is law. The diction that the speaker fashions for Him contains and reconciles all divergent tensions of His being: terror and mercy, aloofness and involvement, secretiveness and openness.[11] "Man shall not quite be lost, but sav'd who will,/Yet not of will in him, but grace in me/Freely voutsaf't" (III.173-175), God says, qualifying His very decree with the subtleties of "not quite . . . but" and "Yet not . . . but" that accommodate man's freedom to His necessity.

Inscrutably different from His creatures, the Father in His omnipotence proposes one role that God and God alone can play. Since man will direct his sin "Against the high Supremacy of Heav'n,/Affecting God-head" (III.205-206), none but God Himself will be able to expiate that sin. The Son, who takes upon Himself the role as expiator and, in turn, man's redeemer, enjoys a total selfhood indistinguishable from the Father's and, like the Father, speaks in a lucid style. His diction, however, is more graceful and flexible than the Father's, marked by lyrical repetitions, assonances, internal rhymes: "I shall rise Victorious," the Son says, "and subdue/My vanquisher, spoil'd of his vaunted spoil" (III.250-51). The harmonious periodicity, the carefully woven echoes of the *i-r-s-v-l* sounds, the bold iteration of *spoil'd-spoil* themselves become part of an epic strategy of rhetorical alienation by which the speaker establishes and maintains the necessary distinction between the human or creatural and the divine.[12]

For each of the angelic characters who deliver lengthy historical and prophetic monologues to Adam, the speaker fashions a rhetoric almost as transparent as God's. Both angels are messengers and spokesmen of God, from whom their clarity and lucidity emanate. They speak in different rhetorical modes, however, owing not so much to their different characters as to the different subject matters they treat and the conditions of the audience they address. Raphael translates God's word into primordial human language for the unfallen Adam to hear, just as God in turn had translated His own word into angelic language for Raphael and the heavenly hosts. The original utterance lies therefore at three removes from the modern English into which the speaker in turn has translated Raphael's discourse for his own audience to comprehend. The speaker empowers Raphael with a classic mode of poetic utterance, replete with elevated diction, controlled hypotaxis, the use of direct discourse, occasional extended comparisons, and other figures of speech and thought associated with the classical epic. Thus, Raphael "in *Adam's* Ear/So Charming left his voice, that he a while/ Thought him still speaking, still stood fixt to hear" (VIII.1-3). The sensuous impact of Raphael's poetry, concerned as it is with events outside of time—the war in Heaven and the creation of the universe—presents no moral problem for the immediate audience, the unfallen Adam who is yet incapable of perverting such a speech. Michael, on the other hand, tells of events within historical time, performed by men shaky from the consequences of Adam's sin; he narrates them, moreover, in an admonitory fashion for the benefit of Adam, his now lapsed and sadly afflicted audience.[13] Thus, midway through his speech Michael confesses how he perceives Adam's weakness: "Much thou hast yet to see, but I perceive/Thy mortal sight to fail; objects divine/Must needs impair and weary human sense" (XII.8–10). The speaker accordingly adjusts his representation of Michael's discourse so that with its muted austerity, its flatfooted parataxis, its avoidance of figural language and its reliance on indirect discourse, the tonal decorum befits the nature of Michael's purpose.

Through both the relative splendor of Raphael's style and the relative drabness of Michael's, then, the speaker manipulates his audience to respond to the singular authority of God's message. As translator and interpreter of Satan's, Adam's, and Eve's speeches, on the other hand, the speaker must bring his audience to detect the flaws inherent in their rhetorical *ethos*. Here the speaker is not entirely a free agent. He must accept the givens of his character's roles and their moral selfhoods, and he must shape for each a language that best represents the individual's dramatic personality.

The speaker, for example, translates Satan's diabolic language by heightening its potential for theatrical effect.[14] As the speaker represents him, Satan is indeed a very theatrical character. At the climax of Eve's temptation scene, he describes Satan metaphorically as an oratorical performer who

> New part puts on, and as to passion mov'd,
> Fluctuates disturb'd, yet comely, and in act
> Rais'd, as of some great matter to begin.
>
> [IX.667–69]

Yet no matter what rhetorical strategy he uses, Satan finds that all his roles constitute variations of one role. Before the revolt in heaven Satan was simply himself, Lucifer (as Raphael tells Adam in VII.131). After the revolt the change of his name to *Satan* signifies the part that he is henceforth destined to play

for all eternity. For *Satan* means "adversary," and Satan functions eternally as the "Adversary of God and Man" (II.629).

The speaker knows that Satan as adversary is serving God's
plan by drawing good out of evil. The tension here originates
in the conflict between the role that Satan thinks he is playing
and the one major role that the speaker shows him actually to
be playing. When Beelzebub questions whether God intends the
fallen angels to "do him mightier service as his thralls . . . /Or
do his Errands in the gloomy Deep" (I.149-52), Satan answers
that henceforth he and all the fallen angels should seek to fulfill
themselves in roles of their own choice:

> If then his Providence
> Out of our evil seek to bring forth good,
> Our labor must be to pervert that end,
> And out of good still to find means of evil.
>   [I.162-65]

Even if, as Satan later decides, he must play the role that God
assigns, he will not alter his selfhood. He brings to hell "mind
not to be chang'd by Place or Time" (I.253). The narrative
speaker, revealing his own rhetorical attitude towards Satan,
plays upon this conviction to disclose Satan's weakness in a
number of decisive ways.

Later, for example, by emphasizing Satan's position as monarch of hell, the speaker exploits the tensions in Satan's *ethos*.
Every role, Satan implies, binds its player to norms that he
cannot alter or reject without changing the role itself:

> Wherefore do I assume
> These Royalties, and not refuse to Reign,
> Refusing to accept as great a share
> Of hazard as of honor?
>   [II.450-53]

The speaker shows, however, that Satan does not realize the full
implications of this commitment until he has well passed the
dangers of plunging through chaos. When the angels apprehend
him inside paradise inspiring "discontented thoughts" (IV.807)

in Eve's dreams, they ask "Which of those rebel Spirits" he is (IV.823). Satan's uncomprehending answer, "Know ye not then said *Satan*, fill'd with scorn,/Know ye not mee?" (IV.827–28), reveals his ignorance of the changes wrought by his fallen state. The angel then obliquely alludes to the lost dignity that Satan can never regain. At this point, and for the first time in the poem,

> abasht the Devil stood,
> And felt how awful goodness is, and saw
> Virtue in her shape how lovely, saw, and pin'd
> His loss.
>
> [IV.846–49]

The speaker hastens to add that more than his loss of heaven and Virtue Satan pines "to find here observ'd/His luster visibly impair'd" (IV.849–50). But the blow to Satan's self-concept has been dealt, and with it comes a weakening of his own epic rhetoric.[15]

The speaker thus justifies his moral condemnation of Satan through the latter's own rhetoric. He dissociates himself and his attitudes relatively easily from Satan and Satan's attitudes, even though, humanly flawed as he is, he is not wholly immune from the adversary's influence.[16] Appealing to his audience to trust his judgment from the very beginning, he asserts his claim to be an inspired bard who knows more than his audience and, with his hindsight awareness of the providence that Satan conspires against, even more than the adversary. He supplements, for example, ancient myth when he associates the origin of wealth with the figure of Mammon ("Let none admire/That riches grow in Hell," I.690–91); and he goes on to stress his own view that even the most vainglorious of modern artisans are outdone by the reprobate spirits of hell ("And here let those/Who boast in mortal things . . ." I.692–93). Within fifty lines he adjusts mythic chronology by conflating the popular account of Mulciber's fall with the story of the war in heaven: "Nor was his name unheard or unador'd/In ancient *Greece*" (I.738–39). And at the very end of book I he corrects the commonplace perspective on demonic size and strength when he foreshortens the devils' "shapes immense" in order to emphasize the breadth of Pandemonium (I.790).

In other more apparently subjective intrusions throughout the poem the speaker misses no opportunity to subvert the audience's response to Satan's activity. Whether he laments the easy accord that Satan makes in hell compared with the shameful disaccord that men create on earth (II.496), or whether he applies to abuses rampant in present-day churches the import of Satan's leap into paradise (IV.193), he is all the while conditioning his audience to respond negatively to Satan's current performance. Less explicitly he undermines Satan's attempted retreat from paradise after Eve's sin with the question, "for what can scape the Eye/Of God All-seeing?" (X.5–6). Moreover, when he interposes a cool and detached "some say" to his report that the fallen angels are transformed into snakes "Yearly enjoin'd, some say, to undergo/This annual humbling" (X.575–76), the speaker is avenging and demeaning Satan's performance. Similarly, when he attacks hypocrites who defame sexual love (IV. 744) and when he praises the innocence of paradise for harboring no sexual jealousy (V.445), or when he has Raphael address Adam on the mischief wrought by the invention of cannon (VI.501) and on the evanescence of man's happiness (VII.625–32), the speaker implicates the audience in the rightness of his own judgment.

Adjustor of false impressions and conjurer of true shapes and sizes, commentator on the action of Satan with sometimes malevolent irony and opponent of wrongdoing in his own day, the speaker hones his talent to move his audience to rethink its own point of view. With regard to Adam and Eve, he feigns no distance. From the beginning he presents them as images of himself and as models for his audience. Nothing is more revealing than his triumphant use of the first-person singular and plural pronouns linking Adam and Eve to himself and his audience. When they retire to enjoy their connubial rites, he compares their simplicity to "These troublesome disguises which wee wear" (IV.740), interjecting on the basis of his own supposition,

"I ween" that Adam did not turn away from Eve all night long. Depicting the beauty of unfallen sexuality, he assails hypocrites who defame sex when they "austerely talk/Of purity and place and innocence," adding that if "Our Maker bids increase, who bids abstain/But our Destroyer, foe to God and Man?" In the epithalamion that follows, "Hail wedded Love, mysterious Law" (IV.750-53), the speaker comments, "Far be it, that I should write thee sin or blame" and concludes with a direct address to Adam and Eve exclaiming how they have found the sum and substance of happiness and knowledge: "Sleep on,/ Blest pair; and O yet happiest if ye seek/No happier state, and know to know no more" (IV.773-75). But the implication that there is a happier state (even if Adam and Eve only think there is) and the ironic repetition and punning of "No . . . know . . . know no" impart a strange twist to the speaker's involvement. Wiser than Adam and Eve, perhaps, in a hindsight knowledge of their fall, but sympathetic to their dilemma, the speaker nonetheless links them to himself and to his first-person plural audience.[17]

Prelapsarian man, created to delight in himself and in God, enjoys like God an integrated selfhood. The speaker, however, shows that Eve, early in her career, itches to begin playing other roles. The fragmentation of her personality—and the beginning of the epic fall which it marks—originate in the conflict between conforming to her assigned role and obeying the impulses of her selfhood. Initially conscious of her relative inferiority to Adam in valor and wisdom, she attributes to him a superior role as guardian of knowledge: "God is thy Law, thou mine: to know no more/Is woman's happiest knowledge and her praise" (IV.637-38). Ironically, she falls through a temptation that appeals to her epic thirst for more knowledge. Satan entices her in her sleep to seek "the Tree/Of interdicted Knowledge" (V.51-52), and she will dream of being transported "among the Gods/Thyself a Goddess, not to Earth confin'd" (V.77-78). On the fateful day, the rhetorical strategy that she uses to argue about leaving Adam's side emphasizes her wish to become a more efficient gardener: "Let us divide our labors . . ." (IX.214).

The attractiveness of each of these roles—becoming Adam's peer in wisdom, a goddess in her own right, or simply a better gardener—dramatizes how Eve's fall was gradual, not the product of a single moment, but the cumulative result of seeking to implement the various aspects of her selfhood.

After the fall the speaker shows how Eve's role-playing options increase significantly. Her soliloquy following the fall reveals her electing to become an idolator when she promises the tree that she "Not without Song, each Morning, and due praise/Shall tend thee" (IX.800–01). It reveals her scheming to withhold her new-found knowledge from Adam:

> shall I to him make known
> As yet my change, and give him to partake
> Full happiness with mee, or rather not.
> [IX.817–19]

And finally, though she is ignorant of the implications, it shows her in the process of earning another role as a jealous wife. When she imagines Adam "wedded to another *Eve*" after her death, she judges such a possibility itself "A death to think." For the first time Eve comes to experience the irony of playing unknown roles, and the unity and integrity of her selfhood are lost forever. In "O much deceiv'd, much failing, hapless *Eve*" (IX.404), the speaker himself laments the loss by addressing Eve directly, one of the rare examples in the poem where he apostrophizes the character.

Adam's fall is also gradual, and the speaker shows how it too implicates him in unfamiliar roles.[18] In the beginning Adam, like Eve, enjoyed an integrated selfhood obedient to God and to nature. What distinguishes Adam from Eve is a characteristic sense of the importance of other persons: first of God, "the Power / That made us," and second of Eve, "Sole partner and sole part of all these joys" (IV.411–413). Significantly, the speaker attributes these lines to Adam as an introduction to his first speech in *Paradise Lost*. Later, in Adam's account to Raphael of his initial days in Paradise, the speaker allows him to stress his creaturely dependence upon God, almost to the point where he obliterates all sense of his own selfhood. In contrast to Eve, he admits to not having known himself at all: "But who I was, or where, or from what cause,/Knew not" (VIII.270–71). He is sure only that he came into life "Not of myself; by some great Maker then" and that he longs for an "other self" to complement his being.

The contrast with Eve's characterization is important. Before the fall, the speaker structures two important scenes to emphasize it. The first occurs when Adam narrates to Raphael his early impressions of Eve. The speaker has allowed Eve in her own words to confess her initial coolness towards Adam as a result of her own self-love: "There had I fixt/Mine eyes till now, and pin'd with vain desire" (IV.465–66). From Adam's point of view Eve's coolness seems the product of her virtue "That would be woo'd, and not unsought be won,/Not obvious, not obtrusive, but retir'd,/The more desirable" (VIII.503–5). Nor is Adam's praise merely rhetorical hyperbole. So impressed is Adam with Eve's "virtue" that he feels nature must have made some mistake: "For well I understand in the prime end/Of Nature her th' inferior" (VIII.540–41). As far as Adam is concerned, Eve rivals God in the perfection of her selfhood: "so absolute she seems/And in herself complete" (VIII.547–48). Ironically Raphael admonishes Adam that Eve only seems so perfect and advises Adam not to abandon confidence in his own selfhood: "Oft-times nothing profits more/Than self-esteem" (VIII.571–72). But despite the warning, Adam persists in diminishing his own worth and the importance of his own role.

The second scene occurs when Adam bickers with Eve about allowing her to depart for a few hours. Here he treads on delicate ground lest he offend her feelings. One can hear Eve's pouting in the repeated *f* sounds of "His fraud is then thy fear, which plain infers/Thy equal fear that my firm Faith and Love/Can by his fraud be shak'n or seduc't" (IX.285–87). Adam replies that he is only trying to shield her from the dishonor of being tempted, "For hee who tempts, though in vain, at least asperses/The tempted with dishonor foul" (IX.296–97). This reply ironically contradicts his earlier declaration when Eve awoke, disheartened after her bad dream, that "unapprov'd" temptation leaves "No spot or blame behind" (V.119). Next he proceeds to give Eve false confidence by portraying himself as needing her more than she needs him: "I from the influence of thy looks receive/Access in every Virtue" (IX.309–10). He further underrates his own *ethos* by citing the authority of Raphael (V.520 40) which in turn echoes the authority of God (III.96–128) that man can resist temptation by appealing to his reason, and he concludes by implying the opposite:

> Seek not temptation then, which to avoid
> Were better, and most likely if from mee
> Thou sever not: Trial will come unsought.
> [IX.364–66]

Suddenly, and for no apparent reason other than that he wants to make Eve happy, Adam reverses his opinion:

> But if thou think, trial unsought may find
> Us both securer than thus warn'd thou seem'st,
> Go; for thy stay, not free, absents thee more.
> [IX.370–72]

He wins the argument but loses the battle. His very permissiveness is an ironic exercise of his own authority, but by exercising it, he surrenders it. Having compromised his rightful role in fact as well as in rhetoric, Adam too enters into the motion of the fall.

To underscore Adam's surrender of authority, the speaker assigns him a soliloquy just before he joins Eve in crime. At the moment of crisis it is all the same to him whether he implements his selfhood as Eve's partner in virtue or in vice. The important thing is that he be Eve's partner. Thus, the speaker orchestrates a contrast between Adam's claim that a "Link of Nature" draws him (IX.914) and Eve's selfish intention to conceal her sin from Adam in order to enjoy the fruit for herself. Even more dramatically he contrasts Adam's rejection of another wife after Eve's death with Eve's jealousy lest he wed again. Eve, of course, will never know the anguish that Adam undergoes in his private soliloquy, and the speaker leaves open the possibility that by keeping his thoughts to himself, Adam is enacting his own kind of selfishness. In the speech that follows, the speaker also allows Adam to echo both God, in speculating that perhaps man shall not die, and Satan, in speculating that perhaps the earthly fruit will ennoble them. Ironically Adam approaches the center of the controversy between God and Satan when he gambles on man's public role as a pawn between them. For God, he speculates,

> Creation could repeat, yet would be loath
> Us to abolish, lest the Adversary
> Triumph and say; Fickle their State whom God
> Most Favors, who can please him long? Mee first
> He ruin'd, now Mankind; whom will he next?
>
> [IX.946-50]

Adam wins the gamble, though only by assigning himself a new role as pawn that all men after him will be destined to play.

In the very last lines of the poem, Adam and Eve "with wand'ring steps and slow" wend through Eden "thir solitary way" (XII.648-49). Their steps are "wand'ring" because the hero and heroine confront a variety of moral options hardly apparent earlier, and striped with the consequences of a sin that has flawed them, they can be expected to falter and err along the mazy roads ahead. At the same time their steps are "slow" because Adam and Eve pause to consider the possible consequences of each intended movement. The hero and heroine have learned reflection, have learned to acknowledge their own limits in accordance with their new and hard-won self-knowledge. Similarly, the audience that has followed the speaker's directions throughout this poem will have yielded to its own "wand'ring steps and slow," both in reading the poem and in encountering moral vicissitudes in life. As models, Adam and Eve take "thir solitary way" for the edification of this audience, "solitary" in the sense that they must find the path that suits them and them alone, accountable to no-one but God and the text the author supplies, and "solitary" perhaps also in the sense that they must accustom themselves (*solitus*, "accustomed") to the state or condition of life that their particular way implies.

However much Adam and Eve provide a moral model for the audience to follow through life, the speaker suggests another model, a rhetorical one, for the reader to follow through the poem. The speaker is very aware that if the charm of its verbal effects becomes an end in itself, the poem's surface texture may distract the audience.[19] He shows in Hell a wrong response to the songs of the fallen angels:

> Thir Song was partial, but the harmony
> (What could it be less when Spirits immortal sing?)
> Suspended Hell, and took with ravishment
> The thronging audience.
>
> [II.552–555]

Of course the fallen angels constitute a defective audience to begin with. The speaker's own audience may yet approach his poem with more objectivity. His problem is to find an apt model. He does censure one faulty response to an artistic performance when he mentions those in Jubal's tribe falling "in the amorous Net/Fast caught" (XI.586–87) by the music of harp and organ. Moreover, he shows how Adam's responses to the angelic discourses are partial, biased, or simply uncomprehending.[20] Thus Adam earns Michael's rebuke: "Judge not what is best/By pleasure, though to Nature seeming meet,/Created, as thou art, to nobler end" (XI.603–05). In all fairness to Adam, however, we must add that he tries hard to be a good audience; his chief problem is that as first man he has no model to follow; he has to learn the art of hermeneutics by himself.

The speaker, on the other hand, aided by Scripture and the teachings of his church, as well as prompted and inspired by heavenly and secular muses, can himself provide an apt model. Like Adam he is an audience to what the angels reveal, but he goes beyond Adam's function. He emerges as an exemplary audience not only of Raphael's and Michael's speeches, but also of the action that he has recorded throughout the poem, the product of divine inspiration and the muses' promptings. Scripture and the teachings of his church provide him a framework for ideas and insights that justify the ways of God to man. Secular poetry, ancient and modern, provides a structure for his own artistic development. In his protean transformation of innumerable literary conventions—from hymn (III.372–415), through landscape description (IV.205–87), to the pastoral mode (IV.288–355), the epithalamion (IV.750–53), lyric meditation (V.153–208), amorous compliment (VIII.540–59), and amorous complaint (X.867–908), to cite only a few—the speaker proves himself an apt audience of Homer and Hesiod, Aeschylus and Lucretius, Virgil and Ovid, Dante and Petrarch, Ariosto and Tasso, Sidney and Spenser, Shakespeare and Donne, and countless others.[21] The reader who would be in turn a truly "fit audience" for *Paradise Lost* must, like the speaker, dispose himself to the Bible and to classical literature, to Christian exegesis and to secular philosophy, and to modern literature in several tongues as much as to the reception of God's grace. The task is formidable, but the speaker shows the way by himself acting as exemplary archetypal audience—of history, of literature, of tradition, of philosophical thought and religious opinion, and of the actions and events performed by his own characters.

The speaker of *Paradise Lost* thus partakes of the epic speaker's conventional role in a challenging, new, and comprehensive way. His heritage comes to him from the Roman literary epic, and it incorporates every major Renaissance influence along the way. Virgil is primary. The speaker of the *Aeneid* accentuated the subjective dimension of his epic speaker's *ethos* not only by the frequency and prominence of his intrusions upon the poem's action in exclamations, apostrophes, and thematically weighted metaphors and similes, but also by the tone of melancholy and regret, privation and denial, all aimed at an audience willing to place its trust in the hands of an imperial architect, but still uncertain of exactly how to proceed or of precisely what to expect. In different ways Ovid and Lucan followed upon Virgil's example, Ovid by his speaker's witty, ironic intrusions throughout the *Metamorphoses* with his appeals to an intelligent, knowledgeable, skeptical, and cynical audience; and Lucan by his speaker's polemical and oratorical tone in *De Bello civili* directed towards an audience receptive to both moralism and sensationalism.

The Roman legacy to the Renaissance epic suggested a special *ethos* for the narrative speaker and a special *pathos* for his relationship with the audience. Thus, Ariosto, while indebted to Virgil's poem and aware of Lucan's, exploited Ovidian wit and irony by devising for his poem a narrative speaker who tries to appear wiser than he is but who often stumbles, forgets, contradicts himself, and yet manages to keep in focus a kaleidoscopic vision of the complexity of human affairs. The audience to which this voice appeals is a varied one whose members the speaker flatters, cajoles, enlightens, entertains, and uplifts all at the same time. D'Aubigné preferred the Lucanian model; without utterly forgetting the Virgilian and Ovidian examples, he appropriated much of the narrator's anger and energy in *De Bello civili* to his own speaker's voice in *Les Tragiques*. And the audience of this voice is composed of unregenerate sinners, deserving of his blame, and preelected saints, worthy of his praise, as well as of members of the vast middle class whom the speaker seeks actively to win over.

Milton, finally, took upon himself Virgil's rhetorical example, which his predecessors had either dismissed or been unable to imitate effectively. Though he avoids Virgil's melancholy questioning of an ideal that he seems to extol, he does respond to his subject with a range of complex attitudes, and the audience that he projects these attitudes upon is a "fit audience" schooled in the Bible and Judaeo-Christian tradition, classical literature, philosophy, history, and all of modern culture.

The epic, then, emerges as pre-eminently the genre presided over by an inspired speaker who is at once an audience of the action that he describes and a mediator between that action and his own audience. In his relationship with this audience the speaker formalizes and codifies the values of the culture that he shares with it, and he does so with a hortatory force, urging contemplation and acceptance of those values, and with a demonstrative force, representing those values in strong images and concrete dramatic action.

Common to all these audiences then is a sense of shared values that give shape and definition to a particular society. Members of that audience may be originators or exemplars of those values (the speaker's patrons and his actual historical models), opponents or champions of them (enemies and allies of the speaker's cause), or detached observers who meditate and contemplate their meaning (the fit audience, including the speaker himself as primal audience of the muses' inspiration). Besides these norms governing the relationships between the speaker and his audience, there are, of course, other norms associated with the epic genre, norms governing the use of conventional themes and motifs as well as of elocutionary devices concerning diction, tropes, schemes, rhythm, and other purely verbal arrangements. Such norms tend to be more variable and idiosyncratic than the ones I have described, and because they can often be found operating in genres other than epic, they are not definitive of any one genre. The strategies characterizing the epic speaker and his relationship with the audience that I have been describing, however, do belong exclusively to the epic genre as essential rhetorical attributes. An examination of these rhetorical strategies leads to a fuller definition of the norms of epic than any more limited consideration of its narrative structure or elocutionary surface alone can provide.

Conclusion

Since literary genre radically affects how author and reader come to terms with the work, a clear understanding of it would seem a prerequisite for any further understanding of meaning and intention, creation and historical evolution in literature. To understand a literary genre and its norms, however, we must understand literary modality and style and their norms. These norms derive from variables that intrinsically complement and modify the system of any given genre. The rhetorical strategies of a mode give way to those of a style, and the rhetorical strategies of both modes and styles in turn give way to those of the genres that accommodate them. If mode is a subdivision of genre which admits to various styles, then the first question to ask when defining any genre is, What modes participate in it, and, within those modes, what styles?

The question of modality proves difficult to explore, however, partly because modality involves many nonaesthetic materials associated with the literary work—theme, motif, world-view, manner, and medium of presentation—and partly because current critical theory offers no universally acceptable critical vocabulary for norms that underlie various modes. I have proposed an approach to modal norms through voice and address. One can partly characterize a mode through the *ethos* that informs both the speaker's and the character's presentation of themselves. One can also partly characterize it through the *pathos* that establishes the speaker's relationship to the author, to the work, and to the audience, as well as the audience's relationship to each of the other agents both as fictive audience and as actual reader. The rhetorical interaction of *ethos* and *pathos* determines the mode.

Such a characterization also illuminates an essential link between the concept of mode and the concept of style, for style itself depends upon the author's manipulations of voice and address. Style, as we have seen, is not just a matter of apt diction, figures of speech, and elocutionary devices; it involves the speaker's concept of himself and the roles that he is playing, as well as his control over the distance between himself and the audience. These aspects of style are implicit in the classical rhetorical concepts of *ethos* and *pathos*, though usually they are not enunciated in the medieval, Renaissance, Baroque, and Neo-classical taxonomies of tropes and figures pertaining to the strategy of *logos*. An emphasis on these strategies in the description of style clarifies the idea of coherence, which modern critics often designate as the distinguishing feature of any given style. Stylistic coherence involves not only verbal texture but also the figure of the speaker and his concept of an audience in their interaction with both each other and their verbal strategies.

The notion of different rhetorical norms cohering in systems of modality and style suggests a larger paradigm for ways in which different rhetorical norms also cohere in a system of genre. A single genre embraces many possible modes and styles and is a composite not only of intrinsic forms and repeated conventions but also of all the modes and styles that participate in the genre. By taking account of the rhetorical qualities informing its various modes and styles, the definition of a genre can reach a level that passes beyond superficial resemblances in structure or technique.

Because systems of mode, style, and genre relate to each other in various ways and can be called intercomplementary, the quality of their relationships affects the pattern of literary history. That pattern extends radically beyond the trajectories of a simple, linear evolution and registers its growth on different levels where adjacent aspects of mode, style, and genre are apt to develop in various directions at unequal rates of speed. It would be naïve to assume that literary history could unfold in any simpler way. On the other hand, an approach to literary history through strategies that I have suggested shows how smaller systems (such as the rhetorical ones) complement each other and generate still larger systems (such as mode, style, and genre). Hence the coherence of these larger systems is a function of the coherence among rhetorical norms animating individual works.

This rhetoric that finally allows us to trace such a literary history frees itself from the currently fashionable linguistic model. It takes into account norms of voice and address that we measure not by transformation of or deviation from an a priori code but by concrete interaction with each other. These norms we can in turn use to describe those of still larger systems like genre, style, and mode. If this conclusion is too broad to stand without further proof (and I would be the first to urge further proof from examples other than those which I have analyzed), I offer it in the spirit of an argument aimed against certain deconstructive tendencies to flatten out literature and literary history to the play of defined verbal antinomies. Perhaps a more temperate conclusion would be to focus on strategies of voice and address as important elements in the concept of rhetoric. Too long subordinated to merely verbal devices in literary analysis, these strategies deserve closer examination on their own as well as in relation to each other. Such an examination will show, after all, how the art of rhetoric transcends the mere embodiment of apt diction, figures of speech, and elocutionary devices, and how it implicates the psychology of the speaker in his roles and in his selfhood as well as the problematic social relationship of the speaker to his audience and of the reader to the author—how, in short, the art of rhetoric nourishes and sustains the nature of the literary creation, which in turn subsumes all the norms of rhetoric into a higher aesthetic synthesis.

Notes

INTRODUCTION: RHETORICAL CRITICISM
AND LITERARY THEORY

1 See E.D. Hirsch, *Validity in Interpretation* (New Haven: Yale University Press, 1967) for a consideration of these approaches.

2 *Wahrheit und Methode* (Tübingen: JCB Mohr, 1960), pp. 154, 290; I quote from the English translation, *Truth and Method*, ed. Garrett Barden and John Cumming (New York: Seabury Press, 1975), pp. 143 and 273. For commentary, see Richard Palmer, *Hermeneutics* (Evanston, Ill.: Northwestern University Press, 1969).

3 The most systematic modern survey of classical rhetorical theory is Heinrich Lausberg's valuable *Handbuch der literarischen Rhetorik*, 2 vols. (Munich: Max Hueber, 1960). For a treatment of the state of the art in various historical periods, see George Kennedy, *The Art of Persuasion in Greece* (Princeton: Princeton University Press, 1963) and *The Art of Rhetoric in the Roman World* (Princeton: Princeton University Press, 1972); both have supplanted Charles Sears Baldwin, *Ancient Rhetoric and Poetic* (New York: Macmillan, 1924), but see the latter's *Medieval Rhetoric and Poetic* (New York: Macmillan, 1928) and *Renaissance Literary Theory and Practice* (New York: Columbia University Press, 1939); for commentary on subsequent theory, see Richard McKeon, "Rhetoric in the Middle Ages," *Speculum* 17 (1942): 1-32; James J. Murphy, *Rhetoric in the Middle Ages* (Berkeley: University of California Press, 1974); various essays by Morris Croll in *Style, Rhetoric, Rhythm*, ed. J. Max Patrick (Princeton: Princeton University Press, 1966); Sister Miriam Joseph Rauh, *Shakespeare's Use of the Arts of Language* (New York: Columbia University Press, 1947); Rosemond Tuve, *Elizabethan and Metaphysical Imagery* (Chicago: University of Chicago Press, 1947); and Thomas O. Sloan and Raymond B. Waddington, eds., *The Rhetoric of Renaissance Poetry* (Berkeley: University of California Press, 1974).

4 For such interpretations, see Roman Jakobson, "Linguistics and Poetics," first printed in *Style in Language*, ed. Thomas Sebeok (Boston: MIT Press, 1960), pp. 350-77; and Julia Kristeva, *Semiotike* (Paris: Seuil, 1969), pp. 75-77.

5 For an acute understanding of the structure of a "double and interlocking dialectic" of speaker and hearer in the rhetorical act, see Walter Ong, S.J., *The Barbarian Within* (New York: Macmillan, 1962), pp.

51 ff., and Father Ong's other writings on the subject in *In the Human Grain* (New York: Macmillan, 1967); *The Presence of the Word* (New Haven: Yale University Press, 1967), especially pp. 214 ff.; *Rhetoric, Romance, and Technology* (Ithaca: Cornell University Press, 1971), and *Interfaces of the Word* (Ithaca: Cornell University Press, 1977). For particular reference to Renaissance Humanism, see Nancy Struever's treatment of rhetoric as "a permanent subjunctive mental mode" in *The Language of History in the Renaissance* (Princeton: Princeton University Press, 1970), p. 155 and passim. For general reference to Renaissance literature, especially in England, see Richard A. Lanham, *The Motives of Eloquence* (New Haven: Yale University Press, 1976).

6 For a link between dramatized voice and role playing, see Father Ong, *The Barbarian Within*, pp. 54 ff. Hugh Richmond has distinguished between "Personal Identity and Literary Personae," *PMLA* 90 (1975): 209–221. Much of modern literary theory concerning "character" applies to the concept of the speaker's persona; see Boris Tomashevsky, *Thematics*, in *Russian Formalist Criticism*, tr. Lee Lemon and Marion Reis (Lincoln: University of Nebraska Press, 1965), especially pp. 87–92; A.J. Greimas, *Sémantique structurale* (Paris: Larousse, 1966), pp. 222–56; Tzvetan Todorov, *Littérature et signification* (Paris: Larousse, 1967); Fernando Ferrara, "Theory and Model for the Structural Analysis of Fiction," *New Literary History* 5 (1974): 245–68; Hélène Cixous, "The Character of 'Character,'" *New Literary History* 5 (1974): 383–402; but for trenchant criticism of the approach represented by the foregoing, see Seymour Chatman, "On the Formalist-Structuralist Theory of Character," *Journal of Literary Semantics* 1 (1972): 57–79.

7 I owe the term "selfhood" to Thomas M. Greene, "The Flexibility of the Self in Renaissance Literature," in *The Disciplines of Criticism*, ed. Peter Demetz et al. (New Haven: Yale University Press, 1968), pp. 241–64. Richard Lanham makes an important distinction between the serious self and the rhetorical self in *Motives of Eloquence*, pp. 66 ff. and passim.

8 In his important discussion of "the radical of presentation" Northrop Frye complains that "criticism ... has no word for the individual member of an author's audience," *Anatomy of Criticism* (Princeton: Princeton University Press, 1957), p. 247. For the fictionality of the audience see Walter Ong, S.J., "The Writer's Audience is Always a Fiction," *PMLA* 90 (1975): 9–21. For an author's constraints upon his audience, see P.F. Strawson, "Intention and Convention in Speech Acts," *Logico-Linguistic Papers* (London: Methuen, 1971), pp. 149–69.

9 "The Fictive Reader and Literary Self-Reflexiveness," in *The Disciplines of Criticism*, pp. 173–91. Instead of the term "reader" I use the more general term "audience."

10 See Wolfgang Iser's phenomenological approach to the reading pro-
    cess in *Die Appellstruktur der Texte* (Konstanz: Universitätsverlag,
    1970) and *The Implied Reader* (Baltimore: Johns Hopkins Univer-
    sity Press, 1974); cf. Stanley Fish, *Self-Consuming Artifacts* (Ber-
    keley: University of California Press, 1972), especially pp. 383-427.
    For a corrective to absolutizing one's own understanding of the text,
    see Roman Ingarden's discussion of indeterminacy and concretiza-
    tion in *The Literary Work of Art*, trans. George Grabowicz (Evan-
    ston, Ill.: Northwestern University Press, 1973), pp. 331-55. See
    also William K. Wimsatt's defense of the "ideal response" of the
    reader in *A Short History of Literary Criticism* (New York: Random
    House, 1957), pp. 546-47, and Geoffrey Hartman's reflection on
    "the extinction . . . of the personal names of *both* author and reader"
    in *The Fate of Reading* (Chicago: University of Chicago Press, 1975),
    p. 255. A vigorous defense of the subjective character of critical inter-
    pretation is David Bleich, *Subjective Criticism* (Baltimore: Johns
    Hopkins University Press, 1978).
11 For the problem of literary evaluation, see René Wellek and Austin
    Warren, *Theory of Literature*, 3rd ed. (New York: Harcourt Brace,
    1962), pp. 238 ff. With reference to evaluation of literary rhetoric,
    see Wayne Booth, *The Rhetoric of Fiction* (Chicago: University of
    Chicago Press, 1961), and for the application of rhetorical genres to
    literary form, A. Kibedi Varga, *Rhétorique et littérature* (Paris:
    Didier, 1970).
12 See Erich Auerbach, *Literary Language and Its Public,* tr. Ralph Man-
    heim (New York: Pantheon, 1965), especially 297-313; and Nancy
    Struever, *Language of History*, pp. 57-58.
13 Edition Guillaume Budé, ed. Alfred Croiset and Louis Bodin (Paris:
    Les Belles Lettres, 1923), with excellent introduction and notes. For
    commentary on the rhetoric of the Sophists, see Mario Untersteiner,
    The Sophists, tr. Kathleen Freeman (New York: Philosophical Library,
    1954), especially pp. 194-205; George Kennedy, *Art of Persuasion in
    Greece*, pp. 74-79, and Nancy Struever, pp. 10-16.
14 Edition Guillaume Budé, ed. Léon Robin (Paris: Les Belles Lettres,
    1933), with excellent introduction and notes. Translation by R.
    Hackforth in *Collected Dialogues*, ed. Edith Hamilton and Hunting-
    ton Cairns, (New York: Pantheon, 1961). See the commentary in
    George Kennedy, pp. 74-79; W.K. Wimsatt, *Short History*, pp. 57-66,
    and Werner Jaeger, *Paideia*, tr. Gilbert Highet, 3 vols. (New York: Ox-
    ford, 1944), vol. 3, pp. 182-196.
15 Aristotle, *The "Art" of Rhetoric*, ed. John Henry Freese, Loeb Classi-
    cal Library (London: Heineman, 1926); I quote the translation of
    Lane Cooper (Englewood Cliffs, N.J.: Prentice-Hall, 1960). For bibli-
    ography, see Keith Erickson, *Aristotle's Rhetoric: Five Centuries of*

Philological Research (Metuchen, N.J.: Scarecrow Press, 1975), and for commentary see Edward M. Cope, *The Rhetoric of Aristotle*, 3 vols. (Cambridge: Cambridge University Press, 1877); Frederich Solmsen, "Aristotle and Cicero on the Orator's Playing Upon Feelings," *Classical Philology* 33 (1938): 390-404; Keith Erickson, *Aristotle: The Classical Heritage of Rhetoric* (Metuchen, N.J.: Scarecrow Press, 1974); and George Kennedy, pp. 82-114.

16 See Heinrich Lausberg, *Handbuch*, pp. 141-45, 552-652.

17 For the history of Aristotle's reception in the Renaissance, see John Edwin Sandys, *A History of Classical Scholarship*, 3 vols. (Cambridge: Cambridge University Press, 1908), vol. 2.

18 E.W. Sutton and H. Rackham, Loeb Classical Library, 2 volumes (London: Heinemann, 1942). For commentary with application to Renaissance theories of rhetoric, see Jerold E. Seigel, *Rhetoric and Philosophy in Renaissance Humanism* (Princeton: Princeton University Press, 1968), pp. 6-17.

19 H.E. Butler, Loeb Classical Library, 4 volumes (London: Heinemann, 1920-22). For commentary, see George Kennedy, *Quintilian* (New York: Twayne, 1969).

20 See Pierre de Nolhac, *Pétrarque et l'humanisme* (Paris: Champion, 1907), pp. 116-19, and Sandys, *Classical Scholarship*, vol. 2, pp. 27, 31, 46, 63, 81, 104. In "Rhetoric of the Middle Ages," Richard McKeon claims the existence as well of two thirteenth-century translations of Aristotle (p. 29).

21 See Francesco Tateo, *'Rhetorica' e 'Poetica' fra Medioevo e Rinascimento* (Bari: Adria, 1960).

22 *Utinensis in librum Aristotelis de arte poeticae explicationes* (Florence, 1548), p. 245.

23 (Lyon, 1561), reprint ed. August Buck (Stuttgart: Friedrich Frommann, 1964), p. 113. Also see below, p. 209, note 5. For a philosophical analysis of the role of *energeia* in Aristotelian rhetoric and metaphysics, see Jacques Derrida, "La Mythologie blanche," *Poétique* 5 (1971): 1-52, especially p. 25; translation in *New Literary History* 6 (1974): 5-74, especially p. 39.

24 (Venice: Valvassori, 1564), ed. Bernhard Fabian (Munich: Fink, 1971), pp. 426, 427.

25 Cesare Vasoli, *La Dialettica e la retorica dell'umanesimo* (Milan: Feltrinelli, 1968), pp. 30-33.

26 See Edmond Faral, *Les Arts poétiques du XIIe et du XIIIe siècles* (Paris: Champion, 1923); and Joseph Miller et al., eds., *Readings in Medieval Rhetoric* (Bloomington: Indiana University Press, 1973), pp. 222-27.

27 "Chiose intorno al Gorgia di Platone" in *Opere* (Bern: 1727), reprint ed. Bernhard Fabian (Munich: Fink, 1969), pp. 288-289.

28 *La Poetica*, reprint ed. Bernard Fabian (Munich: Fink, 1968), pp. 25–26.

29 *Ramus: Method and the Decay of Dialogue* (Cambridge, Mass.: Harvard University Press, 1958), pp. 270–92.

30 *Il Cannocchiale aristotelico*, ed. August Buck (Berlin: Gehlen, 1968), pp. 207, 210–16.

31 *Counter-statement* (New York: Harcourt-Brace, 1931), p. 265.

32 Compare the Russian Formalist equation of poetry with *"attenuated, tortuous* speech," according to Viktor Shklovsky, *Art as Technique,* in Lee Lemon, ed., *Russian Formalist Criticism,* p. 23. But see W. Wolfgang Holdheim on "the inability of the theory of estrangement to account for a literature in which tradition is a positive creative force" in "The Concept of Poetic Estrangement," *Comparative Literature Studies* 11 (1974): 320–25. For general criticism, see Ewa Thompson, *Russian Formalism and Anglo-American New Criticism* (The Hague: Mouton, 1971); and Frederic Jameson, *The Prisonhouse of Language* (Princeton: Princeton University Press, 1972).

33 Ferdinand de Saussure, *Cours de linguistique générale, publié par Charles Bally et Albert Sechehaye,* ed. Tullio de Mauro (Paris: Payot, 1972), pp. 25–30, 38–39; I quote from the translation by Wade Baskin (New York: McGraw-Hill, 1966), pp. 9–13, 20.

34 *Communications* 4 (1964): 2; I quote from the translation by Annette Lavers and Colin Smith, *Elements of Semiologie* (Boston: Beacon Press, 1970), pp. 10–11.

35 See Jacques Derrida, *De la Grammatologie* (Paris: Les Editions de Minuit, 1967), p. 75; translation by Gayatri Spivak (Baltimore: The Johns Hopkins University Press, 1976), p. 51.

36 In *Sémantique structurale* (Paris: Larousse, 1966), A.J. Greimas maintains that all rhetorical use of language, whether on the semantic level of words and phrases or on the combinatory level of narrative and mythic structure, is a function of the linguistic structure; he classifies even larger structural components in *Du sens* (Paris: Seuil, 1970). Tzvetan Todorov, however, characterizes classical rhetoric as a theory which still has relevance in mediating between linguistics and the analysis of literature (*Littérature et signification,* p. 91). In *Poétique de la Prose* (Paris: Seuil, 1971), where he applies rhetorical theory to the analysis of prose fiction, Todorov relies more strongly on linguistic categories. For Jean Cohen, in *Structure du langage poétique* (Paris: Flammarion, 1966), p. 50, rhetoric is less a function of linguistic structures than a deviation from those structures. In response to Cohen, Gerard Genette offers a theory of rhetoric in which the figure functions as a detour through language and calls attention to language by uniting denotation and connotation as an "écart entre le signe et le sens" (*Figures* [Paris: Seuil, 1966], p. 209);

whence the best approach to a text is through a rhetoric structured on the principles of modern linguistics "qui est sans doute la seule discipline scientifique ayant actuellement son mot à dire sur la littérature *comme telle*" (*Figures II* [Paris: Seuil, 1969], p. 16). There is still no proof, however, that linguistics is the only science that can speak of literature *comme telle*, or that rhetoric and poetics can approach the level of scientific models. For a survey of other manifestations of the linguistic hegemony in the semiotic approach, see Lowry Nelson, Jr., "Signs of the Times," *Yale Review* (Winter 1975): 296-320.

37 Jakobson, "Linguistics and Poetics," p. 371. Jakobson stresses the relationship between the speaker and the hearer in his essay on "Linguistics and Communication Theory," *Selected Writings II* (The Hague: Mouton, 1971), pp. 570-79. The most elegant elaboration of this view is by Juri Lotman, *La structure du texte artistique*, tr. Anne Fournier et al. (Paris, Gallimard, 1973), especially p. 99.

38 The members of Groupe μ attempt to construct a general rhetoric along the lines that Jakobson used to define the poetic function of language, "compte tenu de ce que l'effet psycho-esthétique n'est pas fonction de purs mécanismes linguistiques," in *Rhétorique générale*, Jacques Dubois et al. (Paris: Larousse, 1970), p. 27. Inexplicably, however, the authors try to accommodate the ancient theory of *ethos* to a modern terminology by confusing the concept of *ethos* with that of *pathos*, even openly admitting to the confusion when they claim that *ethos* is "assimilable à ce qu'Aristote nomme le $\pi\alpha\theta o\varsigma$ dans sa *Poetique*" (p. 147). In "Semiology and Rhetoric," *Diacritics* 3, iii (Fall 1973): 27-33, Paul de Man rightly assails "the use of grammatical (especially syntactical) structures conjointly with rhetorical structures with no apparent awareness of a possible discrepancy" (p. 28).

39 Thus, for Michael Riffaterre the "average reader" ("l'archilecteur") is in fact "the consciously selected target of the author" (Criteria for Style Analysis," *Word* 15 [1959]: 162, now in *Essais de stylistique structurale*, tr. Daniel Delas (Paris: Flammarion, 1971).

40 According to Julia Kristeva, the text exerts little control over the way in which the audience reads it "intertextually." It functions as a kind of "paragramme" that moves beyond logical norms, as she describes it in *Semiotike*, pp. 270-77. Here Kristeva evokes the reinterpretation of Freudian psychology by Jacques Lacan, for whom "la dominance que nous affirmons du significant sur le sujet" reflects the all important relationship of displacement and inversion. See Lacan, *Ecrits* I (Paris: Seuil, 1966), "Le séminaire sur 'La Lettre volée'," p. 75; "Fonction et champ de la parole et du langage en psychanalyse," pp. 123, 181; and "La chose freudienne," p. 242.

41 See Hirsch, *Validity in Interpretation*; and Michael McCanles, *Dialectical Criticism and Renaissance Literature* (Berkeley: University of California Press, 1975), pp. 228–39.

42 *Literaturgeschichte als Provokation* (Frankfurt: Suhrkamp. 1970), p. 189. I quote from the translation by Elizabeth Benzinger in *New Literary History* 2 (1970): 11 and 30. Rainer Warning has assembled diverse applications in his anthology on *Rezeptionsästhetik* (Munich: Fink, 1975). For criticism from an explicitly sociological perspective that deepens this approach to literary history, see Peter Hohendahl's anthology on *Sozialgeschichte und Wirkungsästhetik* (Frankfurt-am-Main: Athenäum, 1974), whose preface is translated as "Introduction to Reception Aesthetics," *New German Critique* 10 (1977): 29–63; and see his "Prolegomena to a History of Literary Criticism," *New German Critique* 11 (1977): 151–63.

43 See W. Wolfgang Holdheim, "Das Ästhetische und die Zeitlichkeit," *Arcadia* 6 (1971): 237–44, and "The Aesthetic-Historical Paradox," *Comparative Literature Studies* 10 (1973): 1–8, two articles to which I am greatly indebted.

44 They even figure in works of German Romanticism, as Leonard Forster has ingeniously shown in *The Icy Fire* (Cambridge: Cambridge University Press, 1969), without any of the anxiety of influence that Harold Bloom posits in his book of that title (New York: Oxford Press, 1972).

45 For similar reasons neither paradigmatic models, articulated for example by Thomas S. Kuhn in *The Structure of Scientific Revolutions* (Chicago: The University of Chicago Press, 1962), nor analytical models, articulated for example by Arthur Danto in his *Analytical Philosophy of History* (Cambridge: Cambridge University Press, 1965), pp. 201–32, will explain literary history. Hayden White designates the most adequate mode of explanation as "contextualist" rather than "formist," "organicist," or "mechanistic" in his *Metahistory* (Baltimore: The Johns Hopkins University Press, 1973), pp. 1–41. For a defense of exhaustive contextual analysis, see Jack H. Hexter, *Doing History* (Bloomington: Indiana University Press, 1971).

46 For the terms and concepts of historical periodization in literary scholarship and for the need to study them in their own historical development, see the essential articles on Baroque, Neoclassicism, Romanticism, Realism, and Symbolism by René Wellek, collected in *Concepts of Criticism* (New Haven: Yale University Press, 1963) and *Discriminations* (New Haven: Yale University Press, 1970). See also Professor Wellek's views on literary historiography in "Reflections on My *History of Modern Criticism*," *PTL: A Journal for Descriptive Poetics and Theory of Literature* 3 (1977): 417–27.

CHAPTER 1

1 A model for the kind of study that I am suggesting, and a book to which I am indebted on many levels, is Lowry Nelson, Jr., *Baroque Lyric Poetry* (New Haven: Yale University Press, 1962), where the concepts of mode, style, genre, and literary history are fundamental to my own considerations.

2 Propertius, *Poems*, ed. H.E. Butler, Loeb Classical Library (London: Heineman, 1912); see especially I: 7, 11, 15; II: 1, 3, 33, 34; III:11, 17, 19, 21; IV: 3.

3 Ovid, *Heroides and Amores*, ed. Grant Showerman, Loeb Classical Library (London: Heineman, 1914); see especially *Amores* I: 6, 7, 12, 15; II: 5, 10, 16; III: 3, 11.

4 The terminology for the *canzone* which Antonio employs for the sonnet's octave (*pedes*) and sestet (*voltae*) in *Delle rime volgari, trattato di Antonio da Tempo* (1332), ed. Giusto Grion (Bologna: Gaetano Romagnoli, 1869), pp. 73-116, is repeated by Giovanni Giorgio Trissino, *La Poetica* (Venice, 1529), reprint ed. August Buck (Munich: Fink, 1969), IV, xxxvii-xxxx. Ernest Hatch Wilkins studies the relationship of the sonnet to the *canzone* in *The Invention of the Sonnet and Other Studies* (Rome: Edizioni di Storia e Letteratura, 1959). Later Renaissance theorists would associate the sonnet with the classical epigram on the basis of length, subject matter, and style. See Gary Brown, "The Sonnet as Epigram," *Vierteljahrsschrift für romanische Sprachen und Literaturen* 87 (1975): 226-38.

5 Quotation from *Sonetti della Scuola Siciliana*, ed. Edoardo Sanguineti (Turin: Einaudi, 1965).

6 *Le Opere di Dante*, ed. Michele Barbi et al. (Florence: Società Dantesca, 1960).

Petrarch's *Canzoniere*

1 All quotations from Petrarch are from Petrarca, *Rime*, ed. Ferdinando Neri et al., La letteratura italiana (Milan: Riccardo Ricciardi, 1951); See Marga Cottino-Jones's essay on the aesthetics of transformation in "The Myth of Apollo and Daphne in Petrarch's *Canzoniere*" in *Francis Petrarch, Six Centuries Later*, ed. Aldo Scaglione (Chapel Hill: Department of Romance Languages at the University of North Carolina, 1975), pp. 152-76.

2 There are several good articles on the essential formal features of the later Petrarchan sonnet in volume 7 of *Studi Petrarcheschi* (1961) by Fernando Figurelli, "L'architettura del sonetto," 179-86; Giulio Herczeg, "Struttura del antitesi," 195-208; and Emilio Bigi, "La rima del Petrarca," 135-45. Compare the structuralist study of these

features by Giuseppe Sansone, "Assaggio di simmetrie petrarchesche," *Lingua e Stile* 6 (1971): 223-40. See also the attempt to demonstrate the organization of the sonnet form "in a multitude of different coexistent and conflicting patterns—formal, logical, ideological, syntactic, rhythmic, and phonetic" by Stephen Booth, *An Essay on Shakespeare's Sonnets* (New Haven: Yale University Press, 1969), p. ix. Earlier attempts in the same direction include Mario Fubini, *Studi sulla Letteratura del Rinascimento* (Florence: Sansoni, 1948), 1-9; and Norman Stageberg, "Aesthetics of the Petrarchan Sonnet," *Journal of Aesthetics and Art Criticism* 7 (1948): 132-37. Good general discussion is in Thomas Bergin, *Petrarch* (New York: Twayne, 1970).

3 Adelia Noferi in "Da un commento al *Canzoniere* del Petrarca," *Lettere Italiane* 26 (1974): 165-79, calls attention to Castelvetro's note on ambiguity in the use of *voi*; and see Bruce Merry, "Il primo sonetto del Petrarca come modello di lettura," *Paragone* 296 (1974): 73-79.

4 See E.H. Wilkins, *Invention of the Sonnet*, pp. 26-32; Aldo Bernardo studies the evolution of Petrarch's theory of art in "Petrarch and the Art of Literature," in Julius Molinaro, ed., *Petrarch to Pirandello* (Toronto: University of Toronto Press, 1973), 19-43. Christopher Kleinhinz relates Petrarch to his predecessors in "Petrarch and the Art of the Sonnet" in *Petrarch, Six Centuries Later*, pp. 177-91.

5 For the above commentators I cite the following editions throughout: *Petrarcha con doi commenti . . . El primo del ingeniosissimo Miser Francesco Philelpho. L altro del sapientissimo Antonio da Tempo* (Venice: Gregorium de gregoriis, 1508); *Il Petrarca con l'espositione d'Alessandro Vellutello* (Venice: Al segno di Erasmo, 1541); *Il Petrarcha col commento di M. Sebastiano Fausto da Longiano* (Venice: Francesco di Alesandro Bindoni, 1532); *Il Petrarcha colla spositione di Misser Giovanni Andrea Gesualdo* (Venice: Nicolini da Sabio, 1533); *Sonetti, Canzoni, e Triomphi di M. Francesco Petrarca, con la Spositione di Bernardino Daniello da Lucca* (Venice: Nicolini da Sabio, 1549); *Il Petrarca . . . Aggiuntevi breviss. dichiarationi del Sansovino* (Venice: Pietro Ravano, 1546); *Sonetti, Canzoni, et Triomphi di M. Francesco Petrarca con breve dichiaratione e annotatione di Antonio Bruciolo* (Venice: Alessandro Brucioli, 1548); *Il Petraraca* [sic] *con le osservationi di M. Frrncesco* [sic] *Alunno da Ferrara* (Venice: Pauolo Gherardo, 1550); *Il Petrarca, nuovamente corretto da Girolamo Ruscelli* (Venice: Plinio Pietrassanta, 1554); and *Le Rime . . . sposte per Lodovico Castelvetro* (Basel: Pietro de Sedabonis, 1582). For commentary on the commentators, see Luigi Baldacci, *Il Petrarchismo italiano nel cinquecento*

(Milan: Riccardo Ricciardi, 1957), pp. 45–74; Bortolo Tommaso Sozzi, *Petrarca* (Palermo: Palumbo, 1963), p. 154; and Bernard Weinberg, who points out that Antonio was probably not the same Antonio as the author of the fourteenth-century treatise cited above ("The *Spositione* of Petrarch in the Early Cinquecento," *Romance Philology* 13 [1960]: 374–86).

6 Some modern critics feel that the essence of the modality resides in wordplay; see Arnaud Tripet, *Pétrarque ou la connaissance de soi* (Geneva: Droz, 1967), p. 178, and compare Dominque Diani, "Petrarque: *Canzoniere* 132," *Revue des Études Italiennes* 18 (1972): 111–67, whose structuralist analysis emphasizes verbal embroidery. Tripet elaborates upon Petrarch's dialogue with himself in "Pétrarque et le langage" in *Petrarch, Six Centuries Later*, pp. 223–35. Earlier statements by Adelia Noferi, *L'esperienza poetica del Petrarca* (Florence: Le Monnier, 1962), pp. 2, 115, and her recent article, "Scrittura del desiderio e desiderio della scrittura," *Paragone* 296 (1974): 3–23, are illuminating. Compare the extreme position of Guido Almanzi, "Petrarca o della insignificanza," *Paragone* 296 (1974): 68–73, and the article of John Freccero, "The Fig Tree and the Laurel," *Diacritics* 5, i (1975): 34–40, which claims that Petrarch's is "a poetry whose real subject matter is its own act and whose creation is its own author" (p. 35). For a labored "deconstructive" reading that tries to relate Petrarch's verbal practice to his idea of history, see Marguerite Waller, "Historical Theory and Poetic Practice," *Criticism* 18 (1976), 273–94.

7 Damaso Alonso stresses this clash in "La poesia del Petrarca," *Lettere Italiane* 11 (1959): 277–319; compare Silvio Ramat, "Petrarca e la scrittura integrale," *Forum Italicum* 8 (1974): 513–22; Anthony J. Earl, "The Ambiguities of Petrarch's *Rime*," *Modern Languages* 55 (1974): 161–68; and François Rigolot, "The Nature and Function of Paronomasia in the *Canzoniere*," *Italian Quarterly* 69 (1974): 29–36.

8 For the importance of rhythm and prosodic analysis in characterizing the Petrarchan mode, see Mario Fubini, *Metrica e poesia* (Milan: Feltrinelli, 1962), pp. 238–327, and a structuralist approach to the same problems indicated in Stefano Agosti, "I Messagi formali della poesia," *Strumenti critici* 14 (1971): 1–38. Maria Picchio Simonelli offers an inventory of phonic effects in "Strutture foniche nei Rerum vulgarium fragmenta" in *Petrarch, Six Centuries Later*, pp. 66–104.

9 See Thomas Roche, "The Calendrical Structure of Petrarch's *Canzoniere*," *Studies in Philology* 71 (1974): 152–72, and also Adolfo Jenni, "Un sistema del Petrarca nell'ordinamento del *Canzoniere*," *Studi in onore di Alberto Chiari* 2 vols. (Brescia: Paideia, 1973), pp. 721–37, and Mario Santagata, "Connessioni intertestuali nel *Canzoniere*," *Strumenti Critici* 26 (1978): 80–112.

10 Aldo Bernardo studies Laura's role as audience in "Dramatic Dialogue and Monologue in Petrarch's Works," *Symposium* 7 (1953): 92–119; for Umberto Bosco, Laura is the guarantor of Petrarch's posterity through fame (*Petrarca* [Bari: Laterza, 1946], p. 26); see also Georges Güntert. "Modi di sintassi reciproca e speculare in Petrarca," *Giornale Storico della Letteratura Italiana* 151 (1974): 1–20.

11 As though to facilitate such involvement, Renaissance commentators on the poem spent a good deal of time explaining the geography of the river and the region, thus supplying details of the role the reader is supposed to play.

12 Filelfo saw this uncertainty governing even the inherent ambiguity of "anzi laudate lui," in which he interprets *lui* to refer not to God but to death itself; "Più di questo biasmino a la morte anzi nel vero la laudano" (p. 75). But *lui* more probably refers to the divine controller of life and death itself.

13 See Ezio Raimondi, *Metafora e storia* (Turin: Einaudi, 1970), p. 165.

14 For the moral quality of this strategy, see Robert Durling, "Petrarch's 'Giovene Donna,'," *MLN* 86 (1971): 1–20; Kenelm Foster, "Beatrice or Medusa," *Italian Studies Presented to E. R. Vincent*, ed. C.P. Brand (Cambridge: W. Heffer, 1962), pp. 41–56; Mariann Regan, "Petrarch's Courtly and Christian Vocabularies," *Romance Notes* 15 (1974): 527–31; and Riccardo Quinones, *The Renaissance Discovery of Time* (Cambridge, Mass.: Harvard University Press, 1972), p. 138.

15 Thomas M. Greene in "Petrarch and the Humanist Hermeneutic," *Italian Literature, Roots and Branches*, ed. Kenneth Atchity (New Haven: Yale University Press, 1976), pp. 201–24, offers a superb reading of the "archaeology" and "sub-text" of this poem in comparison with its Virgilian model; for an older treatment of the problem of imitation, see Hans Gmelin, who shows convincingly how Petrarch heard in Latin poetry the musicality of the troubadours in "Das Prinzip der Imitatio," *Romanische Forschungen* 46 (1932): 98–99, 173.

Ronsard's *Les Amours*

1 Quotations from Ronsard, *Oeuvres complètes*, ed. Paul Laumonier, completed by I. Silver and R. Lebègue, 20 volumes; Société des textes français modernes (Paris: Droz and Didier, 1914–75); translations are mine. Ronsard has continued to meet with similar criticism in modern times, despite the impressive titles surveyed in Isidore Silver, "Ronsard Comparatist Studies," *Comparative Literature* 6 (1954): 148–73; "Ronsard Studies (1936–1950), *Bibliothèque d'Humanisme et Renaissance* 12 (1950): 332–64; and "Ronsard Studies (1951–55)," *BHR* 22 (1960): 214–68; and by Bodo Richter, "Ronsard Studies (1956–70)," *Neophilologus* 56 (1972): 353–62,

and Raymond Lebègue, "Où en sont les études sur Ronsard," *Cahiers de l'association internationale des études françaises* 22 (1970): 19–23.

2   For Ronsard's Petrarchism, see Franco Simone, *Il Rinascimento francese* (Turin: Società editrice internazionale, 1961), pp. 141–222; Donald Stone, *Ronsard's Sonnet Cycles* (New Haven: Yale University Press, 1966), pp. 25–33; Michel Dassonville, "A propos du pétrarquisme et de Ronsard," *Etudes Critiques* 12 (1972): 178–82; and Henri Weber, *La Création poétique du XVIᵉ siecle en France*, 2 vols (Paris: Nizet, 1956), p. 116.

3   For Muret's commentary, see *Les Oeuvres de Ronsard. Texte de 1587*, ed. Isidore Silver, 3 vols. (Chicago: University of Chicago Press, 1966), from which I quote. For studies of the revisions, see Fernand Desonay, *Ronsard, Poète de l'amour*, 3 vols. (Brussels: Palais des académies, 1952–59) 2: 253; but for a dissenting view that Ronsard did not ruin the poems in revision, see Grahame Castor, "Ronsard's Variants," *Modern Language Review*, 59 (1964): 387–90; the most complete study is Louis Terreaux, *Ronsard, correcteur de ses oeuvres* (Geneva: Droz, 1968).

4   Isidore Silver studies the composition and integration of the cycles in *The Intellectual Evolution of Ronsard: Volume II: Ronsard's General Theory of Poetry* (St. Louis: Washington University Press, 1963), chapter 9; on a lesser scale so do Michel Dassonville, "pour une interprétation nouvelle des *Amours* de Ronsard," *Bibliothèque d'Humanisme et Renaissance* 28 (1966): 241–70; and Jean-Claude Moisan, "L'organisation des *Amours de Cassandre*," *Etudes littéraires* 4 (1971): 175–86.

5   R.A. Sayce comments on Ronsard's use of the *tu* form in "Epilogue," in Terence Cave, ed., *Ronsard the Poet* (London: Methuen, 1973), p. 323; for Ronsard's relationship to the epigrams and other classical poetry, see James Hutton, *The Greek Anthology in France* (Ithaca: Cornell University Press, 1946), and Mary Morrison, "Ronsard and Catullus," *Bibliothèque d'Humanisme et Renaissance* 18 (1956): 240–74.

6   For the question of music in Ronsard's sonnets, see Desonay, vol. 1, p. 166; Nan C. Carpenter, "Ronsard's Préface sur la musique," *MLN* 75 (1960): 126–33; and Brian Jeffery, "The Idea of Music in Ronsard's Poetry," in Cave, *Ronsard the Poet*, pp. 209–37.

7   Alexander L. Gordon in *Ronsard et la rhétorique* (Geneva: Droz, 1970), p. 228, and Louis Terreaux in *Ronsard Correcteur*, (pp. 472–77), confirm the view. For Ronsard's drive towards harmony as a manifestation of Baroque energy, see Marcel Raymond, "Quelques aspects de la poésie de Ronsard," in *Baroque et renaissance poétique* (Paris: José Corti, 1955), p. 104.

8   Ferdinand Brunot, *Histoire de la langue française. Volume II: Le*

seizième siècle (Paris: Armand Colin, 1906), pp. 175-77; cf. Terreaux, pp. 371-87.

9 For myth in Ronsard's poetry, see Terence Cave, "Ronsard's Mythological Universe," in *Ronsard the Poet*, pp. 159-208, and "Ronsard as Apollo," *Image and Symbol in the Renaissance*, ed. André Winandy: Yale French Studies 47 (1972), pp. 76-89; and John Lapp, "The Potter and his Clay," *The Classic Line*: Yale French Studies 38 (1967), pp. 89-108; for a more general presentation, see Helmut Hatzfeld, "Christian, Pagan, and Devout Humanism in Sixteenth-Century France," *Modern Language Quarterly* 12 (1951): 337-52, and "The Role of Myth in the French Renaissance," *Modern Language Quarterly* 13 (1952): 393-404.

10 See Mary Morrison, "Ronsard and Desportes," *Bibliothèque d'Humanisme et Renaissance* 28 (1966): 294-322, and Donald Stone, *Ronsard's Sonnet Cycles*, pp. 173-76.

11 For the role of the beloveds, see Grahame Castor, "Petrarchism and the Quest for Beauty," in Cave, *Ronsard the Poet*, pp. 79-120.

12 Taking the opposite point of view, Mark S. Whitney in *Critical Reactions and the Christian Element in the Poetry of Ronsard* (Chapel Hill: University of North Carolina Press, 1971), stresses "the unique, indispensable contribution that Christian elements bring to his poetry" (p. 52). I feel that the emphasis is more secular, however, as does Brian J. Mallett, "Some Notes on the 'Sensuality' of Ronsard's *Amours de Cassandre*," *Kentucky Review Quarterly* 19 (1972): 433-45; and compare Grahame Castor's explication of "Quand en songeant ma follastre" in Peter Nurse, ed., *The Art of Criticism* (Edinburgh: University of Edinburgh Press, 1969), p. 24, and I.D. McFarlane, "Aspects of Ronsard's Poetic Vision," in Cave, *Ronsard the Poet*, pp. 13-78.

13 The preoccupation would intensify in his poetry to Marie (1555); Desonay sees it as "une chose d'amour propre, et non d'amour" (2:50). Evelyn Vitz makes the point in her "actantial" analysis of "Ronsard's *Sonnets pour Hélène*," *Romanic Review* 67 (1976): 249-67.

14 Ambiguous and controversial owing to the variety of interpretations offered by Renaissance commentators. Antonio da Tempo wrote that Laura foresook the sun when it caused her to squint; Filelfo asserted that Laura surpassed the sun in beauty (this reading is evidently close to Ronsard's interpretation); Bernardino Daniello imagined that a shaft of sunlight shone on Laura in a church. Fausto da Longiano offered the most elaborate account, in which Laura disdains the sun by going indoors, whereupon the sun hides in shame behind a cloud: "il sole sdegnato s'ascose, tanto si spiacque l'esser vinto, sotto nugoletto" (p. 43).

Sidney's *Astrophil and Stella*

1 *A Defence of Poetry*, in *Miscellaneous Prose*, ed. Katherine Duncan-Jones and J.A. van Dorsten (Oxford: Clarendon Press, 1973), p. 95. There is a useful review of criticism on the entire subject in William Gotschalk, "Recent Studies in Sidney," *English Literary Renaissance* 2 (1972): 148-64.

2 Consult Neil Rudenstine, *Sidney's Poetic Development* (Cambridge, Mass.: Harvard University Press, 1967), pp. 150-54.

3 C.f. Theodore Spenser, "The Poetry of Sir Philip Sidney," *ELH* 12 (1945): 251-78; and John Thompson, *The Founding of English Meter* (New York: Columbia University Press, 1961).

4 Quotations from *The Poems of Sir Philip Sidney*, ed. William A. Ringler, Jr. (Oxford: Clarendon Press, 1962), with masterful introduction and notes that have helped me greatly.

5 Richard Lanham admits of no sequence but rather a chronicle of a series of attempts to persuade in "*Astrophil and Stella*: Pure and Impure Persuasion," *English Literary Renaissance* 2 (1972): 100-15; for an older view, see Julius Walter Lever, *The Elizabethan Love Sonnet* (London: Methuen, 1956), p. 70.

6 See David Kalstone, *Sidney's Poetry: Contexts and Interpretations* (Cambridge, Mass.: Harvard University Press, 1965), pp. 105-32. Compare James Scanlon, "'See what it is to love' Sensually," *Studies in English Literature* 10 (1976): 65-74. Andrew Weiner locates an objective point of view on Astrophil's folly in "A Figurative Reading of the Eighth Song," *Texas Studies in Language and Literature* 18 (1976): 341-61.

7 See Ephim Fogel, "The Mythical Sorrows of Astrophil," *Studies in Honour of Margaret Schlauch*, ed. M. Brahmer (Warsaw: Polish Scientific Publishers, 1966), pp. 133-52.

8 Richard Young stresses the complicity between poet and reader on this matter in *English Petrarkhe*, in *Three Studies in the Renaissance* (New Haven: Yale University Press, 1958), pp. 9-10.

9 Among those who comment on the strange mixture of classical and moral tones, Douglas L. Peterson, *The English Lyric from Wyatt to Donne* (Princeton: Princeton University Press, 1967) finds Sidney's poetry "contemplative as well as courtly" (p. 201).

10 Robert L. Montgomery in *Symmetry and Sense* (Austin: University of Texas Press, 1961), p. 31 discusses the motivations animating the formality.

11 For recent studies of the structure of the sequence, see Andrew D. Weiner, "Structure and 'Fore Conceit' in *Astrophil and Stella*," *Texas Studies in Language and Literature* 16 (1974): 1-25; Leonore Brodwin, "The Structure of Sidney's *Astrophel and Stella*," *Modern*

Philology 67 (1969): 25-40; A.C. Hamilton, "Sidney's *Astrophel and Stella* as a Sonnet Sequence," *ELH* 36 (1969): 59-87; and B.P. Harfst, "*Astrophel and Stella*: Precept and Example," *Papers on Language and Literature* 5 (1969): 397-414.

12 Richard Lanham analyzes this rhetorical procedure in "Pure and Impure Persuasion," p. 109.

13 See D.M. Beach, "The Poetry of Idea: Sidney and the Theory of Allegory," *Texas Studies in Language and Literature* 13 (1971): 365-89.

14 I am adapting the terms which Michel Foucault uses to characterize the idea of similitude in the sixteenth century in *Les Mots et les choses* (Paris: Gallimard, 1966); my use of them differs, however, in positing a greater continuity between literary periods and a less radical break between their epistemological fields, or *épistémes*, and in acknowledging the priority of the observing subject in the historical definition. Edward Said applies Foucault's "archaeology" to literary theory in *Beginnings* (New York: Basic Books, 1976), pp. 283-315.

15 For commentary on the Italian Petrarchists, see Luigi Baldacci, *Il Petrarchismo italiano*; Walter Mönch, *Das Sonett* (Heidelberg: FH Kerle, 1955); Carlo Calcaterra, *Nella Selva del Petrarca* (Bologna: Cappelli, 1942); and the articles by Damasco Alonso, "Il poesia del Petrarca e il Petrarchismo," *Studi petrarcheschi* 7 (1961): 73-120; Dante Della Terza, "Manierismo nella letteratura del Cinquecento," *Belfagor* 15 (1960): 462-66; Aldo Scaglione, "Cinquecento Mannerism and the Uses of Petrarch," *Medieval and Renaissance Studies* 5 (1971): 122-53; and James Mirollo, "In Praise of 'La bella mano,'" *Comparative Literature Studies* 10 (1972): 31-43; also relevant is Riccardo Scrivano, *Il Manierismo nella letteratura del cinquecento* (Padua: Liviana, 1959).

16 *Le Rime di Benedetto Gareth detto il Chariteo*, ed. Erasmo Pèrcopo (Naples: Accademia delle Scienze, 1892).

17 Quotations from Tansillo and Della Casa are from *Lirici del Cinquecento*, ed. Daniele Ponchiroli, rev. ed., Guido Davico Bonino (Turin: UTET, 1968); for criticism, see Frank T. Prince, *The Italian Element in Milton's Verse* (Oxford: Clarendon Press, 1954); Philippe Renard, "Travail, poétique, et imitation dans le *Rime* de Della Casa," *Revue des Études Italiennes* 14 (1968): 267-323; Guido di Pino, "L'interpretazione del Petrarca nella lirica del Bembo e Della Casa," *Studi petrarcheschi* 7 (1961): 171-77; Aldo Vallone, "Di taluni aspetti del petrarchismo napoletano," *Studi petrarcheschi* 7 (1961): 355-76; and Pietro Borraro, *Contributo ad una rilettura del Tansillo* (Naples: Società di cultura, 1970).

18 For commentary on French Petrarchism, see Joseph Vianey, *Le Pétrarquisme en France au XVIe siecle* (Montpellier: Coulet, 1909),

208   NOTES TO PAGES 74-77

and Franco Simone, *Il Rinascimento francese*, pp. 141-222; among
the studies of Pléiade poetry one should consult Henri Chamard,
Histoire de la Pléiade, 4 vols. (Paris: Didier, 1939-40); Henri Weber,
La création poétique au XVIᵉ siecle; Grahame Castor, *Pléiade Poetics*
(Cambridge, Cambridge University Press, 1964); Donald Stone, *France
in the Sixteenth Century* (Englewood Cliffs, N.J.: Prentice Hall, 1969);
and for an application of structuralist analysis, Roman Jakobson's
study of Du Bellay's "Si nostre vie est moins qu'vne journée" in *Questions de poétique* (Paris: Seuil, 1973).

19 Consult Walter Mönch, *Das Sonett*, pp. 15-32.
20 See Nicholas Ruwet on Louise Labé's "O beaux yeux bruns" in *Langage, musique, poésie* (Paris: Seuil, 1972), pp. 176-99.
21 See I.D. McFarlane, ed., *The Délie* (New York: Cambridge University
Press, 1965); for representative criticism, see Hans Staub, *Le curieux
désir* (Geneva: Droz, 1967); Jacqueline Risset, *L'Anagramme du désir*
(Rome: Bulzoni, 1971); and Thomas M. Greene, "Styles of Experience in Scève's *Délie*," *Image and Symbol*, ed. Winandy, *Yale French
Studies* 47 (1972): 57-95; for comparative treatment, see Luzius
Keller, "Mélancholie pétrarquienne et mélancholie pétrarquiste,"
Studi Francesi 17, no. 49 (1973): 3-14.
22 *Oeuvres poétiques*, ed. John C. Lapp (Paris: Didier, 1966).
23 *Les Amours d'Hippolyte*, ed. Victor Graham (Geneva: Droz, 1960);
for criticism, see Arnaldo Pizzorusso, "Il petrarchismo di Desportes,"
Studi petrarcheschi 5 (1952): 237-98; and Robert Burgess, "Mannerism in Philippe Desportes," *Esprit Créateur* 6 (1966): 270-81.
24 In the above sonnet, for example, Malherbe not only criticized the
appropriateness of such words as *alme* (2), *appareil* (4), *jouist* (8), and
j'ards (14), but he also questioned the figurative sense of how a cloud
of floating dreams can wash the speaker's thought with waves of forgetfulness; recorded in the footnotes of Victor Graham's edition.
25 For general critical commentary on English Petrarchism, see Hallett
Smith, *Elizabethan Poetry* (Cambridge, Mass.: Harvard University
Press, 1952); Clive Staples Lewis, *English Literature in the Sixteenth
Century* (Oxford: Clarendon Press, 1954); J.W. Lever, *The Elizabethan Love Sonnet;* Jerome Mazzaro, *Transformations in the Renaissance English Lyric* (Ithaca, N.Y.: Cornell University Press, 1970).
Yvor Winters, "The Sixteenth Century Lyric in England," *Poetry* 53
(1939): 258-72, 320-35; 54 (1939): 35-51, the article which began
the revaluation of English Petrarchism, is still provocative.
26 Henry Howard, Earl of Surrey, *Poems*, ed. Emrys Jones (Oxford:
Clarendon Press, 1964). For commentary, see Alicia Ostriker, "Wyatt
and Surrey: Dissonance and Harmony in Lyric Form," *New Literary
History* 1 (1970): 387-405.

CHAPTER 2

1 One of the best studies of style in modern criticism, Erich Auerbach, *Mimesis* (Bern: Francke, 1946), tr. Willard Trask (Princeton: Princeton University Press, 1953) depends upon the high-middle-low distinction, but more recent studies advocate a greater relativism, e.g., Jean Cohen, *Structure du langage poétique*, and Michael Riffaterre, *Essais de stylistique structurale*. The last two conceive of style as a deviation from some norm, an idea at least as old as Quintilian, who urged the use of rhetorical figures which "involve a certain departure from the straight line and have the merit of variation from the ordinary usage" (*Inst. orat.* II, xiii, 11). Erich Auerbach, however, warns against this negative conception and defines style in positive terms as "the unity of all the products of an historical epoch" in *Literary Language and Its Public*, p. 9. See also Seymour Chatman, "On the Theory of Literary Style," *Linguistics* 27 (1967): 13-25, and the collection of papers by various hands (Wellek, Wimsatt, Barthes, Todorov, among others) edited by Seymour Chatman, *Literary Style: A Symposium* (New York: Oxford University Press, 1971). Richard Lanham, finally, offers a challenging approach in *Style: An Anti-Textbook* (New Haven: Yale University Press, 1974), where he defines style as a "response to a situation" (p. 58).

2 See the various essays in Jozef Ijsewijn and Eckhard Kessler, *Acta Conventus Neo-Latini Lovaniensis*, 23-28 August 1971 (Munich: Fink, 1973). For a brief survey of formal treatises on rhetoric in Latin and the venacular, see Aldo Scaglione, *The Classical Theory of Composition* (Chapel Hill: University of North Carolina Press, 1972), pp. 133-58, with good analyses of the anti-Ciceronian current in Poggio, Valla, Politiano, Ermolao Barbaro, and Pico against Ciceronians like Paolo Cortese.

3 *De Latinae linguae elegantia libri sex* (Paris: Simon Colinaeus, 1532), p. 122^r.

4 Erasmus, *On Copia of Words and Ideas*, tr. Donald King and H. David Rix (Milwaukee: Marquette University Press, 1963).

5 *Ciceronianus*, tr. Izora Scott (New York: Columbia University Teachers College, 1908), pp. 87, 121; see Charles Béné, "Erasmus et Ciceron," *Colloquia Erasmiana Turonensia*, ed. Jean-Claude Margolin, 2 vols. (Toronto: University of Toronto Press, 1972), pp. 571-79. For Erasmus's emphasis on oral and visual mimesis, see Terence Cave, "'Enargeia': Erasmus and the Rhetoric of Presence," *Esprit Créateur* 16 (1976): 5-19.

6 Among the many works on the humanist movement, see especially Giuseppe Toffanin, *La fine dell'umanesimo* (Milan: Bocca, 1920);

Storia dell'umanesimo (Naples: Perrella, 1933); *Che cosa fu l'uman-esimo* (Florence: Sansoni, 1929); and *La fine del logos* (Bologna: Zanichelli, 1948); for humanist philosophy, Ernst Cassirer, *The In-dividual and the Cosmos in Renaissance Philosophy*, tr. Mario Do-mandi (New York: Harper and Row, 1964); and for art history, Edgar Wind, *Pagan Mysteries in the Renaissance*, rev. ed. (New York: Norton, 1968).

7 In the *Colloquia Erasmiana Turonensia*, see M.A. Screech, "Folie érasmienne et folie rabelaisienne," p. 441-52, and "Comment Rabelais a exploité les travaux d'Erasmus," p. 453-61; and Sem Dresden, "Erasmus, Rabelais, et la 'festivitas' humaniste," pp. 463-78; for a description of the rhetorical coordinates, see Richard Lanham, *Mo-tives of Eloquence*, pp. 16-20, 165-89.

8 Μωρίας ἐγκώμιον, ed. I.B. Kan (The Hague: Nijhoff, 1898), p. v.

Erasmus's *The Praise of Folly*

1 Quotations from I.B. Kan's edition; translations by H.H. Hudson (Princeton: Princeton University Press, 1941). In "The Metamor-phoses of Moria," *PMLA* 89 (1974): 463-76, Wayne Rebhorn recon-ciles two critical approaches, one concerned with the structural divi-sions of Folly's speech and represented by Hoyt Hudson's introduction to his translation and by Walter Kaiser's chapter in *Praisers of Folly* (Cambridge, Mass.: Harvard University Press, 1963), and another concerned with Folly's psychological composition represented by Leonard Dean's introduction to his translation of the work (New York: Hendricks House, 1946) and by Preserved Smith's comments in *Erasmus* (New York: Harper and Row, 1923), pp. 117-28; except for the first, each of these essays is reprinted, along with others, in Kathleen Williams' useful *Twentieth Century Interpretations of "The Praise of Folly"* (Englewood Cliffs, N.J.: Prentice-Hall, 1969). In *Erasmus and the Northern Renaissance* (New York: Collier, 1965), Margaret Mann Phillips combines these approaches in her discussion, pp. 100-8.

2 Quotations from Frobenius's edition of 1517, *Morias encomium . . . cum Listrij commentarijs* (Basil: Frobenius, 1517). See J. Austin Gavin and Thomas M. Walsh, *"The Praise of Folly* in Context," *Renais-sance Quarterly* 24 (1971): 193-209, and Clarence Miller, "Some Medieval Elements and Structural Unity in Erasmus's *Praise of Folly*," *Renaissance Quarterly* 27 (1974): 499-511.

3 (Basle, 1517), p. 74.

4 See Lynda Christian, "The Metamorphoses of Erasmus' *'Folly*,'" *Journal of the History of Ideas* 32 (1971): 289-94.

5 For commentary on the elocutionary aspect of Erasmus's Latin style,

see D.F.S. Thomson, "The Latinity of Erasmus," in *Erasmus*, ed. Thomas Alban Dorey (London: Routledge and Kegan Paul, 1970), pp. 115-37; the introduction by Jean–Claude Margolin to his edition of *Declamatio de pueris statim ac liberaliter instituendis* (Geneva: Droz, 1966), pp. 465-617; and the brief but suggestive introduction by Margaret Mann Phillips to her translation of the *Adages* (Cambridge: Cambridge University Press, 1964).

6 For the paradoxical combination, see Rosalie Colie, *Paradoxia Epidemica* (Princeton: Princeton University Press, 1966), pp. 15-23; and Sister Mary Geraldine Thompson, *Under Pretext of Praise* (Toronto: University of Toronto Press, 1974).

7 See Richard Sylvester, "The Problem of Unity in *Praise of Folly*," *English Literary Renaissance* 6 (1976): 125-39.

8 For the humanist context implied here, see Jean–Claude Margolin, *Recherches érasmiennes* (Geneva: Droz, 1969), especially "L'idée de Nature chez Erasmus," pp. 9-44; C.A.L. Jarrott, "Erasmus' Biblical Humanism," *Studies in the Renaissance* 17 (1970): 119-52; Paul O. Kristellar, "Erasmus from an Italian Perspective," *Renaissance Quarterly* 23 (1970): 1-14; and Eugenio Garin, "Erasmo e l'umanesimo italiano," *Bibliothèque d'Humanisme et Renaissance* 33 (1971): 7-17.

9 See Clarence Miller, "Some Medieval Elements."

10 See Johan Huizinga, *Erasmus*, tr. F. Hopman (New York: Scribners, 1924); Roland Bainton, *Erasmus of Christendom* (New York: Scribners, 1969); James Tracy, *Erasmus, The Growth of a Mind* (Geneva: Droz, 1972).

11 See Gavin and Walsh, "*The Praise* in Context," p. 207.

More's *Utopia*

1 See Edward Surtz, S.J., *The Praise of Pleasure* (Cambridge, Mass.: Harvard University Press, 1957), p. 21; R.J. Schoeck, "On Reading More's *Utopia* as Dialogue," *Moreana* 22 (1969): 19-32; André Prévost, "*L'Utopia*: Le genre littéraire," *Moreana* 31-32 (1971): 161-68; David Bevington, "The Dialogue in *Utopia*," *Studies in Philology* 58 (1961): 496-509; and Louis Martz, "Thomas More's Tower Works," in Richard Sylvester, ed., *St. Thomas More, Action and Contemplation* (New Haven: Yale University Press, 1972), p. 61.

2 Quotations and translations from *The Yale Edition of the Complete Works of St. Thomas More*, vol. 4, *Utopia*, ed. Edward Surtz, S.J., and J.H. Hexter (New Haven: Yale University Press, 1965).

3 For interpretations of Hytholdaeus's character, see Edward Surtz, S.J., *The Praise of Wisdom* (Chicago: Loyola University Press, 1957), p. 182; and Elizabeth McCutcheon, "Thomas More, Raphael Hythlodaeus, and the Angel Raphael," *Studies in English Literature* 9 (1969): 21-38.

212   NOTES TO PAGES 96–105

4 See Edward Surtz, S.J., "Vocabulary and Diction" in *Utopia*, Yale
   Edition, pp. 577–82; and his "Aspects of More's Latin Style in *Utopia*," *Studies in the Renaissance* 14 (1967): 93–109; also R. Monsuez,
   "Le latin de Thomas More dans *Utopia*," *Caliban* 3 (1966): 35–78;
   Elizabeth McCutcheon, "Denying the Contrary: More's Use of Li-
   totes," *Moreana* 31–32 (1971): 107–21; and Ulrich Mölk, "Philolo-
   gische Bemerkungen zu Morus *Utopia*," *Anglia* 82 (1964): 309–20.
5 For the distinction between "Thomas More" and Thomas More, see
   H.W. Donner, *Introduction to "Utopia"* (London: Sidgwick and Jackson, 1945); Russell Ames, *Citizen Thomas More and His "Utopia"*
   (Princeton: Princeton University Press, 1949); Richard Sylvester, "A
   Part of His Own: Thomas More's Literary Personality in His Early
   Works," *Moreana* 15–16 (1967): 29–42; and Dana McKinnon, "Marginal Glosses in *Utopia*: The Character of the Commentator," *Renaissance Papers* (1970): 11–19.
6 See Alan Nagel, "Lies and the Limitable Inane," *Renaissance Quarterly* 26 (1973): 173–80; and for a counterargument, Robert Coogan,
   "Nunc Vivo vt Volo," *Moreana* 31–32 (1971): 29–45.
7 See J.H. Hexter, *More's "Utopia": The Biography of an Idea* (Princeton: Princeton University Press, 1952), and his restatement of approach
   in "Inventions, Words, and Meaning," *New Literary History* 6 (1975):
   529–41.
8 For the idea of nature in the work, see Wayne Rebhorn, "Thomas
   More's Enclosed Garden," *English Literary Renaissance* 6 (1976):
   140–53.
9 See Robert Elliott, *The Shape of Utopia* (Chicago: University of
   Chicago Press, 1970); A.R. Heiserman, "Satire in the *Utopia*," *PMLA*,
   78 (1963): 163–74; and T.S. Dorsch, "More and Lucian," *Archiv
   für das Studium der neueren Sprachen und Literaturen* 203 (1967):
   345–63. William Nelson's useful *Twentieth Century Interpretations
   of "Utopia"* (Englewood Cliffs, N.J.: Prentice–Hall, 1968) reprints
   Dorsch's essay along with others.
10 See Harry Levin, *The Myth of the Golden Age in the Renaissance*
   (Bloomington: Indiana University Press, 1969), for the ironic component of the dialogue. Timothy Reiss discusses its circular self-
   referentiality in *"Utopia* and Process: Text and Anti-Text," *Substance* 8 (1974), 101–25.
11 For the importance of the letter, see Peter Allen, "*Utopia* and European Humanism," *Studies in the Renaissance* 10 (1963): 91–107;
   David Bleich, "More's *Utopia*: Confessional Modes," *American Imago*
   28 (1971): 24–52; and Andrew Weiner, "Raphael's Eutopia and
   More's *Utopia*," *Huntington Library Quarterly* 39 (1975): 1–27.

Rabelais's *Gargantua and Pantagruel*

1 For especially helpful commentary on the role of the narrative speaker,

see Thomas M. Greene, *Rabelais: A Study in Comic Courage* (Englewood Cliffs, N.J.: Prentice-Hall, 1970); Dorothy Coleman, *Rabelais: A Critical Study in Prose Fiction* (London: Cambridge University Press, 1971), p. 62; and Ruth Mulhauser, "The Fictional World of Alcofribas Nasier," *Romanic Review* 64 (1973): 175-83.

2 For helpful commentary on phenomenological correspondences, see Alfred Glauser, *Rabelais créateur* (Paris: Nizet, 1966), p. 117; and Jacques Ehrmann, "La temporalité dans l'oeuvre de Rabelais," *French Review* 37 (1963): 188-99.

3 Quotations from the critical editions in the *Textes litteraires français* series: *Gargantua*, ed. Ruth Calder and M.A. Screech (Geneva: Droz, 1970); *Pantagruel*, ed. Verdun L. Saulnier (Geneva: Droz, 1959); *Le Tiers Livre*, ed. M.A. Screech (Geneva: Droz, 1964); and *Le Quart Livre*, ed. Robert Marichal (Geneva: Droz, 1947); translations are by John Cohen (Baltimore: Penguin Books, 1955).

4 The stylistic contrast is often linguistic. According to Brunot, Rabelais initiated the movement that legitimized the use of *patois* other than Parisian; owing to his extensive travels Rabelais came into contact with an extraordinary range of *patois*; see *Histoire de la langue française* 2: 174. But the stylistic contrasts are not just linguistic; they are rhetorical and dramatic as well. See Pierre Jourda, *Le Gargantua de Rabelais* (Paris: Nizet, 1969), p. 172; and Volker Roloff, "Zeichensprache und Schweigen," *Zeitschrift für romanische Philologie* 90 (1974): 99-140.

5 See William Frohock, "Panurge as a Comic Character," *Yale French Studies* 23 (1960): 71-77; Robert Griffin, "The Devil and Panurge," *Studi Francesi* 47-48 (1972): 329-36; Jerome Schwartz, "Panurge's Impact on Pantagruel," *Romanic Review* 67 (1976): 1-8; and M.A. Screech, *The Rabelaisian Marriage* (London: Edward Arnold, 1958), pp. 57-62.

6 Compare Donald Frame, "Interaction of Characters in Rabelais," *MLN* 87 (1972): 12-23.

7 For the social implications of style, see Alban J. Krailsheimer, *Rabelais and the Franciscans* (Oxford: Clarendon Press, 1963), pp. 237-38; François Rigolot, "Les Langages de Rabelais," *Etudes Rabelaisiennes* 10 (1970): 9-183; and Jean Larmat, *Rabelais* (Paris: Hatier, 1973), p. 184.

8 Stanley Eskin analyzes the episode in "The Idea of Nature in Rabelais and Calcagnini," *Comparative Literature* 14 (1962): 167-73; on the theme of generation, see Ricardo Quinones, *Renaissance Discovery of Time*, p. 189.

9 Verdun L. Saulnier offers a comprehensive interpretation of the irony in *Le Dessein de Rabelais* (Paris: Société d'édition d'enseignement supérieur, 1957); see also Florence Weinberg, *The Wine and the Will* (Detroit: Wayne State University Press, 1972); Wayne Rebhorn,

214 NOTES TO PAGES 110-21

"The Burdens and Joys of Freedom," *Etudes Rabelaisiennes* 9 (1971): 71-90; Charlotte Costa Kleis, "Structural Parallels and Thematic Unity in Rabelais," *Modern Language Quarterly* 31 (1970): 403-23; Stanley Eskin, "Mythic Unity in Rabelais," *PMLA* 79 (1964): 549-53; and Margaret Spanos, "The Function of the Prologues," *Etudes Rabelaisiennes* 9 (1971): 29-48.

10 Mikhail Bakhtin charts the social and anthropological significance of these roles in *Rabelais and His World*, tr. Helene Iswolsky (Cambridge, Mass.: MIT Press, 1968).

11 The history of Rabelaisian criticism charts an uneven path of attempts to find deeper meanings in the fiction beginning in the sixteenth century; see Marcel de Grève, *L'interprétation de Rabelais au XVIᵉ siècle* (Geneva: Droz, 1961); for modern attempts see G. Mallary Masters, *Rabelaisian Dialectic* (Albany: SUNY Press, 1969), and Claude Mettra, *Rabelais secret* (Paris: Grasset, 1973); for the art of deep interpretation in the Renaissance in general, see Edgar Wind, *Pagan Mysteries in the Renaissance* and Jean Seznec, *La survivance des dieux antiques* (London: Warburg Institute, 1940).

12 According to some critics, even Gargantua's letter to Pantagruel in *Pantagruel* VIII is parodic; see Gerald Brault, "Gargantua's Letter to Pantagruel," *Bibliothèque d' Humanisme et Renaissance* 28 (1966): 615-32.

13 See Michel Butor and Denis Hollier, *Rabelais, ou c'était pour rire* (Paris: Larousse, 1972), pp. 112-21.

14 Louis Marin studies the rhetoric of the Thélème episode as a self-referential play of language in "Les corps utopiques rabelaisiens," *Littérature* 21 (1975): 35-51. For Rabelais's attitudes towards religion, see the conservative position of Etienne Gilson, "Rabelais franciscain," in *Les Idées et les lettres* (Paris: Vrin, 1955), pp. 197-240, and A.J. Krailsheimer, *Rabelais and the Franciscans*; for a radically liberal position, see Lucien Febvre, *Le problème de l'incroyance au XVIᵉ siècle* (Paris: Albin Michel, 1942); for a political position, see Nicole Aronson, *Les idées politiques de Rabelais* (Paris: Nizet, 1973), pp. 160-65.

15 The best analyses of the prologue are Walter Kaiser, *Praisers of Folly*, pp. 120-21; and Alice Berry, "Apollo versus Bacchus," *PMLA* 90 (1975): 88-95.

16 Floyd Gray studies these effects in *Rabelais et l'écriture* (Paris: Nizet, 1974), pp. 168-98; Jerry Wasserman comments on them in "The Word as Object," *Novel* 8 (1975): 123-37.

17 Note his presence in the episode of Pantagruel's account of the death of Pan (chapter 28), the war with the Andouilles (chapter 38), and the frozen words (chapter 55).

18 See Michel Beaujour, *Le Jeu de Rabelais* (Paris: l'Herne, 1969), pp. 132-40.

19 See Michel Foucault, *Les mots et les choses*; and Nancy Struever, *The Language of History in the Renaissance*.

20 See William K. Wimsatt: "At the fully cognitive level of appreciation we unite in our own minds both speaker and audience. This principle, though it has to remain largely implicit in most rhetorical discussion, is actually that by which the various levels of the poem's meaning are integrated.... The appreciation of that structure is that total experience or that total knowledge of which the critics speak" (*The Verbal Icon* [Lexington: University of Kentucky Press, 1954], p. xvi).

21 *Mémoires*, ed. J. Calmette and G. Durville (Paris: Champion, 1924–25) 2: 319; see Jeanne Demers, *Commynes memorialiste* (Montréal: University of Montreal Press, 1975).

22 *Oeuvres*, ed. J. Stecher, 4 vols. (Louvain: Lefever, 1882-91) 1: 135.

23 Edmond Huguet, *Etude sur la syntaxe de Rabelais* (Paris: Hachette, 1894), p. 445. The investigation of Rabelais's language in its historical context yields many possibilities, and it is no wonder that the masters of twentieth-century stylistic criticism have plied their craft on it. Many regard Erich Auerbach's *Mimesis* as the finest work of criticism in this century, and some regard its chapter on Rabelais as its finest. Leo Spitzer wrote his doctoral dissertation on Rabelais's formation of words in farcical, burlesque, and grotesque ways in *Die Wortbildung als stylistisches Mittel an Rabelais* (Halle: Max Niemeyer, 1910), as well as two later articles, "Le prétendu réalisme de Rabelais," *Modern Philology* 37 (1939): 139-49, and "Rabelais et les 'rabelaisants',," *Studi Francesi* 4, no. 12 (1960): 401-23, which deflate facile assumptions about the realism of Rabelais's style by stressing his "poésie de la langue." Helmut Hatzfeld wrote a doctoral dissertation on *Rabelais* (Leipzig: Teubner, 1923), which reasserts claims for Rabelais's sharp realism.

24 *La Précellence du langage françois*, ed. Edmond Huguet (Paris: Colin, 1896), p. 105.

25 Quotation from the Pléiade edition by Albert Thibaudet and Maurice Rat (Paris: Gallimard, 1962); translation by Donald Frame (Stanford University Press, 1957). For comparison with Rabelais, see Michel Jeanneret, "L'écriture comme parole," *Esprit Créateur* 16 (1976): 78-94. For general criticism see Auerbach, *Mimesis*; Albert Thibaudet, *Montaigne* (Paris: Gallimard, 1963); Walter Kaiser's "Introduction" to his edition of Florio's translation (Boston: Houghton Mifflin, 1964); Anthony Wilden, "A Reading of Montaigne," *MLN* 83 (1968): 577-97, and "Montaigne's *Essays* in the Context of Communication," *MLN* 85 (1970): 454-78; and Richard A. Sayce, *The Essays of Montaigne* (London: Weidenfeld and Nicolson, 1972).

CHAPTER 3

1 (New Haven: Yale University Press, 1963), p. 9. But see also Stephen

G. Nichols for supplemental remarks in "The Spirit of Truth: Epic Modes in Medieval Literature," *New Literary History* 1 (1970): 365–86. Other treatments of epic form are in Käte Friedemann, *Die Rolle des Erzählers in der Epik* (Darmstadt: Wissenschaftliche Buchgesellschaft, 1969 reprint of 1910 edition); Adalbert Dessau, "Zum Problem der epischen Kunst," *Beiträge zur Romansichen Philologie* 1 (1963): 52–69; Cecil Maurice Bowra, *From Virgil to Milton* (London: Macmillan, 1945), and *Heroic Poetry* (London: Macmillan, 1952); Albert Cook, *The Classic Line* (Bloomington: Indiana University Press, 1966); Josephine Waters Bennett, "Genre, Milieu, Epic Romance," *English Institute Essays 1951*, ed. Alan S. Downer (New York: Columbia University Press, 1952); Jeremy Ingalls, "The Epic Tradition: A Commentary," *East-West Review* 1 (1964): 42–69, 173–211; and 2 (1965): 271–305; Maurice McNamee, *Honor and the Epic Hero* (New York: Holt, Rinehart, Winston, 1960); and Georges Dumézil, *Mythe et épopée*, 3 vols. (Paris: Gallimard, 1968–73), and W. Wolfgang Holdheim, *Die Suche nach dem Epos.*
2 New Haven: Yale University Press, 1967, p. 76.
3 Claudio Guillén, *Literature as System* (Princeton: Princeton University Press, 1971); but see René Wellek's review in *Yale Review* 61 (1972): 254–59, and Ciriaco Morón-Arroyo's discussion of "System, Influence, and Perspective," *Diacritics* 3 (1973): 9–18, for important qualifications; and Rosalie Colie, *The Resources of Kind* (Berkeley: University of California Press, 1973); see also Klaus Hempfer, *Gattungstheorie: Information und Synthesee* (Munich: Fink, 1973).
4 The classifications of genre in Oswald Ducrot and Tzvetan Todorov, *Dictionnaire encyclopédique des sciences du langage* (Paris: Seuil, 1972) are exemplary of the trend. There, to cite the particular treatment of epic, the authors refer to the genre only once (p. 198), and even then they destroy the notion of generic form by making epic synonymous with novel, romance, and narrative in general. Broadly speaking, the structuralist position on genre is a negative one; each text constitutes a genre unto itself which requires its readers to learn to read anew; see Julia Kristeva, "Problemes de la structuration du texte," *Tel Quel: Théorie d'ensemble* (Paris: Seuil, 1968), pp. 297–316.
5 *Beyond Genre* (Ithaca, N.Y.: Cornell University Press, 1972), p. 9.
6 Illustrating a variety of methods and approaches are *The Making of Homeric Verse: The Collected Papers of Milman Parry*, ed. Adam Parry (New York: Oxford University Press, 1971); W.F. Jackson Knight, *Roman Virgil* (London: Faber and Faber, 1944); William Whallon. *Formula, Character, and Context* (Cambridge, Mass.: Harvard University Press, 1969); Fredi Chiappelli, *Studi sul linguaggio del Tasso epico* (Florence: Le Monnier, 1952); Imbrie Buffum, *Agrippa d'Aubigné's Les Tragiques* (New Haven: Yale University Press, 1951);

Paul Alpers, *The Poetry of "The Faerie Queene"* (Princeton: Princeton University Press, 1967); and Christopher Ricks, *Milton's Grand Style* (New York: Oxford University Press, 1963), among others.

7 For major revaluations of the classical epic, see W. Ralph Johnson, *Darkness Visible* (Berkeley: University of California Press, 1976); Brooks Otis, *Ovid an Epic Poet* (Cambridge: Cambridge University Press, 1966); and Frederick Ahl, *Lucan* (Ithaca, N.Y.: Cornell University Press, 1976).

8 Quotation from *Rime*, ed. Ferdinando Neri; for criticism see Ezio Raimondi, *Metafora e storia*, pp. 163-88, with its emphasis on tradition and conventional emblems in the portrait of Sofonisba.

9 For criticism on Sannazaro, see Thomas M. Greene, *Descent from Heaven*, pp. 144-70; on Vida, see Mario di Cesare, *Vida's Christiad and Virgilian Epic* (New York: Columbia University Press, 1964).

10 Quotations and translations from *The De arte poetica of Marco Girolamo Vida*, ed. and trans. Ralph G. Williams (New York: Columbia University Press, 1976).

11 Though an earlier Greek text in the Aldine *Rhetores Graeci* appeared in 1508, and a Latin translation by Giorgio Valla appeared in 1498, de' Pazzi's text directed attention to the *Poetics* in an unprecedented. way; later came the influential critical edition and commentary by Francisco Robortello in 1548 and the first Italian translation by Bernardo Segni in 1549; see Sandys 2: 133.

12 Sandys 2:103.

13 Quotation from the partial translation by Allan Gilbert, *Literary Criticism from Plato to Dryden* (Detroit: Wayne State University Press, 1942), p. 266; there is a complete translation by Henry Snuggs, *Cinthio on Romances* (Lexington: University of Kentucky Press, 1968).

14 *L'Arte poetica* (Venice: Valvassori, 1564), reprint ed. Bernhard Fabian (Munich: Fink, 1971), p. 27; quotation from Gilbert, p. 278.

15 *Prose*, ed. Ettore Mazzali (Milan: Riccardo Riccardi, 1959), p. 386; Tasso repeats the substance of these remarks in the *Discorsi del poema eroico* (1594), in Mazzali, p. 587, translated by Gilbert, p. 499.

16 For classical references in Milton, see Davis Harding, *Milton and the Renaissance Ovid* (Urbana: University of Illinois Press, 1946) and *The Club of Hercules* (Urbana: University of Illinois Press, 1962); in d'Aubigné, see Jacques Bailbé, *Agrippa d'Aubigné: Poète des Tragiques* (Caen: Association des publications de la Faculté des Lettres et Sciences Humaines de l'Université de Caen, 1968); and in Ariosto see Pio Rajna, *Le Fonti del Furioso* (Florence: Sansoni, 1900).

Ariosto's *Orlando Furioso*

1 The best general criticism of the poem is Thomas M. Greene, *Descent from Heaven*, pp. 104-43; A. Bartlett Giamatti's chapter on the Alcina

episode in *The Earthly Paradise and the Renaissance Epic* (Princeton: Princeton University Press, 1966), pp. 137-64, and his essays "Headlong Horses, Headless Horsemen" in *Italian Literature, Roots and Branches*, ed. Kenneth Atchity and Giose Rimanelli, pp. 265-308, and "Sfrenatura: Restraint and Release in the *Orlando Furioso*," in *Ariosto 1974 in America*, ed. Aldo Scaglione (Ravenna: Longo, 1976), pp. 31-39, have aided my interpretation greatly. Italian criticism tends towards extremes, whether in Walter Binni's emphasis on Petrarchan lyricism and metaphysical subtlety in *Metodo e poesia di Ludovico Ariosto* (Messina: G. d'Anna, 1947), or in Antonio Piromalli's emphasis on the earthy realism of Boccaccio and the popular tradition in *Motivi e formi della poesia di Ludovico Ariosto* (Messina: G. d'Anna, 1954), or in Raffaello Ramat's emphasis on Renaissance pessimism in *Per la storia dello stile rinascimentale* (Messina: G. d'Anna, 1953), or in the idealist reading by Benedetto Croce in *Ariosto, Shakespeare, e Corneille* (Bari: Laterza, 1920), perpetuated In Giuseppe Raniòlo, *Lo spirito e l'arte dell'Orlando Furioso* (Milan: Vallardi, 1929) and Emilio Santini, *La poesia del Furioso* (Palermo: Denaro e la Fauci, 1952). Accounts of the reception of Ariosto through modern times are in Walter Binni, *Storia della critica ariostesca* (Lucca: Lucentia, 1951); Raffaello Ramat, *La critica ariostesca dal secolo XVI ad oggi* (Florence: La Nuova Italia, 1954); and Aldo Borlenghi, *Ariosto: Storia della critica* (Palermo: Palumbo, 1961), with an anthology of excerpts.

2 For Ovid's epic technique, see Brooks Otis, *Ovid an Epic Poet*, and also Richard Lanham, *Motives of Eloquence*, pp. 48-64. For divergent views on the status of Ariosto's poem as epic, see Josphine Waters Bennett in *English Institute Essays, 1951*, and C.P. Brand, *Ariosto* (Edinburgh: Edinburgh University Press, 1974), p. 87.

3 Quotations from *Orlando Furioso*, ed. Lanfranco Caretti (Milan: Riccardo Ricciardi, 1954); translation by Allan Gilbert (New York: S.F. Vanni, 1954).

4 For the speaker's role in relation to his material and his audience, see Robert Durling, *The Figure of the Poet in the Renaissance Epic* (Cambridge, Mass.: Harvard University Press, 1965); also Giorgio di Blasi, "L'Ariosto e le passioni," *Giornale storico della letteratura italiana* 129 (1952): 318-62, and 130 (1953), 178-203; and Franco Pool, *Interpretazione dell'Orlando Furioso* (Florence: La Nuova Italia, 1968), with an emphasis on the role of the poet as "arbitro assoluto delle intricate vicendi dei suoi personaggi" (p. 17).

5 Useful for understanding the thematic principles of characterization is Attilio Momigliano, *Saggio su l'Orlando Furioso* (Bari: Laterza, 1928); for a psychoanalytic approach see G. Resta, "Ariosto e i suoi personaggi," *Rivista di psicoanalisi* 3 (1957): 59-83; Marcello Turchi criticizes both of these approaches in "Sui personaggi del *Furioso*,"

Rassegna della Letteratura Italiana 79 (1975): 129–45; in *Ludovico Ariosto* (New York: Twayne, 1974), Robert Griffin points to the thematic contrast between *volere* and *potere*, p. 59.

6 Cesare Segre studies the accretions to the poem, as well as other linguistic revisions before the final edition of 1532, in *Esperienze ariostesche* (Pisa: Nistra-Lischi, 1966), pp. 29–44.

7 See my article, "Ariosto's Ironic Allegory," *MLN* 88 (1973): 44–67. The episode in Alcina's garden stimulated a wealth of commentary in the sixteenth century, both in extended treatises on Ariosto's "allegory" such as *La spositione di M. Simon Fornari da Rheggio sopra l'Orlando furioso*, 2 vols. (Florence: L. Torrentino, 1549–50) and Orazio Toscanella's abridgment of the poem with moralizing commentary and connecting notes, *Bellezze del Furioso* (Venice: Pietro de i Franceschi, 1574); and in printed editions of the entire poem with headnotes to each canto explaining the "allegoria" therein, of which *Orlando Furioso . . . con le annotationi, gli auuertimenti, e le dichiarationi di Girolamo Ruscelli* (Venice: V. Valgrisi, 1556) and *Orlando Furioso . . . con nuove allegorie e annotationi di M. Thomaso Porcacchi* (Venice: Girolamo Poso, 1568) provided the central models imitated, echoed, and plagiarized by Horologgio (1563), Valvassori (1567), and Bonomone (1584). There are of course differences in intention which mark the various allegorizers' approaches. Fornari produced his long commentary out of a conviction that Ariosto equalled the ancients in scope and invention, even if he transgressed the Aristotelian rules: "dico secondo il mio debol guidicio che si come egli non cede à gli antichi poeti nelle ingeniose" (II.8). Ruscelli offered his annotations in opposition to overly pious or zealous readers who might condemn Ariosto's fictions out of hand as profane inventions: "chi domanda dubiti, ò mostri di dubitare, se quelle cose steno ben poste, ò nò, essi rispondono più da reliogiosi che da intendenti" (p. 5). Toscanella proceeded from the most extreme belief in the poem's allegorical significance: "Questa opera adunque è uno specchio, nel quale si veggono le attioni de gli huomini di laude, ò di biasmo meritevoli" (p. 3b). Porcacchi on the other hand took his allegories far less seriously, urging recalcitrant readers to ignore them: "queste Annotationi son fatte solamente per coloro, c'hauranno voglia di leggerle: e chi non potrà hauerui gusto, ò patientia: sia contento di lasciarle stare" (p. ii^v).

8 One may refer to the ambiguous allegorical emblem printed on the final page of the 1532 edition, "dilexisti malitia sur benignitatem," thus framing the author's entire presentation; Raffaello Ramat interprets a good portion of the poem from that perspective in *Per la storia*, pp. 72–73.

9 C.P. Brand comments on Ariosto's audience and readers, both fictive and real, in his chapter on "Dynastic and Political Themes" in *Ariosto*,

pp. 107-25. With regard to this courtly audience, Giuseppe Toffanin made the definitive statement in *La Vita e le opere di L. Ariosto* (Naples: Libreria scientia, 1959), pp. 122 f. Dieter Kremers studies the poet's patronage in *Der "Rasende Roland": Aufbau und Weltbild* (Stuttgart: Kohlhammer, 1973), pp. 130-60.

10 Quotations from Pulci, *Il Morgante*, ed. Giuseppe Fatini, 2 vols. (Turin: UTET, 1964).

11 See Luigi Blasucci, "Riprese linguistico-stilistiche del *Morgante* nell'*Orlando Furioso*," *Giornale storico della letteratura italiana* 152 (1975): 199-221.

12 Quoted from Boiardo, *Orlando Innamorato*, ed. Aldo Scaglione, 2 vols. (Turin: UTET, 1963).

13 An excellent history of Ariosto's verse form adapted from Boiardo, Pulci, and Boccaccio appears in Alberto Limentani, "Struttura e storia dell'ottava rima," *Lettere Italiane* 13 (1967): 20-77. See also Luigi Blasucci, "Osservazioni sulla struttura metrica del Furioso," *Giornale storico della letteratura italiana* 139 (1962), 169-218.

14 Eduardo Saccone discusses Ariosto's use of "alienation effects" to orient his audience towards his own moral vision in his essay on "Cloridano e Medoro" in *Il soggetto del "Furioso" e altri saggi* (Naples: Liguori, 1974); compare Marcello Turchi's modern emphasis on the complexity of Ariosto's moral vision in *Ariosto o della liberazione fantastica* (Ravenna: A. Longo, 1969), pp. 51 and 107. See also Mario Santoro's essay on "Ecco il giudicio uman come spesso erra" in *Letture ariostesche* (Naples: Liguori, 1973), pp. 51-80. For the Ovidian basis of these effects, see Daniel Javitch, "Rescuing Ovid from the Allegorizers," *Ariosto 1974 in America*, pp. 85-98.

15 Nino Cappellani studies the interlacing and ordering of the episodes as they reflect a self-conscious artistic control in *La sintassi narrativa dell'Ariosto* (Florence: La Nuova Italia, 1952), especially p. 77; there are also good comments in Lanfranco Caretti, *Ariosto e Tasso* (Turin: Einaudi, 1961), pp. 36-39; D.S. Carne Ross, "The One and the Many," *Arion* 5 (1966): 195-234; Eugenio Donato, "Desire and Narrative Structure in Ariosto's *Orlando Furioso*," *Barroco* 4 (1972): 17-34; and Daniela Del Corno Branca, *L'"Orlando Furioso" e il romanzo cavalleresco medievale* (Florence: Olschki, 1973), pp. 68-98.

16 Such a conception of variety as a central artistic norm is typically Ovidian. With regard to the image of weaving as a metaphor for the work of a poet, see Ovid's statement on the nature of the artistic process in his account of Arachne in *Metamorphoses*, VI. 1-145. In Ariosto, as in Ovid, the narrator's control over the varied materials of his art is essential.

Agrippa d'Aubigné's *Les Tragiques*

1 See Jacques Bailbé's definitive thesis, *Agrippa d'Aubigné: Poète des*

Tragiques, p. 169; and also Henri Weber, *La création poétique au XVIe siècle*, pp. 632, 642-44, 707.

2 Among reassessments of these qualities are Ahl, *Lucan*, and M.P.O. Morford, *The Poet Lucan* (Oxford: Basil Blackwell, 1967).

3 Marc Bensimon interprets the poem as "le portrait d'un poète souffrant, au seuil du tombeau en exile" in "Essai sur Agrippa d'Aubigné," *Studi Francesi* 7, no. 21 (1963): 418-37; see also the romantic biography by Jeanne Galzy, *Agrippa d'Aubigné* (Paris: Gallimard, 1965).

4 See the excellent essay by J.A. Walker, "*Les Tragiques*: A Genre Study," *University of Toronto Quarterly* 33 (1964): 109-24, and compare Michel Jeanneret, "Les styles d'Agrippa d'Aubigné," *Studi Francesi* 11, no. 32 (1967): 246-57; for biblical references, see Jean Trenel, *L'Elément biblique dans l'oeuvre poétique de d'Aubigné* (Paris: Leopold Cerf, 1904); Marguerite Soulié, "L'inspiration biblique dans *Les Tragiques*," *Europe* 563 (1976): 68-78; and Marie-Madeleine Fragonard, "Les noms divins dans *Les Tragiques*," *Europe* 563 (1976): 91-98; and for the very important history of the development of the text over a period of forty years, see Giancarlo Fasano, *Una Epopea della Morte*, 2 vols. (Bari: Adriatica, 1970) 2: 9-78.

5 "Tout cela est pour l'escholier de Limosin," p. 8; all quotations are from *Les Tragiques*, ed. A. Garnier and J. Plattard, 4 vols. (Paris: Droz, 1932-33); translations are mine.

6 *Pages inedites d'Agrippa d'Aubigné*, ed. P.P. Plan (Geneva: Droz, 1945), p. 168; see Jacques Bailbé, "Lucain et d'Aubigné," *Bibliothèque d'Humanisme et Renaissance* 22 (1960): 320-37.

7 For the role of the audience, see Jacques Bailbé, *d'Aubigné: Poète des Tragiques*, pp. 186-87, and compare Richard Regosin, *The Poetry of Inspiration* (Chapel Hill: University of North Carolina Press, 1970), pp. 30-31, 37.

8 For the speaker's sense of his mission, see Giancarlo Fasano, *Una Epopea della Morte*, 1: 193-270; see also Henry Sauerwein, *D'Aubigné's "Les Tragiques"* (Baltimore: Johns Hopkins University Press, 1953), pp. 148-72, and Henri Weber, "Conflit sociale et genèse poétique," *Europe* 563 (1976), 7-20.

9 In *d'Aubigné's "Les Tragiques"* (New Haven: Yale University Press, 1951), Imbrie Buffum discusses the effect of Baroque theatricality (p. 49); Odette de Mourgues defines it as lacking "in any apparent care for proportions or balance," in *Metaphysical, Baroque, and Precieux Poetry* (New York: Oxford University Press, 1953), p. 74; but see Lowry Nelson's criticism in *Baroque Lyric Poetry*, pp. 6-15.

10 I.e., how often have I betrayed my poetic talent for lesser ends; an alternate rendering of these lines could be "how often have I kindled for the sake of truth the lamp which was extinguished": i.e., how often have I used poetry for nobler ends than others, who have virtually extinguished it.

11 For discussions of style, see Thomas M. Greene, *Descent From Heaven*, p. 262; and Henri Weber, *La création poétique au XVIe siècle*, pp. 715-27.

12 Giancarlo Fasano discusses the Calvinist mentality in *Una Epopea della Morte*, 1: 193-270; for a mythopoetic approach see Claude Gilbert Dubois, "Les images de parenté," *Europe* 563 (1976), 27-42, and compare Greene, *Descent*, pp. 277-84, and Bailbé, *d'Aubigné*, pp. 263-66.

13 See Eduard Fraenkel, *Lucan als Mittler des antiker Pathos* (Leipzig: Warburg Institut, 1924), pp. 229-57, and Konrad Seitz, "Der patetische Erzählstil Lucans," *Hermes* 93 (1965): 204-32.

14 For the correspondence of function and audience in this instance to those of the Bible, see Giancarlo Fasano, *Una Epopea della Morte*, 1: 193-270, and Weber, *La création poétique*, pp. 705-15.

15 See Michel Jeanneret, "Les tableaux spirituals d'Agrippa d'Aubigné," *Bibliothèque de Humanisme et Renaissance* 35 (1973): 233-46.

16 Robert Griffin comments on this idea in "D'Aubigné and Sixteenth Century Occultism," *Romanische Forschungen* 79 (1967): 114-32.

Milton's *Paradise Lost*

1 Ed. J.C. Smith and E. de Sélincourt, 3 vols. (Oxford: Oxford University Press, 1909-10); see my article on "Rhetoric, Allegory, and Dramatic Modality in Spenser's Fradubio Episode," *English Literary Renaissance* 3 (1973): 351-68.

2 Chief spokesmen for this point of view are Arthur John Alfred Waldock, *"Paradise Lost" and Its Critics* (Cambridge: Cambridge University Press, 1947) and William Empson, *Milton's God* (London: Chatto and Windus, 1961); to refute this line of interpretation Anne Ferry calls attention to the speaker's controlling framework in *Milton's Epic Voice* (Cambridge, Mass.: Harvard University Press, 1963) and Stanley Fish even more emphatically to the reader's participation in *Surprised by Sin* (New York: St. Martin's Press, 1967); both Professors Ferry and Fish demonstrate the necessity of understanding the strategies of voice and address.

3 Quotations from John Milton, *Complete Poems and Major Prose*, ed. Merritt Y. Hughes (New York: The Odyssey Press, 1957).

4 For analysis of the prologue, see Anne Ferry, p. 45 and Louis Martz, *The Paradise Within* (New Haven: Yale University Press, 1964); for general analysis of style, see Christopher Ricks, *Milton's Grand Style*, especially pp. 81-87 and 66-77, and also F.T. Prince, *The Italian Element in Milton's Verse* (Oxford: Clarendon Press, 1954); and Isabel MacCaffrey, *Paradise Lost as "Myth"* (Cambridge, Mass.: Harvard University Press, 1959).

5 On the dramatic relevance of Milton's blindness, see especially Kenneth

Muir, "Personal Involvement and Appropriate Form" *Etudes Ang-laises* 27 (1974): 425-35; and Franklin Baruch, "Milton's Blindness: Conscious and Unconscious Patterns of Autobiography," *ELH* 42 (1975): 26-37; for "The Rhetor as Creator," see John Shawcross's article of that title in *Milton Studies* 8 (1975): 209-19.

6 See Stanley Fish, p. 4 and passim; for assessments of Fish's reader-oriented approach, see Leslie Brisman's review of *Self-Consuming Artifacts* in "Critical Priorities," *Diacritics* 4, ii (Summer 1974): 24-27; Robert Crossman, "Some Doubts About 'the Reader of *Paradise Lost*,' *College English* 37 (1975): 372-82; and Burton Weber, "The Non-Narrative Approaches," *Milton Studies* 9 (1976): 77-103. For earlier views on the involvement of the reader, see Joseph Summers, *The Muse's Method* (Cambridge, Mass.: Harvard University Press, 1962), pp. 30-31 and 120-21, and Douglas Knight, "The Dramatic Center of *Paradise Lost*," *South Atlantic Quarterly* 63 (1964): 44-59; for the importance of the audience in Milton's poetics, see Irene Samuel, "The Development of Milton's Poetics," *PMLA* 82 (1977): 231-40, with emphasis on "readers of native good sense with some experience of good poetry" (p. 235).

7 The phrase is quoted from Milton's essay *Of Education*, Hughes ed., p. 637. See B. Rajan, "Simple, Sensuous, and Passionate," *Review of English Studies* 21 (1941): 289-301; for the typological and prophetic aspects of Milton's poetics, see Jon S. Lawry, *The Shadows of Heaven* (Ithaca, N.Y.: Cornell University Press, 1968) and William G. Madsen, *From Shadowy Types to Truth* (New Haven: Yale University Press, 1968).

8 See W. Ralph Johnson, *Darkness Visible* for an excellent summation of this approach to Virgil.

9 Jackson I. Cope identifies Urania and her role in *The Metaphoric Structure of Paradise Lost* (Baltimore: The Johns Hopkins University Press, 1962), pp. 149-63; compare Maurice Kelley, *This Great Argument* (Princeton: Princeton University Press, 1941), pp. 117-18; and Sanford Budick, *Poetry of Civilization* (New Haven: Yale University Press, 1974), pp. 68-69.

10 See Edward Said, *Beginnings*, pp. 279-81.

11 Margaret Shaklee analyzes the way God's abstractions reinforce the notion of abstract law in "Grammatical Agency and the Argument for Responsibility in *Paradise Lost*," *ELH* 42 (1975): 518-30; for the opposite point of view that similar abstractions demonstrate Satan's evasions of responsibility, see Seymour Chatman, "Milton's Participial Style," *PMLA* 83 (1968): 1386-99; for the theological background of Milton's concept of God, see Denis Saurat, *Milton: Man and Thinker* (London: Dial Press, 1925), p. 107; for comparison with other epic presentations of divinity where the poet "both praises and subverts values," see Joan Webber, "Milton's God," *ELH* 40 (1973):

514-31, and Judith Kates, "Revaluation of the Classical Hero in Tasso and Milton," *Comparative Literature* 26 (1974): 299-316.

12 For analysis of the Son's rhetoric, see Irene Samuel, "The Dialogue in Heaven," *PMLA* 72 (1957): 601-11; compare Arnold Stein, *Answerable Style* (Minneapolis: University of Minnesota Press, 1953), p. 131; J.B. Broadbent, *Some Graver Subject* (London: Chatto and Windus, 1960), p. 162; and George Miller, "Stylistic Rhetoric and the Language of God," *Language and Style* 8 (1975): 111-26.

13 See the excellent analysis by Christopher Grose, *Milton's Epic Process* (New Haven: Yale University Press, 1973), pp. 192, 242-43. Compare Michael Murrin's speculations in "The Language of Milton's Heaven," *Modern Philology* 74 (1977): 350-65.

14 See Northrop Frye, *The Return of Eden* (Toronto: University of Toronto Press, 1965), pp. 116-17; and for the role of Satan as rhetorician, see John Steadman, *Milton and the Renaissance Hero* (New York: Oxford University Press, 1967), p. 70, and *Milton's Epic Characters* (Chapel Hill: University of North Carolina Press, 1968), pp. 227-40 and 281-319.

15 For a reading of Satan's development, see John Diekhoff, *Milton's Paradise Lost* (New York: Columbia University Press, 1946), p. 79; Leonora Brodwin relates "The Dissolution of Satan" to heretical eschatology in *Milton Studies* 8 (1975): 165-207. For a "deconstructive" interpretation of Satan as a literary critic, see Donald Bouchard, *Milton: A Structural Reading* (Montreal: McGill University Press, 1974), p. 72. For an interpretation of Satan as an antihumanist conservative, see Wayne Rebhorn, "The Humanist Tradition and Milton's Satan," *Studies in English Literature* 13 (1973): 81-93.

16 See Hugh Richmond, *The Christian Revolutionary* (Berkeley: University of California Press, 1974), p. 25; and William Riggs, *The Christian Poet in "Paradise Lost"* (Berkeley: University of California Press, 1972), pp. 24, 44. For a fine interpretation of echoes and repetitions in Milton's meaning, see Michael McCanles, *Dialectical Criticism and Renaissance Literature*, pp. 143-54.

17 Dennis Burden comments on this linking in *The Logical Epic* (Cambridge, Mass.: Harvard University Press, 1967), p. 95.

18 For a fine contrast between Adam's roles and Satan's, see Geoffrey Hartman, "Adam on the Grass with Balsamum," *ELH* 36 (1969): 168-92.

19 See D.C. Allen, *Harmonious Vision* (Baltimore: The Johns Hopkins Press, 1954), p. 101; and Christopher Grose, pp. 43-45.

20 In *Milton's Poetry of Choice and Its Romantic Heirs* (Ithaca, N.Y.: Cornell University Press, 1973), p. 177, Leslie Brisman indicates Adam's need to achieve "the impersonality of the epic artist."

21 For the mixing of genres, see A.K. Nardo, "The Submerged Sonnet as Lyric Moment in the Miltonic Epic," *Genre* 9 (1976): 21–35; and Harold Toliver, "Symbol-Making and the Labors of Milton's Eden," *Texas Studies in Language and Literature* 18 (1976): 433–50 and "Milton's Household Epic," *Miltonic Studies* 9 (1976): 105–20. Walter Ong, S.J., comments brilliantly on Milton's shift from epic epithet to logic and the dissolution of the genre in *Interfaces of the Word*, pp. 189–212.

Index